ALL-AGE LECTIONARY HOMILIES

BRINGING THE GENERATIONS TOGETHER

SUSAN SAYERS
WITH FATHER ANDREW MOORE

Kevin Mayhew

First published in 2000 by KEVIN MAYHEW LTD
Buxhall, Stowmarket, Suffolk IP14 3BW

All-age Lectionary Homilies is taken from *Living Water*, Years A, B and C, first published in 1998, 1999 and 2000.

The publishers wish to express their gratitude to Phoenix House, a Division of the Orion Publishing Group, for permission to use the extract from *The Solitaire Mystery* by Jostein Gaarder, translated by Sarah Jane Hails, copyright © 1996.

0 1 2 3 4 5 6 7 8 9

ISBN 1 84003 589 7
Catalogue Number 1500371

Cover Design by Jonathan Stroulger
Edited by Katherine Laidler
Typeset by Louise Selfe

FOREWORD

All-age homilies are not the same thing as talks for children, with the adults present. They are aimed rather at the whole worshipping community, when children, young people and adults from 18 months to 98 are in church together.

Naturally that poses some problems. What on earth have all these different age groups got in common? How can we possibly preach the gospel in a meaningful way to such a broad age and culture range? How will anyone benefit? Won't we end up by devaluing the gospel and teaching no one?

All these fears are valid and it is essential that they are asked. I ask them regularly myself.

However, I wonder if, when we ask such questions, we have in our minds a school image of what we are about on Sundays, rather than a family or household image. In educational terms there is much to be said for splitting the age groups and organising the curriculum accordingly, whereas in a family or household it is expected that all the different age groups are living together, along with the affection and irritations, the shared jokes, worries, celebrations and memories. Through such living together, we are given the practice for learning to love. It seems appropriate, then, for the household of faith to gather, to celebrate and to explore the gospel.

People will be at different stages as well as ages; there may be adults who are hovering on the brink of faith or rejection of it, and children who enjoy God's love and talk to him every day. There may be middle-aged adolescents and adolescents with profound maturity. Our joy as the people of God is knowing that we are all accepted and loved wherever we are at the moment, and that we are all in the process of learning to love, however many years have passed since our birth and whatever our choice in clothes.

The profound truths of the gospel need to come across in how we speak as well as in what we say. The all-age talk gives the church a wonderful opportunity to enjoy unpacking the gospel together, sometimes playfully, sometimes in a very moving or challenging way. In Christ we are all brothers and sisters. Whatever family we have or don't have biologically, as Christians we are family members, and the all-age talk takes that truth and celebrates it.

The talks in this book are from the *Living Water* parish programme, published separately for the convenience of those given responsibility for this part of the worship on any particular Sunday. Accordingly, the appropriate lectionary readings are given, together with the thought for the day. In preparing to give a talk, prayerful reading of these passages is vital. The suggested talks can then be used either as written, or as a springboard to set you off expressing your own insights, in the light of the needs of your congregation.

Practise the talk aloud, and ensure that any signs or posters are clearly written and well produced. Be fair in who you choose as volunteers, and include different age groups; it doesn't always have to be the children. Prepare well in advance, so that there is time to contact any 'experts' whose help may be needed, and adapt the talks in any way you want to. They are provided as a help, not a straightjacket.

The whole point of speaking during the liturgy like this is to help people get to know God better; to excite them into deepening their faith, their understanding of God's love, and their response to God. I pray that God will speak through you to get in touch with each of those in your congregation, and that their hearts and minds will be open to receive his love.

SUSAN SAYERS

CONTENTS

FEASTS OF THE LORD

ORDINARY TIME

YEAR B

ORDINARY TIME

YEAR C

ADVENT

SPECIAL FEASTS – YEARS A, B, C

APPENDIX

YEAR A

FIRST SUNDAY OF ADVENT

Isaiah 2:1-5
Psalm 121:1-2, 4-5, 6-9
Romans 13:11-14
Matthew 24:37-44

We are to wake up and make sure we stay ready for the second coming.

All-age talk

Begin by explaining that today is Advent Sunday, the first Sunday of the year as far as the Church is concerned. Advent means 'coming', and over the next four weeks we will be getting ourselves ready for the coming of Jesus which we celebrate on Christmas Day.

Today's readings tell us to keep ourselves ready and alert for God's coming, which happens all the time and will happen in a very dramatic way at the end of time when Jesus returns in all his glory. The children will be helping to show us all how to make sure we don't miss out by being unprepared for this.

Invite all the children and young people to walk quickly around the centre aisle, changing direction every time you clap your hands or blow a whistle. Two claps or whistle blows means stand still and listen to a new instruction. Give them a few goes at changing direction, and then make the standing-still and listening signal. Explain that one clap will now mean change direction, two will mean walk backwards, and three will mean stand still and listen. Try this out for a short while and then, when they are standing still and listening, thank them for their demonstration and ask them to sit down where they are.

Explain that if we are to keep ourselves ready and alert while we get on with our lives, it will mean listening out all the time for the good and loving direction that God whispers to us to follow, just as the children were doing so well. As they walked about their lives, they were listening out, so that whenever there was a need to change direction, they were ready to do it straightaway. If they hadn't listened so carefully, they wouldn't have been able to do it nearly so well.

Tell the children that this time when they hear the signal it will mean 'Go back to your seat'. As you start them moving about the aisle again, remind everyone to keep listening to God's loving direction as they walk about through life, so they are always ready. Make the last signal, and thank the children for their help as they go back to their seats.

All-age ideas

- At the beginning of the service tell everyone that at some point the first candle of the Advent ring will be lit. It won't be announced, so everyone is to watch out for it. When anyone sees it happening, they raise their hand, until everyone has noticed. (Arrange beforehand for the candle to be lit at an appropriate time, and as soon as everyone has raised their hand the usual short prayer can be said.)

- Read the Isaiah passage chorally, using the voices of men, women and children. Work through the reading together, trying out different voice combinations, and finish with verse 5 spoken all together.

- As an introduction to the Gospel reading, have small groups of people miming various everyday activities in different parts of the church during the Gradual hymn, and have the Bible, or book of the readings, held high just before the Gospel is read. Some of those miming notice straightaway and turn to face the reader, walking towards them and standing attentively. Gradually the others follow.

13

SECOND SUNDAY OF ADVENT

Isaiah 11:1-10
Psalm 71:1-2, 7-8,
   12-13, 17
Romans 15:4-9
Matthew 3:1-12

Get the road ready for the Lord!

All-age talk

In the aisle lay down some 'holes' (cut from black paper) and some blocks (chairs with cardboard boxes or trays leaning against them).

Talk about John the Baptist coming out of the desert and urging everyone to 'Get the road ready!' Some people may have seen a new road being built, with some parts being banked up and others tunnelled through, in order to cut out the steep hills. Most people will at some time have been stuck in traffic jams while roads are being mended, or widened.

John the Baptist was imagining us getting a nice new road ready so that God can travel straight into our lives without finding any holes to fall down, or blocks in the way. He was saying to the people, 'You need to get yourselves ready like a good straight road.'

Ask a couple of volunteers to inspect the 'road' in the aisle, finding all sorts of blocks and holes along it that need putting right. This is a bit like our lives, and the lives of the people John was talking to about two thousand years ago. There are 'holes' of selfishness and meanness, and gaping holes in our loving. They need to be filled in with loving kindness and thoughtfulness. Perhaps there are gaps in our honesty, because we don't always tell the truth, or live the truth. These holes need filling up with truthfulness and integrity. There are perhaps holes of superiority, because we sneer at people who aren't like us, or as clever or handsome or rich as us.

Then there are those roadblocks which block God from getting through to us: blocks such as 'I

14

don't need God', 'I'm fine as I am, thanks', 'I don't want to change', and 'It's not my fault I'm bad tempered so you'll have to put up with it'. (The blocks can have these labels written on them clearly.)

When today we hear John the Baptist rushing out of the desert and shouting, 'Get the road ready for our God!', it's a good idea to listen to him, look at our own life-road, see where the holes and blocks are, and ask God to help us put them right straight-away, so that God can come to us easily without any hold-ups.

All-age ideas

- For the Penitential Rite, give everyone a piece of paper and a pencil so they can draw their road and ask God to help them make it ready. Other people will only see the holes and blocks; what these stand for will be known only by the person drawing them.

- Read the Isaiah passage chorally. This helps to bring out both the meaning and the poetry.

- Act out the Gospel with someone dressed up as John the Baptist. This person can then light this week's Advent candle.

THIRD SUNDAY OF ADVENT

Isaiah 35:1-6, 10
Psalm 145:6-10
James 5:7-10
Matthew 11:2-11

Great expectations. Jesus fulfils the great statements of prophecy.

All-age talk

Beforehand wrap some objects as presents. Some should be obvious, such as a tennis racket, a balloon and a bottle of wine. Others should be harder to guess from the shape, such as a boxed toy and a book.

Display the wrapped presents, and talk about the way Christmas is getting nearer and we're all getting our presents ready. Perhaps some of us are really hoping for a particular present, even though we know it's the thought that counts and we'll be happy with whatever we get because it means someone has thought of us.

Draw attention to the wrapped presents you have brought in, and pick up the first group of obvious presents, asking people to guess what is inside. Then go on to the second group, discovering that some things are harder to guess – we might look at the parcel and expect something completely different to be inside.

John the Baptist knew that God was coming to his people, and he had done a good job of getting them ready. But exactly how this would happen was like a wrapped present – still hidden from view because it hadn't happened yet. Perhaps John was expecting Jesus to be more of a mighty warrior, judging everyone and destroying those who didn't make the grade.

What *did* Jesus do? We heard about it in the first reading from the prophet Isaiah: he was going around healing the sick, making the deaf hear again, the blind see again and the lame walk again. He was letting the weak and downtrodden know that God was on their side and loved them.

16

Once Jesus pointed out that he was doing these things, John could see that it really did fit in with the 'shape' he had been expecting, even though it wasn't quite the same, rather like our wrapped-up bottle of red wine which we had perhaps been expecting to be white wine, or sherry. Or like the boxed game that you might have expected to be 'Guess Who' and it turned out to be 'Mr Pop'.

As we wrap our presents, let's remember that God's ways are often hidden and unexpected – he is a God who sometimes takes us by surprise. But the surprises will always be true to his good and loving nature.

All-age ideas

- On banners or posters have the words of Isaiah 35:1-6, 10 celebrated and decorated, so that the very building proclaims them.

- The Isaiah reading contains wonderful poetry. Think how best to bring this out; you could try choral reading, or a combination of reading and music to give the words 'soaking in' time.

FOURTH SUNDAY OF ADVENT

Isaiah 7:10-14
Psalm 23:1-6
Romans 1:1-7
Matthew 1:18-25

Through the willing participation of Mary and Joseph, God is poised to come among his people as their Saviour.

All-age talk

Ask for two volunteers. Stand one on a chair and have the other lie down on the floor. Talk with the volunteers about what they can see from their particular viewpoint. Although nothing else in the church has changed, the descriptions will be different because of where the volunteers are.

You could also suggest that everyone looks at something central, first through one eye and then the other. They can then all notice the change of view even when looking out from the same head!

What our readings today are reminding us is that we need to get into the habit of looking at everything from God's point of view. What we then see may sometimes come as a surprise to us, because we are so used to looking from our own point of view. Take Joseph, for instance. He was in for a surprise. He thought he had worked out the kindest way of dealing with the embarrassing problem of Mary expecting a baby before they were married. He had it all worked out. He'd divorce Mary without a big fuss, so that she needn't be noticed too much.

But through the dream God helped him look at things from another point of view. Joseph saw that Mary's baby was all part of God's plan, and, rather than divorcing her, he had an important job to do – to look after Mary and this very special baby. Joseph must have been a very brave man, as well as a good and kind one. He knew people would think he was stupid; perhaps they would stop being friends with him; his life would never be nice and

18

straightforward again. But he did that brave, good thing because he had seen the situation from God's point of view and was happy to go along with that.

It was the same with Mary. If she had only seen the angel's message from her own point of view she might have refused to go along with God's plan, which was bound to turn her own hopes and dreams upside down. But she saw it from God's point of view – that the people of our earth needed a Saviour; God needed to be born as a human baby so he could rescue humans as an insider. And a baby needed a mum. So she agreed and that made Christmas possible.

All-age ideas

- Use nativity play costumes and dress people up as Joseph and Mary, who can then mime the actions as the Gospel is read.

CHRISTMAS DAY

Isaiah 52:7-10
Psalm 97:1-6
Hebrews 1:1-6
John 1:1-18

The Word of God is made flesh. In the birth of Jesus we see God expressed in human terms.

All-age talk

Begin by getting different people to say, 'Happy Christmas, everyone!' in whatever way they like. A group of friends might like to shout it together; someone might like to stand at the front; others will choose to say it quietly to their neighbour.

Point out how all the 'Happy Christmas!' messages are much appreciated, and they all show the wonderful way we're all different. You don't have to be a particular sort of person to be a Christian. The only sort of person you have to be is yourself! God loves you that way.

Today we've been expressing ourselves when we spoke our Christmas messages, and Christmas is about God expressing himself: Jesus being born as a human baby is God saying to all of us, 'I love you!'

All-age ideas

- Gather the collection in a model manger (made from a box and filled with straw) and use different age groups to do the collecting.

- Ask everyone to bring bells and ring them at the Gloria.

- Gather the children round the crib during the intercessions.

FIRST SUNDAY OF CHRISTMAS: THE HOLY FAMILY

Ecclesiasticus* 3:2-6,
12-14 (* also called
Sirach)
Psalm 127:1-5
Colossians 3:12-21
Matthew 2:13-15,
19-23

Jesus, the expression of God's love, lives as a vulnerable boy in the real and dangerous world we all inhabit.

All-age talk

If you have a member of the congregation whose job involves rescue (for example in the fire, ambulance, lifeboat or mountain rescue services), ask if they would be willing to take part in a brief interview before the talk. Talk with them about the kind of dangers they themselves have to accept in order to rescue people, and the way they get alongside the people who need rescuing in order to help them. If you are not having a live interview, talk briefly about these rescuers.

Explain how Jesus is a rescuer, who comes in person to save us and help us. Stand someone on a paper island in the middle of a flood. God doesn't stand a long way off and shout to us. (Stand a long way off and shout to them to get into a boat and sail away.) That's no good, because the person feeling drowned by sadness or guilt or evil can't do what you are shouting even if they wanted to. We can't rescue ourselves; only God can set us free by accepting us, loving us and forgiving us. So instead of being a long way off and telling us what to do, God came in person to rescue us. (Pretend to row over to the person and then rescue them.) That's what happened at Christmas – God came to live among us in the person of Jesus, and he is still with us now. We are all his brothers and sisters.

21

All-age ideas

- Have the first reading read by a parent who is carrying a young child.

- During the Gospel, have the holy family moving from one place to another, settling down, and then setting off again.

- Have a collection of money or gifts for homeless families or refugees, with some pictures and figures to help people understand the problems experienced.

SECOND SUNDAY OF CHRISTMAS

Ecclesiasticus 24:1-4,
  12-16
Psalm 147:12-15,
  19-20
Ephesians 1:3-6, 15-18
John 1:1-18

The grace and truth revealed in Jesus show God's freely given love; through Jesus, God pours out his blessings on us and gives us real freedom.

All-age talk

Bring something with you to offer as a small gift – a chocolate bar, a sticker, a few flowers or a piece of fruit, perhaps.

Over Christmas we have all been busy giving one another presents. Explain that you have brought something with you to give away today, so that we can understand a bit more about God's Christmas present to us. In Jesus we see God giving himself to set us free from sin and evil because he loves us so much.

Show everyone what your gift is, and ask them to put their hands up if they would like to be considered for it. Choose someone using some random method, such as their name being first in the alphabet, or their birthday coming up this week. When God gives us his present no one has to get left out. Everyone who asks, gets.

Stand a short distance away from the person chosen, and hold out the gift. Can they receive the gift without moving? No, they can't. If we are going to receive a gift we have to change our position a bit. (The person can demonstrate this and receive the gift.) It's the same with us all receiving God's gift – we are bound to change if we receive Jesus into our daily living.

Just as Joseph and Mary's lives changed when Jesus was born into their family, so our lives will change. As we reach out to receive Jesus, we shall find we are able to reach out to one another in a more loving, positive way; we shall find we are more

23

concerned about justice and mercy being written into our social system; we shall find we are wanting to be more truthful to others and ourselves.

So be prepared – if you don't want to change into a happier, more loving person, freed from guilt and able to be truly yourself, then don't take God up on his offer!

All-age ideas

- At the same time as the collection plate is passed around, have a basket of coloured shapes with the reference to John 3:16 written on them. These are given to everyone, so that they are given a message which they can then decide to receive.

- Just before the Gospel is read, have a single candle carried by a young child ahead of the Bible, or book of readings, into the centre of the congregation.

THE EPIPHANY OF THE LORD

Isaiah 60:1-6
Psalm 71:1-2, 7-8,
    10-13
Ephesians 3:2-3a, 5-6
Matthew 2:1-12

Jesus, the hope of the nations, is shown to the world.

All-age talk

Beforehand arrange for a knitter to bring a completed garment to church, together with a ball of wool and needles. Also prepare a large paper cut-out of a similar garment, which is folded up so that the first bit that would be made is the only piece showing. Alternatively use the actual garment, folded up at that point.

Begin by showing everyone the wonderful garment that the knitter has made and asking how long it took to make and who it is for. What did it look like at first, when they started making it? The knitter can show the ball of wool and needles, and do a couple of stitches. Hold up the needles with these stitches and point out that it doesn't look much like a jumper/scarf yet! But the knitter went on working at it, knowing that one day it would be ready.

God knew that one day everything would be ready for Jesus to come into the world, but he, too, took a long time making things ready. He started by calling one person, Abraham. (Show the folded garment, but don't refer to it – it is there to be visual reinforcement of what you are saying.) Over the years God went on to prepare all Abraham's family. (More of the garment is revealed.) Until over more years that family became one nation. (Reveal some more of the garment.) But God's plan still wasn't finished. He went on to include not one nation but all the nations and everyone in them. (Shake the whole garment out and display it.) Today is called the Epiphany because the word 'epiphany' means 'showing' or 'revealing' or 'manifesting', and

25

when those wise men arrived at Bethlehem with their presents, God was showing or revealing himself not just to Abraham or his family, not just to the whole nation of Israel, but to all the rest of us in the world as well.

Whatever country you come from, whatever you look like and whatever language you speak, God is saying to us today that he is there for you and no one is left out. You don't have to have the right ancestors to know God. You don't have to pass any exams to know God.

We sometimes get so interested in the presents the wise men were bringing to Jesus that we forget what brought them there in the first place. It was God who called these wise men from other nations to be there when Jesus was still a baby, so he could welcome them as well. They were there representing all the nations, so when God welcomed them he was welcoming each of us.

All-age ideas

- Today's Gospel can be acted out, preferably with costumes, as these may well be available from a nativity play. I am not suggesting a full-blown production with hours of rehearsal. All that is needed is a sensitive narrator, and the characters to mime what the narrator says.

- The wise men can take the collection and offer the gifts today. This emphasises their role as representatives of all the nations coming to be welcomed and offer their gifts. A globe can be offered at the same time.

- Have a bowl of burning incense, gold and myrrh arranged among flowers as a display either as people come in or near where they will come to receive communion.

THE BAPTISM OF THE LORD

Isaiah 42:1-4, 6-7
Psalm 28:1-4, 9-10
Acts 10:34-38
Matthew 3:13-17

As Jesus is baptised, the Spirit of God rests visibly on him, marking him out as the One who will save his people.

All-age talk

Ask various children if they know what job they would like to do when they grow up. Ask various adults what they wanted to be when they were children, and whether they did it or not. Ask some of the children if they have seen pictures of their mums and dads when they were babies and toddlers. Do they look anything like that now? Ask some of the mums and dads if they can imagine what their children will be like in twenty years' time.

A week or two ago we were thinking about when Jesus was a baby. Now, suddenly, we're looking at what he was like when he grew up. Here he is at about thirty years old. He's a carpenter, so he's probably quite strongly built. He's heard that his cousin, John (do they remember John?), is washing people in the River Jordan as a sign that God has forgiven their sins. We wash to get our bodies clean. John baptised people to show they were getting their souls clean. They were all getting ready for the Messiah, or Christ.

And now here comes Jesus, wading into the river, and wanting John to baptise him as well! (We know that Jesus is the Christ they were waiting for, but the people didn't know that yet.) John realises who Jesus is, and is shocked that he wants to be baptised. 'It ought to be the other way round!' says John. '*You* ought to be baptising *me!*'

Jesus insists. 'No, it's right for you to baptise me. God's work of putting things right all through the centuries is coming together now in this Baptism.' So John agrees to baptise Jesus. He pushes Jesus down under the water in the river, and when Jesus comes up out of the water, something amazing happens.

It's as if the heavens are opened up, and Jesus sees the Spirit of God coming to him and resting on him. Matthew tells us it looked something like a dove flying down to him. Jesus hears God his Father speaking to him deep into his being. God is saying that Jesus is indeed his well-loved Son, chosen and marked out for a special life that will save the world.

So that tiny baby, born in the stable, visited by shepherds and wise men, looked after by Joseph and Mary all through his childhood, is now at the start of his important work on earth. His job is to show the world God's love.

All-age ideas

• Use the Rite of Blessing and Sprinkling Holy Water in place of the Penitential Rite.

• Decorate the font today, and have the renewal of baptismal promises displayed beside it. Suggest that people go and visit it after the service or during the week, thinking over their own Baptism as being the start of their Christian ministry.

• Have some floating candles in a shallow tray of water incorporated in an arrangement that people will see as they come up to receive communion.

First Sunday of Lent

Genesis 2:7-9; 3:1-7
Psalm 50:3-6, 12-14, 17
Romans 5:12-19
Matthew 4:1-11

Jesus knows all about temptation; and he can deal with our sin.

All-age talk

Talk about some of the rules we are given, such as 'Wear your seat-belt', 'Don't lean out of the window of a moving train', 'Don't play on the railway line' or 'Don't keep poisons in old lemonade bottles'. Gather ideas about why they are good, sensible rules which are worth keeping. Point out that they are good rules whether we actually know the reasons or not.

Now ask for some volunteers to stand around as trees in the garden of the story from Genesis. Give the volunteers real or paper fruits to hold. God's rule for Adam and Eve was 'Don't eat fruit from this tree'. Hang this rule round the tree in the centre of the garden. Now God has very good reasons for making this rule, based on his love for Adam and Eve and his concern for them. And since God is God, that rule is the most important thing for Adam and Eve to remember. However tasty the fruit looks, whatever they may be told it will do to help them, they are always to keep hold of God's rule (what was it?), and stick to keeping that. Anything that cuts across God's rule must be wrong.

Ask two people who think they will be able to keep to God's rule without disobeying it. These two are going to be Adam and Eve. Show them how tasty the fruit looks and try to persuade them to try it. Tell them that it will do wonderful things for them, and make them wise like God. When they (hopefully) manage to resist the temptation to do what God's rule told them not to, praise them, and then point out that they managed it this time, but we are always being tempted to be disobedient to God's rule of love, and when it next happens we

29

need to stick close to God, and remember his rule: 'Love God and love one another'.

Adam and Eve in the story stand for all of us who are human. And humans tend not to be very good at resisting temptation. God loves us and understands what it is like to be humans being tempted. We know that because Jesus was tempted during his life on earth. He will give us the strength we need to resist those pressures of temptation, but that doesn't mean it's going to be easy. Resisting temptation is *very hard*, and that's why Jesus told us to pray about it every day of our life: 'Lead us not into temptation but deliver us from evil.' Let's use the strength God offers; we need all the help we can get!

All-age ideas

- The Genesis reading can be accompanied by a group of people miming the action.

- Have different voices to read through the Gospel, either using the *Dramatised Bible* or simply going through the text together and deciding how the meaning and drama can best be brought out.

- Give everyone a cut-out paper shape of a bitten apple, and during the Penitential Rite ask them to hold it and look at it as they bring to mind the times they have gone along with temptations instead of holding on to God's rule of love. The shapes can be collected and placed at the foot of the cross as the words of forgiveness are proclaimed.

SECOND SUNDAY OF LENT

Genesis 12:1-4a
Psalm 32
2 Timothy 1:8-10
Matthew 17:1-9

The disciples witness the glory of God revealed in Jesus. It is a glimpse of the glory which will be the great hope for all nations of the world.

All-age talk

Bring along a family photograph album with snaps of holidays or celebrations in it, and if possible a camera which takes instant pictures. Also have two cards to hold up, one with a large plus sign on and the other a large minus sign.

If you have an instant camera, begin by taking a picture of some people or the day's flower arrangement. Show the album and talk about the way we all like to snap away to capture the moments when we are on holiday or at a special celebration, or when our children and grandchildren are growing up. We want to hang on to the moment and cherish it for years to come, because we know the moment itself won't last. The children will soon grow up, and we may never have the chance to visit the Eiffel Tower or Southend illuminations ever again!

The 'plus' side of taking pictures like this (encourage everyone's suggestions) may be that we will remember better if we look back at the picture – it may help us see the importance of the occasion, it helps us pass on the family tradition to the next generation, and it lets us enjoy more at our leisure later than we were able to take in at the time.

The 'minus' side may be that we're so busy taking pictures at the time that we aren't able to concentrate properly on the actual moment.

In the Gospel we heard about something amazing which happened on a mountain in Galilee. Three of Jesus' friends – Peter, James and John – saw Jesus shining with God's glory as he prayed. It was one of those times when Peter wanted to reach for the

31

camera (except that cameras hadn't been invented then) so they could hold on to the wonderful moment for ever. Perhaps they had never before felt God quite so close to them! They even heard God's voice. He wasn't saying, 'I hope you're watching carefully and I'm sorry cameras haven't been invented yet or you could have got a pretty dramatic picture here today!' He was helping them understand the real, actual experience they were in, assuring them that Jesus really was God's Son, and wanting them to listen to Jesus in a way they had never listened before.

God doesn't just want Peter, James and John to know – he wants St Peter's church and St James's and St John's and all the other churches to know. He wants all the people in all the world to know who Jesus is, and he wants us all to pay attention to what Jesus says, and really listen to him with our hearts and minds as well as our ears.

All-age ideas

- Have some A4 sheets of paper printed with single words in big letters, such as 'Life', 'Love', 'Joy' and 'Peace'. Print them out in black and again in colour. Make a display with the black words next to the coloured words as a visual way of seeing how God can transform life with shining richness and love.

THIRD SUNDAY OF LENT

Exodus 17:3-7
Psalm 94:1-2, 6-9
Romans 5:1-2, 5-8
John 4:5-42

God both knows us completely and loves us completely; meeting us where we are, he provides us with living water, to satisfy all our needs.

All-age talk

You will need some paper cups, one with holes poked in it, a washing-up bowl or bucket and a jug of water.

Remind everyone of the way the people in the desert were very thirsty, and Moses asked God how their thirst could be quenched. He also told God how grumpy everyone was getting – they were so grumpy that Moses began to think they might take their anger out on him physically! God answered by providing water tumbling out of a rock, fresh and pure and delicious. There's nothing more wonderful when you're thirsty than the refreshing sound and taste of water. Now pour some water out and enjoy the sound of it. Invite some thirsty person to drink some from the proper cup. The people wanted to be back in the past, but God wanted to lead them on into the future.

We heard about two more water supplies today. Did anyone notice what they were? One was a well, where a woman had come to collect water, and where Jesus was sitting, feeling thirsty. Perhaps his own thirst reminded him of the people getting grumpy with Moses in the desert, and the way God had given them the flowing, living water they needed.

The other water supply is a bit unusual. Jesus told the woman about some water which would quench her thirst completely, and become a spring of water inside her welling up to give her life that lasts for ever. At first the woman thought this

33

sounded too good to be true! What Jesus was doing was explaining the way God fills our lives, and leads us into the future, satisfying us all the way along, and refreshing us when we are sad and longing for good and right and fair and helpful things to happen in our world. The more we go to God to be filled with his living water of life and love, the more we shall find that we too are becoming sources of love and comfort and fairness and truthfulness for other people.

Let's see what happens when we pour some water into this cup with holes in it. (Station some people around with proper cups.) Pretend this hol(e)y cup is a Christian drinking the living water of life and love from the living, loving God. Can you see how the Christian then pours out that love to other people he or she meets? There's no problem that God will suddenly dry up, because God is living, flowing, for ever. And the other people may well want to become hol(e)y themselves, drinking that eternal supply which they can see is changing us for the better.

So if your life feels rather dry or thirsty or stuck in the past, go to Jesus; keep going to Jesus; and let him fill you up with the living spiritual water that really satisfies. And don't keep it all to yourself – pass it on!

All-age ideas

- Make streamers for the children from green and blue crepe paper, and have them sweeping and twirling like water during one of the hymns.

- Have the Gospel read as a conversation between a man and a woman.

FOURTH SUNDAY OF LENT

1 Samuel 16:1, 6-7,
  10-13
Psalm 22
Ephesians 5:8-14
John 9:1-41

Jesus gives sight to the man born blind and exposes the blindness of those who claim to see.

All-age talk

Beforehand prepare a message on a piece of paper which will only be visible from the other end of the church through a pair of binoculars. The message is: 'People look at the outward appearance, but the Lord looks at the heart.' Also ask someone with strong glasses if they would mind helping with the talk today.

Ask the person with glasses to come and talk about one or two of the difficulties of poor physical vision; perhaps they wouldn't mind taking off their glasses and saying what they can see without them, contrasting that with their vision when wearing their glasses. So many of us would be forced to live very different lives if we were not helped to see by special lenses, and all that research and developed skill is something to be very thankful for.

Now blindfold a volunteer and ask everyone for ideas about how this lack of vision would make life very difficult. Thankfully there are aids to help those who are blind, and many blind people get really skilled at coping in their lives; but blindness still makes extremely difficult things that sighted people take for granted, and we all need to make sure that we notice the needs, and don't leave our bikes lying on the pavement or anything that might make it dangerous for those who can't see very well.

Today we heard about a man who had been born blind, so he had never seen anything in his whole life. And when Jesus made some mud and put it on his eyes, and told him to wash it off, that man was suddenly able to see for the very first time. (Remove the blindfold from the volunteer as you say this.) Can you imagine how that felt! All the colours and faces and new meaning to the textures he knew from touch alone! It's not a bad idea for us all to spend today looking at everything as if we have just been given our sight – as if we are seeing all the beauty and variety of God's world for the very first time. That will make us freshly thankful to our loving God; and it will help prevent us from being so used to seeing it all that we take God's gift of sight for granted.

Being given your sight is so obviously the work of goodness, and the man born blind is not prepared to go along with what the Pharisees are suggesting – that Jesus is not from God. He hasn't only been given physical sight, but spiritual in-sight as well. And we all need both sorts of sight. Sometimes, like the Pharisees, we think we are seeing everything clearly, so we stop looking.

Ask a volunteer to go to the back of the church and hold up the piece of paper. From the front it just looks like a piece of paper. But if we take the trouble to look at it through binoculars (give the volunteer a pair) you find truths you hadn't noticed before. (Ask them to read out the message they can now see.)

So today we are reminded of the wonder of sight, and encouraged to thank God for all we see. And we are challenged to keep seeking God, keep looking for him, and not shut our spiritual eyes to the light of his truth and goodness.

All-age ideas

- Have a 'still life' collection of glasses, binoculars, telescope, kaleidoscope and various other items designed to help us see clearly, together with a Bible and a cross. Give it a title: 'The blind receive their sight.'

- The Gospel is already written like a script and lends itself particularly well to being acted out.

FIFTH SUNDAY OF LENT

Ezekiel 37:12-14
Psalm 129
Romans 8:8-11
John 11:1-45

Jesus is the resurrection and the life. He can transform death and despair, in any form, into life and hope.

All-age talk

You will need an inflatable ball or a balloon, and, if possible, a dummy used for teaching mouth-to-mouth resuscitation. Otherwise, bring along a large baby doll.

Begin by asking everyone to breathe in deeply, hold their breath while you count to twenty and then let their breath out. They will all have noticed how much we need that air. By the end of just twenty seconds we're getting desperate! Most of the time we breathe in and out without even thinking about it. Although it's such a vitally important thing to do, we're designed so that the breathing mostly goes on automatically so we can do lots of other things at the same time. Yet without that breathing we wouldn't be able to do any of those other things because we would be dead. That's how important breath is – it's a matter of life and death.

Ask a volunteer to demonstrate what we have to do if we come across someone whose breathing has stopped. Point out that what is happening when we are doing mouth-to-mouth resuscitation is that we actually do the breathing for the other person. With our living breath we can save someone's life.

Today in the Gospel we have heard an amazing story of Jesus actually bringing someone back to life. It was his friend Lazarus, and when Jesus' voice, as the Lord of life, broke into the place of death, Lazarus heard his name being called and walked out into life again towards that voice.

Jesus calls each of us by name. He calls into the place we are, even if that place is full of darkness and sadness, or if the noise of unimportant things

37

we like wasting our time on nearly drowns his voice, or if we're running as fast as we can away from God's way of living. Wherever we are, Jesus keeps calling because he wants to bring us out into new life. He knows his breath in us will transform our time in this life, and beyond that into the time after our physical death. As Jesus breathes his life into us it will make such a difference to us that we'll wish we'd gone for it ages ago!

Ask someone to blow up the ball or balloon, and as they do so point out what a difference it is making to have that breath inside. Once they are filled with our breath they have a whole new dimension – they're much more useful and they're much more their true selves. It's the same with us. When we let God breathe his life into us every minute of every day, we become much more our true selves, our life has a whole new dimension, and we are of more use to God in caring for the world he loves.

All-age ideas

- Have the Gospel read through by a group, with people taking the different parts, so that the different conversations in the story are brought out.

- Ask some of the creative people in the congregation to make a poster or banner about God's power to renew us, using the 'dry bones into living people' image.

PALM (PASSION) SUNDAY

Liturgy of the Palms:
Matthew 21:1-11

Liturgy of the Passion:
Isaiah 50:4-7
Psalm 21:8-9, 17-20,
   23-24
Philippians 2:6-11
Matthew 26:14-27:66
or Matthew 27:11-54

Jesus rides into Jerusalem cheered by the crowds. Days later, crowds will be clamouring for his death.

All-age talk

Have the London Underground map printed out on the weekly sheet, or have some larger versions available to show everyone.

Look at the plan and talk about the way it is simple sign language to help us make sense of a huge complicated network of rails and tunnels criss-crossing under the streets. The whole thing is so enormous to understand that we need this simple map.

But when we travel on the underground it only works because, as well as the simple map in our hand or on the station wall, the real massive tracks are laid in all those dark tunnels, and the electrical power is surging through all the thick cables, and the tilers have been busy fixing tiles on the station walls, and the computers are busy checking where each train is so that they don't bump into one another, and those moving stairs, the escalators, are well oiled and running smoothly. Although all this doesn't show up on our plan of coloured lines and blobs, we only have to look at it and we know that all the real stuff is right there.

In a way the cross shape is like one of those plans. Draw people's attention to the crosses they can see around them in church. It is only a simple shape, and we can all make it ourselves by placing one index finger across the other. (Do that now.) When people say 'fingers crossed' what do they do? (Ask some people to show this.) Today it usually means hoping we'll be lucky, but a long time ago it was people making the sign of the cross as they prayed about something they were worried about. (We could go back to using the sign that way!)

Now if the shape of the cross is like the underground train plan, what is all the real, deep stuff that the cross reminds us of? Ask everyone to find or make a cross and look at it, as you tell them about the deeper meaning: God loves the world so much that he was willing to give up everything, and come and live with us in person as Jesus. That loving led him to a cross where he gave up his life for us, taking all the selfishness and sin on himself, and stretching out his arms in welcome and forgiveness, because he so longs for us to be free.

All-age ideas

- The reading of the Passion can be sung by the choir, or dramatised using different voices, with the whole congregation joining in the crowd's words.

- A drama group could prepare a short mime to bring out the meaning of the crucifixion. Rather than having set movements to follow, give them some familiar religious keywords to pray about, unpack and express, such as *Saviour, Redemption* or *Justification*.

EASTER DAY

Acts 10:34-43
Psalm 117:1-2, 16-17,
   22-23
Colossians 3:1-4
John 20:1-9

It is true. Jesus is alive for all time.
The Lord of life cannot be held by death.
God's victory over sin and death means
that new life for us is a reality.

All-age talk

Bring along a few fresh eggs in a carton, and a chocolate egg.

Begin by reminding everyone that we are here for an exciting celebration. Draw attention to all the flowers, and the cleaning that has been going on, and the Paschal Candle or other special Easter decorations and symbols. What is it we're celebrating? That Jesus had died on the cross and is now alive – alive for ever!

Introduce the chocolate egg. For some reason we've been seeing a lot of these at Easter. No doubt some people gave some away. No doubt some ate one before breakfast! What have they got to do with Jesus? Why do we all like to give one another eggs at Easter time?

One reason is that people were giving one another eggs around the time of Easter long before they had heard about Jesus. This is springtime, and eggs are all part of the spring, with its promise of new life.

New life! That's interesting – we've been hearing about the new life that Jesus gives us. When people came to our country and told us about Jesus, they thought the egg was a very good way of explaining the Gospel, so they kept it.

How does an egg help us to understand the Easter story? Show everyone the carton of ordinary eggs, and hold one up on its own. What is it? (An egg.) What comes out of a fertilised egg like this? (A chicken.) Yes, it's a new life – in this case a chicken. An egg is the way new creatures come into being. And Easter is about Jesus being alive in

41

a new way and making it possible for all of us to be given new life.

What does the inside of an egg look like? (It's got yellow yolk and some thick runny stuff which is white when it's cooked.) What are some favourite ways of eating an egg? (Gather suggestions.) So what is inside the shell turns into something quite different. Jesus' life now, as from the first Easter Day, is different. For a start, he's never going to die again; his new life isn't a life that runs out.

Now break one of the eggs. When we enjoy eating an egg the shell needs to be broken; otherwise we wouldn't be able to get at the white and the yolk. When a chick is ready to live in the big wide world it has to crack the eggshell before it can climb out. What does that tell us? Sometimes we want to hang on to things just as they are. We don't always want to change, even if change in our lives is for the best.

Will we let our shells be broken ready for the new life Jesus wants us to have? God is calling us out of our shells into a whole new, different way of living. It is the loving way of living, trusting in God with our heart and soul and mind and strength, and loving one another. That may mean that some of our habits and fears may, like shells, have to be broken before we can live freely in the loving way. The good news of Easter is that Jesus has already broken through death and sin, so if we hold on to him, he can bring us through the shell breaking and out into the light and space of day – a daylight which lasts for ever.

All-age ideas

- If part of the children's worship on Good Friday has involved art and craft work, such as banners or posters or Easter gardens, these can be used to decorate the church today.

- Make a celebration arch of flowers at the entrance of the church, either by attaching oasis in chicken wire around the doorway, or actually constructing an archway using three ladders, lashed together and fastened securely. Weave plenty of greenery in and out of the ladder rungs to hide the main structure, and then decorate with flowers and ribbons.

- Bells may be rung in a burst of praise, together with the organ or music group at the beginning of the Gloria.

- Rather than a traditional Easter garden, consider a cross made of wire and deadwood, which has flowers in oasis fixed into it.

SECOND SUNDAY OF EASTER

Acts 2:42-47
Psalm 117:2-4, 13-15,
  22-24
1 Peter 1:3-9
John 20:19-31

Through the risen Jesus we have a living hope which will never spoil or fade.

All-age talk

Ask for one volunteer who is brave and one who is more scared and timid. Tell the timid one that you are asking them to fall backwards. You promise them they won't come to any harm (but you don't say you will catch them). Suggest that they watch the brave volunteer to try it first, so they can see what happens. Now ask the brave volunteer to fall backwards, and make sure you catch them, or arrange to have someone strong to catch them.

Now ask if the timid person is able to try it, now that they have seen that it is safe. If they are, let them try it, making certain they are safely caught!

Sometimes it is very hard to know whether we can trust something or not unless we have seen it in action. Perhaps we have bought a tape recorder, or a jigsaw puzzle at a boot sale or a jumble sale, and it looks fine, and we are assured that it's in good working order. But when we get home we find the tape recorder chews up our favourite tape, and the jigsaw puzzle has two or three pieces missing.

It's all very disappointing to be let down like that. And the longer we live, and the more we are let down by things or by people, the more disappointed we get, and the more determined we are not to trust anyone or anything in case we are let down again. Thomas was a bit like that. He had probably been badly let down by people during his life. Like lots of us, it made him scared to trust good news. We and Thomas would love good news to be true, but we'd rather not trust it at all than trust it and risk being let down.

44

Now Jesus himself knows that he is alive, and will stay alive for ever. He knows it would be quite safe for us to believe this, because he knows it's true! He hopes very much that we will be able to believe, because he knows it will make such a wonderful difference to our lives – we'll be able to live in a new kind of freedom, and become more and more our real selves.

So what does he do about it? In our Gospel reading today we heard how Jesus came into the room, joining his friends as they were praying, so that they knew he was there. And Jesus still does that, nearly two thousand years later. He is here now, with us, his friends. Whenever we gather in Jesus' name, he joins us. When we live on the lookout for him, we'll find we start noticing him more and more. We won't see him with our eyes, but we'll feel his love and peace, and suddenly know he is there.

All-age ideas

- Try this short sketch to alert people to the way we don't see what we aren't expecting, or what doesn't seem relevant.

  Phil and Robert are waiting with their coats on at a bus stop. Both have briefcases. Robert is reading his newspaper. Phil is checking his watch.

  Phil   Excuse me, but has the 7:42 gone yet? The 25A?

  Robert   The 25A? I wouldn't know. I'm waiting for the 26. That's the bus I catch.

  Phil   Well, how long have you been waiting?

  Robert   Oh, since 7:40. But it isn't due till 7:50, and it's always late.

  Phil   Is the 7:42 ever late? *(Checks watch.)*

  Robert   I wouldn't know. I wait for the 26, you see.

  Phil   Well, have any other buses come since you've been waiting?

  Robert   Oh yes, there's been a few others, I think.

45

Phil   What numbers were they?

Robert I wouldn't know. I wait for the 26 you see. That's the bus I catch.

Phil   Oh. Thanks. *(Folds arms in resignation and looks the other way.)* Hey there's a bus coming . . . It's the 25A! So I haven't missed it! *(Checks watch.)* And it's only two minutes late. *(Sticks out arm to stop it.)*

Robert The 26 is due at 7:50, you know. That's the bus I catch.

THIRD SUNDAY OF EASTER

Acts 2:14a, 22-28
Psalm 15:1-2, 5, 7-11
1 Peter 1:17-21
Luke 24:13-35

Jesus explains the scriptures and is recognised in the breaking of bread.

All-age talk

Bring in some kind of game or piece of equipment which needs putting together and setting up properly before it can be used. This could be anything from a computer to a folding bed – it all depends on what is available and the interest area of the group. It needs to have a set of instructions to go with it.

Begin by introducing your item of equipment. We are continuing to look at the resurrection stories, when one person after another is astonished by amazing events. The congregation may well be astonished to see one of these brought into church for the sermon! Pretend that you are having a real problem with this thing because you don't understand it at all. You don't understand how to get it to work.

Have a primed helper who comes up at this stage and shows you the instruction leaflet. They tell you that if you read that it will tell you how the thing works and how to use it. Be surprised, but set to reading some of the instructions, without relating them to the equipment. They don't make much sense to you, and you get fed up. It's no good – you don't understand and it doesn't make sense.

Explain that this is rather like the way the two disciples felt as they walked sadly back home on the very first Easter Day. They didn't understand anything any more. They had great hopes about Jesus, but now he was dead, so their hopes were dead as well. They had heard about the women saying they had seen Jesus alive early that morning, but that didn't make any sense to them either. How on earth could someone be dead as dead and now be alive? It couldn't possibly be true!

47

Just then, as we read in today's Gospel, someone joined them and asked what they were so sad about. And when they told him, he started to show them how it actually did make a lot of sense. (Break off as the helper comes and offers to take you through the instructions and sort the equipment out. Accept their help and marvel as gradually, step by step, it starts to come together, and eventually works. Be excited about this and thank the helper. Then come back to the Emmaus story.)

Well, it certainly helps to have someone who really understands to help you when you are in a muddle! That's how those disciples felt when the stranger explained that it was all there in the scriptures (pick up a Bible) about the promised Messiah having to suffer and die before there could be new life. When they reached their home they invited the helpful stranger in to stay with them, and when their guest took the bread and blessed and broke it (mime this) . . . what do you think they suddenly realised?

It was Jesus!

And that is still what Jesus does. He walks along with us where we are walking. He helps us understand about God through the words of scripture (pick up the Bible again), he helps us make sense of life and its problems (stand beside the working piece of equipment), and (move to the altar) he makes himself known to us in the breaking of bread.

All-age ideas

- Have the Gospel mimed as it is narrated, using the centre aisle as the road and the sanctuary as the house, so that the breaking of bread is mimed at the altar. Have Jesus wearing an alb so that the links are there with the breaking of the bread in the Eucharist.

- Have a display of Bible reading notes and various Bibles suitable for different age groups, so as to encourage people to get to know the scriptures better and deepen their understanding.

FOURTH SUNDAY OF EASTER

Acts 2:14, 36-41
Psalm 22:1-6
1 Peter 2:20-28
John 10:1-10

Jesus, the Good Shepherd, has come so that we may have life in rich abundance.

All-age talk

Using chairs, build a circular sheepfold, with a gap for the entrance. Ask for some volunteer sheep to go inside. Explain that this is what a sheepfold was like in Jesus' day, except that it was made of stones, not chairs. Is there a door? No, there isn't. That's because the shepherd himself was the door. Ask a volunteer shepherd to come and be the door of the sheepfold. (You could even give the shepherd a stick or crook from the Nativity costumes, and a shepherd's sling.) Why is this living door likely to be a good safe one for the sheep? Because the shepherd would hear any dangers, such as wolves, or bears, or sheep stealers, and take action to protect the sheep, using his staff or sling. (The shepherd can pretend to frighten off a dangerous wolf.)

Another thing about sheep is that they get very frightened by lots of things, but when they hear the voice of the shepherd at the door they know they can trust him, and they feel safe. They will even follow him when he calls them and leads them off to some good juicy grass. (The sheep can try this.) And then they will follow the shepherd back home at the end of the day. (They do this.)

Now why are we getting a lesson in sheep farming this morning? What has all this got to do with Jesus? Or us?

In the Gospel today we hear Jesus telling the people that he is the sheep-door. (And you know what that means, now.) He told them all about the sheep being safe when the shepherd is the door, and the sheep knowing the shepherd's voice and following him. (You know about that too.) But the

49

people didn't have a clue why Jesus was talking to them about sheep and shepherds. So they asked him to explain.

Jesus said he was trying to tell them something important about God. (Can anyone think what it was?) He was telling the people that they were a bit like sheep and Jesus was like the good shepherd who lies down in the doorway to keep the sheep safe. He was saying that God looks after us and defends us with his life because he loves us so much. He hates the thought of us coming to harm, and fights off evil. We can trust God's voice when he calls us, and follow him without any fear because we know God is always faithful and good and loving.

So whenever you are scared to face a bad problem, or bad ideas and temptations keep coming at you, stand there in the sheepfold behind Jesus, the sheep-door, and you will be safe. And whenever you are muddled about whether to do something or not, or whether to be selfish or not, listen out for the quiet calling of the Good Shepherd (you won't hear it with your ears, but you will know it in yourself) and follow him into the way that is right and good and kind and loving.

All-age ideas

• Include some model or toy sheep and lambs, or a shepherd's crook in one of the flower arrangements, which could make use of wild meadow flowers and grasses.

• Consider making a parish photograph album, scrap book or a video which aims to capture something of the real Christian identity of your church community, based on the portrait of the Early Church given to us in Acts. This may well be a year-long or an ongoing project, and could include prayers and excerpts from special service sheets, as well as pictures.

FIFTH SUNDAY OF EASTER

Acts 6:1-7
Psalm 32:1-2, 4-5,
  18-19
1 Peter 2:4-9
John 14:1-12

Jesus is the Way, the Truth and the Life, through whom we can come into the presence of God for ever.

All-age talk

Ask two or three experts to come and explain the way they do whatever it is they are good at. (The actual areas of expertise depend on the interests of your congregation, but try and choose people from representative age and interest groups. The skill should be capable of being demonstrated in front of everyone, so it could be ironing, juggling, dribbling a football, doing a cartwheel or skipping, for example.)

First ask each one to explain it to you, placing them out of sight of everyone as they do so. Share with the group how it all sounds incredibly complicated, and difficult to follow, even though it is obviously expert advice. That's rather how it is with the Old Testament Law – everyone respects it highly and it's very good advice for living, but somehow we never seem to manage to follow the instructions or get the hang of them. They help us to know how to live a good life, but they don't change us so that we are able to do it. Some of the prophets had told everyone that one day it would be different. People wouldn't need those instructions any more, because they would already know, in their hearts, how to behave properly.

Let's find out if we can understand our experts any better if we can actually see them doing these clever things. (Invite them to demonstrate, one by one.) Ah, that's much clearer! We may not be able to do it ourselves, yet, but at least we have their example in front of us, to learn from and copy. (Someone might like to try copying one of the skills.)

When Jesus came, it was like being able to see God's way of living – in person. 'So that's what it

51

means to love God and love one another!' people thought. 'So that's what God's love for us is like!' And even though we may not yet be able to do it very well, at least we have a wonderful example to learn from and copy.

If we're still full of bitterness about something that happened to us long ago, we can look at Jesus and copy his forgiving. If we're looking down on someone because they aren't as clever or rich as us, we can look at Jesus and copy his way of enjoying people and accepting them for what they are. If we are always worrying about clothes and possessions, we can look at Jesus and copy his simple way of living, and spend our energy cultivating the treasures that we can take with us to heaven. So Jesus is like a living 'Way' – he's a walking, talking Way to live.

In fact that's what Jesus called himself in our Gospel today; he said, 'I am the Way, the Truth and the Life'. With Jesus we go one better than having his example to copy – since the Resurrection we can have his life living in us! That would be rather like our experts being able to fill us with all that makes them able to do those clever things. Imagine what a skilled parish we would be if that were possible! We'd all be expert ironers, football dribblers, jugglers and cartwheelers! Well, I have to tell you that we can't do that. As humans we have to pass on our skills the hard way, by teaching and learning. But with Jesus it's different. He really can live in our lives, enabling us to love God and one another. All we need to do is invite him into our personal lives and our church, and be prepared to be gradually transformed.

All-age ideas

- On a wall or pillar display a very large speech bubble made of paper, on which is written: Lord Jesus, receive my spirit!

- Incorporate rocks and stones and a builder's trowel in one of the flower arrangements today.

SIXTH SUNDAY OF EASTER

Acts 8:5-8, 14-17
Psalm 65:1-7, 16, 20
1 Peter 3:15-18
John 14:15-21

The Spirit of truth, given to us, enables us to discern the living, risen Christ.

All-age talk

Start by displaying a fairly simple equation, such as $2x+3=x+10$, or $y(5+2)=21$, or $x+4=6$ (difficulty depends on your group), perhaps on a blackboard. Provide chalk, and ask someone mathematical to take us through the stages of solving the mystery of this unknown value of x or y.

When we tried to solve our x mystery, we worked it out, step by step, gradually getting a clearer idea of what x meant, until, in the end, it was quite clear to us (or some of us!).

That's rather like the way we can look at the beauty and order of our world, and all the physics and chemistry of it, and all the variety and colour and shape in it, and begin to work our way towards discovering what God is like. We can work out that he must be clever and thoughtful, and imaginative and faithful, for instance.

But with Jesus coming, and showing us exactly what God is like, it's more like this.

Set up the same equation as before, using solid shapes, like building blocks. Each x is a bag, filled with the correct number of blocks. We could still work out what x is, but if the bag is opened, we can actually see what it is. (Do this.)

With Jesus' life there in front of us through reading the Gospels, and through living in his company every day, we can have a very clear idea of what God is like. We can see that he is forgiving and totally honest and good, that he is responsible and stands up for what is right, whatever happens to him and however much people sneer. We can see that he looks for the good in people and doesn't condemn them or give up on them. We can see that his love has been proved stronger than death.

If we put our faith in that God, whom Jesus has revealed to us in a new and clear way, and if we claim to love him, then we will have to start doing what he says. Who finds it easy to be obedient? Most of us find it very hard. We don't want to do what we are told; we want to do what we like!

Jesus says that the way you can tell if someone really does believe in him and love him, is by whether they are obedient to him, and obey what he says. That means listening to God and saying yes to him, whether it's what we want to do or not.

That is a *very hard* thing to learn, but it's worth learning, because being friends with Jesus is the best and happiest thing that could ever happen to us.

All-age ideas

- Have a group of dancers (these can be mixed ages and gender) to work on expressing in movement the truth that we are brought through the waters of death into new life, and given the guiding Spirit of Truth to lead us onwards. They could use waving silver and blue cloth or streamers to represent the flood water as they pass through. They need to make it clear that they are turning their backs on the old life, and going willingly into this 'drowning', from which they emerge, with the Spirit to hold their hands and guide them, first to an attitude of praise and worship, and then out, through the congregation. Suitable music would be something like *Amazing grace*.

- If you have an OHP, make up an acetate which has in the centre: 'Our God is . . .', and invite people to tell you characteristics about God that they know to be true. Write the suggestions up and then invite everyone, in their own time and order, to read out these truths – Our God is faithful, our God is forgiving . . . – so that there is a general noise of praising God for who he is. As the voices die away, finish by a single voice saying just the centre words: 'Our God is. Amen.'

THE ASCENSION OF THE LORD

Acts 1:1-11
Psalm 46:2-3, 6-9
Ephesians 1:17-23
Matthew 28:16-20

Having bought back our freedom with the giving of his life, Jesus enters into the full glory to which he is entitled.

All-age talk

Imagine staging a Mexican wave, which runs through the whole church. Point out how it could only work well because all of us as individuals would work together as a unit of energy.

Remind everyone of the events leading up to today, giving them a whistle-stop tour of Jesus' life, death, Resurrection and post-Resurrection appearances. Explain how the disciples needed that time to get used to Jesus being alive and around, though not always visible or physically present.

Now they were ready for the next stage in the plan. Jesus leads them out of the city and he gives them his blessing, telling them to hang around Jerusalem without rushing off to do their own bit of mission work. (Enthusiasm is wonderful but it can sometimes make us race off to start before we've got everything we need.) The disciples have got to wait because God is going to send the Holy Spirit to empower them and equip them for the work they will be doing. It will make it possible for the news of God's love to spread out through the world like our Mexican wave.

When Jesus had finished giving the disciples their instructions and his encouragement, we are told that the disciples watched him being taken into heaven, until a cloud hid him from their sight. Those are the only practical details we have, so we don't know exactly how it happened. But we do know that the disciples were in no doubt about where Jesus had gone, and they were full of joy and excitement as they made their way back to the city to wait for the Holy Spirit, as Jesus had told them to.

55

A lot of years have gone by since Jesus ascended into heaven – nearly two thousand years. But that isn't much if you aren't stuck in time as we are, and God isn't stuck in time. He's prepared to wait to give us humans the chance to turn to him in our lives, and we don't know the date when Jesus will return. We do know that in God's good time he will come back, and everyone will see his glory together, both the living and those who have finished the earthly part of their life.

In the meantime, we have been given the Holy Spirit, so that God can be with us in person every moment of our life, helping us and guiding our choices, steering us safely through temptations, and teaching us more and more about our amazing God. All he waits for is to be invited.

All-age ideas

- Any artwork or writing that the children have done on what the Ascension is about can be displayed around the building.

- Have a beautiful helium balloon at the ready. Write on it an Ascension message that the children would like to send. After the service two representative children can let the balloon float away.

Seventh Sunday of Easter

Acts 1:12-14
Psalm 26:1, 4, 7-8
1 Peter 4:13-16
John 17:1-11

God's glory is often revealed in the context of suffering and failure in the world's eyes.

All-age talk

Before the talk, use the short sketch in the all-age ideas section.

Begin by talking about saying goodbye. The kind of goodbye it is depends on how well we know each other, whether we love or hate each other, and whether we are saying goodbye for a short time, a long time or for ever. Today in our first reading we were with the disciples as Jesus said goodbye to them. Since Easter we have been looking at various times when he had been meeting up with them after the Resurrection. Sometimes he had met them when they were all together, sometimes on their own. They would suddenly recognise him, or he would suddenly be there among them, and the disciples had begun to get used to Jesus being with them even when they couldn't see him with their eyes.

Now, here they are, all together with Jesus, and this is going to be their last goodbye to him as a person whom they see with their eyes, because he is going back to heaven. He tells them two things: (show a picture of rushing wind and flames) that they are going to be given power when the Holy Spirit comes upon them, and (show a picture of an empty speech bubble) that they are going to tell lots of people all over the world about the Jesus they know and love so well.

Then we are told that he was lifted up, while they watched, and a cloud took him from their sight so that they couldn't see him any more. So they stood there, peering up into the sky, rather like you do when you've just let a balloon go, and you watch and watch until you can't see it any more. What happened next?

They realised that two people, dressed in white, were standing next to them. 'Why are you standing here looking up into the sky?' they asked. They told the disciples that one day Jesus would come in the same way they had seen him go. But what they wanted them to know was that there wasn't any point in hanging around in that one place for a glimpse of Jesus, because he had gone on to the next phase, where he would be with all his friends, including us, all the time, not in a way that we can see, but in new ways. Just as real, just as much alive, but in a form which makes him free to be in all kinds of different countries and places and dates and times all at once!

What he said to the disciples that day, he says to us as well: we will be given power when the Holy Spirit comes upon us (show the first picture again) and we are going to tell lots of people about the Jesus we know and love (show the second picture).

All-age ideas

- *A goodbye sketch.* This works with either a number of different pairs of people, of different ages and gender, or one pair who keep changing style and props. They simply walk on, say goodbye (it can be a wordy or a one-word goodbye) and walk off, but in several different roles. Here are some suggestions:

  1. A mother and her son at his first day at school.
  2. Lovers at a station.
  3. Host and unwelcome visitor who has overstayed his welcome.
  4. Two friends after school.
  5. Daughter with well-loved elderly parent in hospital or nursing home.

- Incorporate some horse chestnut blossom in one of the flower arrangements. It is traditionally known as the candle tree, in flower to celebrate the Ascension.

PENTECOST

Acts 2:1-11
Psalm 103:1, 24, 29-31
1 Corinthians 12:3-7,
   12-13
John 20:19-23

With great power the Spirit of God is poured out on the expectant disciples.

All-age talk

Bring along an electrical appliance and, if necessary, an extension lead. Alternatively, have a torch or game powered by batteries, and keep the batteries separate at first.

Refresh everyone's memory of today's dynamic event, with the disciples praying and waiting on God, and the early morning experience of his power coming to them like a rushing wind, or flames, searching out each one of them and touching them with the touch of God.

It quite overwhelmed them, and left them fired up with excitement at what God is capable of doing in people. They were bursting to tell everyone else about it, and wanted everyone to share this sense of God actually living in them. It was quite different from knowing about God; it was even different from walking about in the company of Jesus. This was like being flowed through with new life that set them living, talking and working in a new way.

Show the electrical appliance you have brought. Explain what this thing is capable of doing, but point out that at the moment it can't do any of those things. It has everything in place to work in that lively way, but something is missing at the moment – it isn't linked up to the power supply. Would it help if the appliance knew exactly how electricity works? Not really. However much is known about electrical circuits and the power grid, that won't bring this appliance to life. What it needs is this. (Plug the appliance into the power supply and switch on.)

Now the thing springs into life, and all kinds of

potential are activated. That's what it's like having God's Spirit living in us and flowing through us. It makes that much difference! Just think what our world could be like if we were all full of the power of God's Spirit. Just think what a difference it would make in the world if all those in churches today all over the world asked God, seriously and openly, for a fresh outpouring of the Holy Spirit!

So often we are like well-finished appliances or games, knowing all about God's power, but not wanting to have the power switched on in us, just in case. Just in case what? Our God is the true, living God of love and compassion and mercy. Which means that any power he sends to touch us and affect us, will be only and entirely good for us. God is longing for his Church to be 'live' with the active power of his Spirit; we may be in good working order, but we also need to have the power, so that we actually 'work'!

All-age ideas

- This is a day to bring out those flame-coloured banners, flags and streamers.

- Lots of flame and white colours in the flower arrangements, with the swirling sense of movement and power.

TRINITY SUNDAY

Exodus 34:4-6, 8-9
Daniel 3:52-56
2 Corinthians 13:11-13
John 3:16-18

The mystery of God – Creator, Redeemer and Sanctifier all at once – is beyond our human understanding, yet closer to us than breathing.

All-age talk

Produce a jacket or sweater of a young child's size, and invite a much larger volunteer to get into it. (It should be obvious that they won't be able to, even though they try.) Agree that it is impossible to get Ben into Justin's jacket – he's simply too big to fit!

Sometimes we expect God to be able to fit into our human-sized minds. We start to think about God, and say things like, 'But how can he possibly be able to hear us all praying at once?' when what we really mean is that we know humans couldn't do that, so it must be impossible for God as well. Or we say, 'God *must* have had a beginning sometime, because *everything* does!'

When we do this we are holding out a small human shape (hold out the little jacket) and expecting God to climb into it. And of course he doesn't fit, because being God is much bigger and deeper and wider than being a human being. God is so great that he is always going to be full of wonderful mystery for us, however much we learn about him. As humans we cannot hold his nature and understand it, any more than this small jacket will hold a big boy like Ben.

So does that mean that we can't really know God? Not at all! Invite Ben and Justin to come up and shake hands, and say hello to each other. You could have Ben asking Justin some questions, so that everyone can see that both boys are able to have a conversation.

Just because God is God and you are human

doesn't mean you can't be good friends. There are lots of people here today who talk with God every day (it's called praying) and know that he is the person they love and trust best in their whole life.

We have been given a lifetime to get to know God really well and live as his friends. Sometimes we waste that time, and sometimes we suddenly realise that nothing else is quite so important. Sometimes we don't bother to tell other people about our loving God, or we let our behaviour tell them that we don't think he is worth very much at all. And other times we feel such love for our God that we can't wait to let other people know about him. And then our loving behaviour tells them as well as our words.

Our God is wonderful and all-knowing. He is the maker of our universe and of us all, he is the one who came as Jesus to die for love of us and save us, and he is present with his people, living in us as the Holy Spirit. How could we possibly ever expect to completely understand a God as amazing as that!

God being so great that he is full of holy mystery should make us excited, not frustrated. Let's enjoy being friends with the God who is so amazing that no human can ever explain what he is really like! And let's lavish our worship on him; any god smaller, or knowable, wouldn't be worth worshipping anyway.

All-age ideas

- Have a length of lining paper on which are drawn several outlines of a Celtic expression of the Trinity, shown opposite. Provide green crayons and invite some people (they do not have to be children – adults would benefit from it just as much) to come and draw round the lines continuously, following their path of inter-relatedness so that they sense, rather than understand, the harmonious community of the One God. This could be done during the singing of *St Patrick's breastplate (I bind unto myself today)*.

- In the flower arrangements use evergreen for eternity, shamrock and clover leaves, and three colours blending in and out of one another to make a unified whole.

CORPUS CHRISTI

Deuteronomy 8:2-3,
  14-16
Psalm 147
1 Corinthians 10:16-17
John 6:51-58

Jesus Christ is the living bread; as we feed on him we share his life.

All-age talk

Bring along some examples of junk food, such as crisps and sweets and various snacks. Talk about how many of us enjoy eating this kind of thing, and read out some of the ingredients. Although we like eating them, they have very little real food value, and if we tried to live entirely on junk food our health would soon suffer.

For our bodies to grow and repair and be kept in good working order, we need good, wholesome feeding at regular intervals. Give some examples of 'real' meals, and ask others for examples of their favourites. We can feel the difference when we are properly nourished; we have more energy, and we don't find ourselves needing so many snacks between meals.

Sadly, there are many living today in areas of drought and war who are not able to give their children adequate feeding, and must watch them growing weak from lack of nourishment. Good feeding is a shared responsibility, and we cannot pray, 'Give us this day our daily bread' with any real meaning unless we are doing all we can to right the injustices and wrongs which make for terrible hunger and the suffering of starvation.

Our need for spiritual feeding is just as urgent and vital. In our world we are offered lots of spiritual junk food, and many try to survive on this. The sentimental and tinselled religion of Christmas and the themed chocolate eggs and cards with baby rabbits and lambs at Easter are the only spiritual feeding many are getting. Other things, like human relationships, music and art, football and shopping,

64

may be good in their own way but make poor value substitutes when they are used as spiritual food.

What God offers us is *real* food – feeding which will nourish and sustain us in our life with all that we have to face in the way of problems and sorrows, joys and challenges. This feeding provides for our deep spiritual needs so that we can journey through life well fed, with spiritual energy and inner resources to deal with the problems. This feeding is nothing less than being fed with Christ, who loved us so much he was ready to die for us. As we share the bread and wine, we are nourished with his life and love and forgiveness and hope. That is real feeding.

All-age ideas

• Make a flower arrangement around a loaf of bread and a carafe of wine, with some grapes and wheat amongst the flowers.

• Read the last two paragraphs from Donald Nicholl's book, *The testing of hearts*.

SECOND SUNDAY OF THE YEAR

Isaiah 49:3, 5-6
Psalm 39:2, 4, 7-10
1 Corinthians 1:1-3
John 1:29-34

Jesus is recognised and pointed out by John to be God's chosen one.

All-age talk

Start by hiding some treasure while a volunteer 'seeker' covers their eyes. Everyone else needs to know where it is hidden. Now set the treasure-seeker off to search, with everyone else guiding them by calling out whether they are colder or hotter. With all this help it shouldn't take too long for the seeker to find.

Lots of people are truth-seekers. They want to find out the truth about life and about God and about the reason we are here. These are the deep questions that humans have always asked, and it is important that we ask them. Questions are good things; never stop asking them, just because you're grown up. Grown-ups need to learn from the children here – children are very good at asking important questions!

When we are seeking for the truth about God, it helps if there are people who have already found him, who are happy to tell us when we're getting nearer or drifting further away. John the Baptist is one of those who is calling out to us, 'Warmer! You're getting warmer . . . you're boiling hot!' That's what he was doing to his disciples when Jesus came by. 'Look!' he said. 'That's the one I was telling you about – this is the one you've been waiting for! This is the Son of God!'

Think about whether you ever help other people find the truth about God. Think about whether other people help you, and how they do it. And if you don't think you've been doing much helping, today's readings are giving you some ideas as to how to start:

- telling people what you have noticed and found out about God;

- mentioning that he's worth spending time with;
- suggesting that they come with you to find out more;
- and introducing them to God by the way you live.

All-age ideas

- Have a display of different Bible reading schemes for people to browse through and order after the service.

THIRD SUNDAY OF THE YEAR

Isaiah 8:23-9:3
Psalm 26:1, 4, 13-14
1 Corinthians 1:10-13, 17
Matthew 4:12-23

The prophecies of Isaiah are fulfilled in a new and lasting way in Jesus of Nazareth.

All-age talk

Out of strong card (or a wooden broom handle) make a demonstration yoke to show, on a brave volunteer, how conquerors used to subdue their captives. When you release the volunteer captive, talk to them about how good it feels to be free of the yoke.

Explain how in our first reading today we heard from a man called Isaiah. He was a prophet – someone who clearly speaks out God's words to the people. At the time, the people he was speaking to were being threatened by another country. It looked as if Assyria might well come and yoke the people up as captives, and take them far away from their own homes and their temple and their country, to live in exile in the country of their conquerors.

Isaiah showed the people that if they went on turning away from him by treating the poor unfairly, and spoiling themselves while others starved, then God would not save them from this attack. They were already 'yoked' up as slaves to their greed and selfishness, and their worries about the Assyrians.

Through Isaiah the prophet, God spoke to his people. He told them that he loved them, and that he longed for them to sort their lives out and trust him again. God would then be able to look after them and keep them and their holy city of Jerusalem safe. It would be like their yokes being broken in pieces, so they would be completely free.

Show the demonstration yoke again on another volunteer. Do any of us wear invisible yokes and need to be set free? We may be wearing yokes of selfishness, or resentment; we may be always wishing for things we can't have. We may still feel guilty about something we did. We may need healing of some emotional damage which is holding us back from living freely.

Jesus came so that we could be set free from all these yokes. He's an expert 'yoke shatterer'! He's the kind of light that makes all the darkness in our lives and minds and hearts disappear. If we let him in to walk around our own lives, as well as the lake of Galilee, he will set us free from all those yokes that hold us captive. And then we'll be able to walk through life with a new spring in our step, full of hope.

All-age ideas

- Gather as mixed a group as possible to work on this mime about Jesus setting captives free. First have the line of captives, wearing card yokes and roped together, walking dejectedly up the aisle, sometimes flinching as if from a captor's whip. At the front of the church stands the Christ figure with arms outstretched, both in welcome to the captives and also in the shape of a cross. As the others approach they stretch out their hands towards the human cross, and begin to line themselves up against its shape. As they do this the Christ figure unties their yoke and sets them free. Eventually the captives are helping each other until all are free. Then all stretch out their arms (this time because they want to, and not because the yoke makes them) towards one another and the whole congregation.

- Have a light arrangement, rather than a flower arrangement, using lots of different containers and candles, perhaps in conjunction with a mirror.

- Use this prayer of penitence:
  All Father, forgive us, for we have sinned.
  A Into the darkness of our selfishness
  All shine with the light of love.
  B Into the darkness of our thoughtlessness
  All shine with the light of love.
  A Into the darkness of our unkindness
  All shine with the light of love.
  B Into the darkness of our greed
  All shine with the light of love.
  Father, forgive us, for we have sinned.

FOURTH SUNDAY OF THE YEAR

Zephaniah 2:3;
   3:12-13
Psalm 145
1 Corinthians 1:26-31
Matthew 5:1-12

Happy are the poor in spirit, who are aware of their need of God.

All-age talk

You will need a jug of water, a tumbler and a bowl. Have these hidden (not too well!) in different places around the church.

Begin by reminding everyone of the words of the prophet Zephaniah, telling us to seek or search for the Lord in our lives. If we are going to search for something, it helps to know what we are looking for, and the prophet suggests seeking God's ways, like truth and humility. Hidden around the church are three things to be found. We'll ask three people to seek them, and, to make it easier, we'll tell them what they are looking for. (Tell one to look for each item. While they are looking, ask everyone to notice how they search.)

When the volunteers return with the objects, collect observations about how they searched, with their eyes looking around, with concentration and attention on the task, listening out for helpful clues from the congregation. That's how we are to seek for God, giving the job our full attention and concentration, and listening out for helpful clues from one another and from the Bible and other books. That way we will be sure to find him and get to know more about what God is really like.

As we get to know God better we shall start to realise that we need that godly love very badly. It's as if we are empty tumblers coming to be filled up with God's life and love. (Ask one of the volunteers to hold the empty tumbler as you pour water into it.) We can pass that love on to the world (pour the tumbler of water into the large bowl) and the more

70

of us there are doing that, the more full of God's love the world will be.

But sometimes we don't realise we need filling with God's love; that's like putting our hand over the top of the tumbler when God offers to fill us and saying, 'No, thanks, I'm full already.' We block ourselves off from receiving God's gifts to us if we think we don't need them. That's why Jesus said in today's Gospel, 'How happy are the poor in spirit' – those who know their need of God. As soon as we know our need of God, we shall come to him in our emptiness, without our hands in the way (the volunteer removes his hand), and God can fill us up with goodness and love, truth and wisdom, courage and strength (fill the tumbler up again as you speak), not just for our good, but the good of the whole world.

All-age ideas

- Use the following alternative to the Penitential Rite:
  We have failed to seek you with our whole heart;
  Lord, have mercy
  Lord, have mercy.
  We have failed to recognise how much we need you;
  Christ, have mercy
  Christ, have mercy.
  We come to you now in our emptiness and need;
  Lord, have mercy
  Lord, have mercy.

- Have some very small, simple arrangements of wild flowers with the Beatitudes printed beside them.

FIFTH SUNDAY OF THE YEAR

Isaiah 58:7-10
Psalm 111:4-9
1 Corinthians 2:1-5
Matthew 5:13-16

We are commissioned to live so that we shine like lights which direct others on to God, the source of Light.

All-age talk

You will need a large saucepan, a pack of spaghetti, a jar of Italian sauce and a large carton of salt, a jug, a teacup and a tablespoon. You will also need a table lamp and a bright spotlight.

Produce the first set of items, setting them out and talking about cooking pasta. Invite a good cook from the congregation to supervise! Explain that the best cookery books say that pasta can't be seasoned after it's cooked, so we need to add the salt to the cooking water. Pick up the salt, and wonder aloud how much salt to use. A jugful? Get the cook to explain what would happen if you put in that much salt. A teacupful? Still too much! A tablespoonful? Still too much. If we use that much all we will taste will be the salt, and the whole idea of salt is that it isn't really noticed but brings out the flavour of the other ingredients.

That's what we are called to do as Christians: not to take over and dominate or possess people, or want to control them, but in humility to make ourselves available and useful in helping to give other people the freedom and the confidence to be themselves. That may mean more listening and less speaking; it may mean being less concerned about being thought important and more concerned about other people's needs being recognised. It is the way of quiet, loving service.

Now flash the spotlight around so that it goes in people's eyes (but don't overdo this!). Explain that Jesus also calls us to be light. That doesn't mean trying to blind people with our natural brilliance, or trying subtly to impress others, so that we're

72

more like disco lights, designed for a flashy effect. The kind of light we are called to be is a much more practical sort, rather like a table lamp, perhaps, which simply helps people to see better, so they don't bump into things and hurt themselves, and so they can get on with living more effectively.

Salt and light are just simple things, but they are things which can make a great difference. As Christians we are called to be like that – just our ordinary selves, but through our faith in God, able to make a difference.

All-age ideas

- Have a salt mill and a table lamp included in one of the flower arrangements today.

- Read the Isaiah passage chorally, with a group of men, women and children.

- Include actions with this penitential meditation:

  We have used our words selfishly.
  (touch lips)
  We are sorry. Lord, have mercy.
  We have used our hands selfishly.
  (look at open hands)
  We are sorry. Christ, have mercy.
  We have used our minds to think selfishly.
  (touch heads)
  We are sorry. Lord, have mercy.

SIXTH SUNDAY OF THE YEAR

Ecclesiasticus 15:15-20
Psalm 118:1-2, 4-5,
    17-18, 33-34
1 Corinthians 2:6-10
Matthew 5:17-37

To live God's way is to choose the way of life.

All-age talk

Begin by drawing attention to the direction everyone is facing in church. Obviously this will vary according to your architecture and the age of the building. The architecture reflects a focus and a general direction which the planners thought of most importance. Perhaps if you were all about to start planning from scratch, you might arrange things slightly differently!

Once you have established the general seating focus, move to another part of the church, such as the baptistry. If people are going to continue facing you, they will all have to turn round. That is because at the moment the important thing going on is you speaking, and that takes over in importance from the general focus of the building.

Now move somewhere else so that everyone has to turn round again. Today we heard Jesus teaching about the Law, which is summed up in the ten commandments. Have these displayed on card, or on an OHP, or walk to the part of the church where they are written on the wall. They are good rules to live by and our whole law system is still based on them. But with all rules there is a problem. Jesus wanted his followers (and that includes us) to remember that the really important thing is to stay focused on God in everything we do.

Perhaps you haven't ever killed someone. But the spirit of the law means more than that, just as our focus is more than just sitting facing the front. It also means making sure we haven't got unkind or destructive thoughts about people, that we're

74

not making people feel stupid or useless, that we aren't putting other people down or running them down behind their backs, because those things are in the destructive spirit of hate, which is the opposite of God's law of love. As you mention each of these, move around the building so people have to move their 'attitudes' to see you.

What we need to do is keep our eyes fixed on Jesus, and whatever we are doing we can think to ourselves, 'Does this thing I'm doing or saying or thinking make Jesus happy? Is it a loving thing to do or think or say?'

And if it is, carry on. If it isn't, stop and change direction.

All-age ideas

- Have two people standing in different places in the church, calling out the following contrasting attitudes alternately:

I want!

What do you need?

Me first!

Let's share!

Why should I?

I'll help!

I believe in freedom so I can do whatever I like!

If we think of one another we can all be free!

You've got to look after number one. Never mind anyone else.

Love God – and love your neighbour as yourself.

This is the way of death.

This is the way of life.

- Fix to the floor four footprints with the letters L, I, F and E on them, so that people can read them as they come in.

SEVENTH SUNDAY OF THE YEAR

Leviticus 19:1-2, 17-18
Psalm 102:1-4, 8, 10,
    12-13
1 Corinthians 3:16-23
Matthew 5:38-48

We are called to be holy; to be perfect in our generous loving, because that is what God our Father is like.

All-age talk

Bring along a rubber stamp and ink pad, making sure it isn't permanent ink. Begin by putting the stamp on a number of volunteers. Talk about the way we sometimes get stamped at theme parks or discos to show that we have a right to be there because we have paid our entrance fee.

When we are baptised we have the sign of Jesus Christ marked on our foreheads. (What is that sign? It's the cross.) It's as if we've got God's stamp on us. (You could get everyone to trace a cross on their foreheads with their thumb to feel it freshly.) We are marked out as his children, whether we are one-day-old children, twenty-three-year-old children or ninety-seven-year-old children, and we have been freely given the right to belong in God's kingdom, which is a kingdom full of love and peace and joy, patience and kindness, goodness, gentleness and self-control.

As well as us belonging in God's kingdom, God's kingdom now belongs in us! As we've got God's stamp on us we will be wanting to behave like him, and he will help us to do that. Our behaviour will then be a visible sign to other people that we really do belong to God as his children. When they see us being honest and kind and patient and joyful, loving and working for peace and justice, they will be able to say, 'That must be a child of God – look how generous he is, even when he isn't going to gain anything by it!' And, 'That must be a child of God – look how loving she is with those difficult people!'

The whole point is this: we don't work to behave

nicely so that God will love us. We don't need to do that, and we can't ever earn his love anyway. God simply loves us! He thinks we're really special, and he always wants the best for us.

When we love him back, and let him work in us, we will find we are beginning to behave more like our God. The closer we get to God, the more generous loving we will find ourselves doing. Instead of looking out for what we can get all the time, we'll find we're looking out eagerly for ways we can give instead! Instead of making sure we are doing whatever *we* want, we'll find we are looking to check if other people are OK. And that is actually a much happier and more fulfilling way to live.

All-age ideas

- Print out in large letters: 'Love your friends, hate your enemies!' with a line crossing through the second part and the alteration written in: 'Love your enemies too!'

- Express God's extravagant generosity by having some lavish flower arrangements with garlands and cascades.

EIGHTH SUNDAY OF THE YEAR

Isaiah 49:14-15
Psalm 61:2-3, 6-9
1 Corinthians 4:1-5
Matthew 6:24-34

God is creative and good; seeking his rule, as our priority, will mean that everything else falls into place.

All-age talk

Beforehand prepare some large speech bubbles from thin card, with the typical worries of those in the congregation written clearly on them. Here are some suggestions:

- My hair's going grey/thin on top!
- What can I wear?
- Weetabix or cocopops or toast?
- Suppose they don't like me?
- Brut or Denim – and how much of it?
- I'm the wrong shape!

Ask some volunteers to hold these worries up high. They're the kind of things we all waste our time and energy worrying about. Jesus was sad to see people worrying their lives away, and he wanted them to be free of this constant worrying. Point out that the volunteers will start to get aching arms if they have to go on holding the worries up for too long.

In our Gospel reading today Matthew tells us that Jesus says to us, 'Put all those worries down – they're heavy to carry and are making your arms ache.' Let the volunteers put the worries down, and talk about what a relief it is to have our worries sorted out.

Jesus wants us to know that although life is bound to be full of difficult and uncomfortable times as well as easy and happy times, we don't need to worry about it as well as live through it! That makes it twice as bad for us. The way to be free of worry is not to be massively rich or refuse to grow up, or bury your head in the sand and pretend not to see the problems. The way to be free of worrying yourself sick is to trust that your Parent God loves you, likes you, and is well able to help you cope with everything you'll face in your life.

Jesus suggests we live one day at a time, instead of worrying about things that might never happen, or which are bound to happen, and God will bring us safely through it all to heaven, where we will be safe with God for ever.

All-age ideas

- To celebrate the way God looks after us as a loving parent, have a display of photographs showing young children being fed, washed, cared for and played with; young children simply being absorbed and happy in what they're doing. Mount them all on the wall or on a display board and have various scriptures written out among the pictures. Here are some possible texts to use: Matthew 6:9, Genesis 1:27, Genesis 1:31, 1 Corinthians 3:16.

- Have some banners or posters illustrating God's creative love displayed on banners or the wall, and flower arrangements that include fruit and vegetables.

NINTH SUNDAY OF THE YEAR

Deuteronomy 11:18,
    26-28
Psalm 30:2-4, 17, 25
Romans 3:21-25, 28
Matthew 7:21-27

*Wise listeners build their lives up on
the strong rock of the word of God.*

All-age talk

Set up some young children and an adult or two to
build with Lego, building blocks or a variety of
cartons. Draw attention to the building they are
involved with and explain that today we have heard
Jesus advising us on a wise building policy in our
lives. We are also concerned that we do as much as
possible to ensure that our faith is passed on faithfully to our young children, and their children yet
to come. Having them building here in front of us
will serve as a memory jogger to remind us both of
our life building, and our responsibility to the
young ones entrusted to our care.

The passage from Deuteronomy goes on to talk
about passing on our faith. We are not to expect
our children to pick up the faith all by themselves –
we are to talk to them about it in all kinds of situations, so that they get to realise that it is relevant
and valuable, of great importance for the whole of
life. What does that mean in practice?

- It means that our children will not see God as the
  firm, secure rock he is unless they see the adults
  around them trusting that rock and building
  their lives on it. They need to see adults living
  their faith, every day of the week.

- It means that if our children see the adults in
  their Christian community saying they believe
  in God, coming to church and behaving in ways
  which are selfish, prejudiced, unforgiving or
  without loving respect for everyone, they may
  get the impression that God is not strong rock at
  all, but sand; that he is not to be taken seriously.

Heaven forbid that we should lead any of our little ones astray by the inconsistency of our life.

- It means that we need to get over our embarrassment in talking about God, and chat about him with our children as we would talk about all the other things that are important and excite us.

- It means that we need to start praying aloud with our children, and praying daily with them, so they learn what it is to talk over everything with the loving God, sharing both the lovely times and the sad ones with him. We need to get back the habit of thanking God – aloud – for our food before we eat. Our homes need to become places where it is natural to pray. How else will our children learn to pray naturally?

Of course, this is not going to be easy, especially if we live in a community where only part of the family are believers. But that makes our church community particularly important. Children can cope with the fact that one of their parents believes and one doesn't. It is the hypocrisy of conflicting words and behaviour that confuses them. All our families need the support of the whole Christian community in the precious work of parenting. We are all part of that, whether we have young children ourselves or not.

So let us watch how we build. When we hear Jesus' words, let's really start acting on them, changing our behaviour and our habits to sing out those words in all we do. And then we shall be taking seriously our charge to nurture our little ones, and pass on to them faithfully the Gospel that sets us free to live abundantly, even through storms and floods.

All-age ideas

- In one of the flower arrangements incorporate bricks, a trowel and a spirit level.

TENTH SUNDAY OF THE YEAR

Hosea 6:3-6
Psalm 49:1, 8, 12-15
Romans 4:18-25
Matthew 9:9-13

Jesus' life of healing and compassion acts out God's desire for mercy rather than empty sacrifice.

All-age talk

Beforehand work with one or two people who don't mind acting. They are going to say 'Hello' to one another in various different ways that mean:

- I was really hoping I wouldn't meet this person here.
- I have no respect for this person whatsoever.
- This person is of no interest to me at all.
- This person has a swimming pool and I'd like to be invited round, so I'll suck up to them.
- I'm really glad to see this person.
- I respect and love this person very much.

Begin the talk by getting the actors to say 'Hello' to one another in each different way, and each time follow their greeting with the interpretation, read like a label.

We all show what we think of each other by the greeting we offer one another. (Incidentally, does the way we offer the Sign of Peace tell the other person that they are really valued, or are we looking at someone more our type or more interesting while we greet some people?)

Today we have come to meet together as Christians for a reason. Why have we come here? We haven't come just to see our family or friends (though that is always nice to do!) and we haven't come just to play with the Noah's ark, or to get out of mowing the grass. We have come to greet our God in worship and to greet one another in his name. What kind of 'Hello' are we giving to God by our worship?

Perhaps we are hoping that we won't actually meet God here, in case he asks of us something we don't want to give. We glance in his direction, but don't want to make eye contact, so to speak. Today we are reminded that to worship God beautifully we need to COME TO GOD HONESTLY, JUST AS WE ARE. (Display this.)

Perhaps we nod in his direction, but have really got our thoughts on the people coming for dinner and whether the bathroom should be white or pale green. Or we are thinking more of the piece of chewing gum under the seat in front of us, or the behaviour of the young, or the middle-aged or the elderly, or how many candles need replacing. Today we are reminded that to worship God beautifully we need to GIVE GOD OUR FULL ATTENTION. (Have that written up.)

Perhaps we are here thinking God will notice and tick off our names for good attendance, so that when we die we will have a pre-booked place in heaven. We intend to join in with all the hymns and prayers in church, but for the rest of the week we plan to carry on with the real life in the real world, where Christian values are not actually practical. Today we are reminded that to worship God beautifully we need to KNOW THAT GOD IS NOT FOOLED, and MATCH UP OUR WORDS WITH OUR LIFE (or WALK THE TALK).

Our God is the God of compassion and healing. He does not want our empty words, dry habit worship or closed-up prejudice. He does not want pretence or hypocrisy. God loves us and delights in his people coming to meet with him in worship, Sunday by Sunday. Wherever we are in our spiritual journey he can work with us, and he will never turn anyone away who is genuinely seeking. But whether we greet him in worship with our faces scratched and bruised, as we lie sprawled in the dust of life, or whether we greet him as we stop for breath from running away from him, or whether we greet him timidly but bravely, what we must do is greet him honestly, openly and expectantly.

Suggest that, not out loud but in the silence of

their hearts, everyone says their own 'Hello' to God, honestly, openly and expectantly.

All-age ideas

- Draw up a short list of the people you would like to invite to your house. Draw up a second list of the sort of people you would not like to have in your house. Now think of reasons why those on the second list should be added to the first list.

ELEVENTH SUNDAY OF THE YEAR

Exodus 19:2-6
Psalm 99:2-3, 5
Romans 5:6-11
Matthew 9:36-10:8

Jesus sends his ambassadors out to proclaim God's kingdom and bring hope and peace of mind to the harassed and lost in every age.

All-age talk

Ask everyone to place their hand flat on their tummy. This is often the place where we can tell if we are anxious or stressed, because it feels 'uptight'. When we are at peace, and not tensed-up, this place is where we feel calm and relaxed, and contented. (In fact, one way of calming yourself down is to do what you are doing now, and breathe slowly in and out a few times.)

Recently we have been looking at what religion *isn't*. We've found that it isn't telling God he is Lord of our life and then behaving as if he is not important. And it isn't going through the motions of worshipping him without showing his love and compassion to other people.

Today we are looking at what religion *is*. It is all about being at peace with God. Ask for two people who are really good friends to come to the front, and talk to them about what it feels like to be with each other. How does being together make them feel? Do they feel worried about how the other friend will treat them? Would they trust their friend with a secret?

Best friends are good news. You are contented and happy to be with them, and are not worried all the time that you might say the wrong thing and offend them, or that they may start being nasty to you, so you need to be ready to hit them back if necessary. You know you can trust them with your secrets, and they won't laugh at you or think you are stupid. Even going through bad experiences isn't as bad if you are both in it together, because you know you will help one another along.

Well, that's what being at peace with God is like, and it has the spin-off effect of making us deeply happy and calm inside – a feeling that, whatever happens, all will be well. We heard today how Jesus wanted everyone to know this sense of calm assurance and peace and joy in their lives. He knew there were lots and lots of people going around worried and lost, with no peace inside them because they were not at peace with God. And he sent his disciples off to tell them that the kingdom of God was coming very soon, and soon they would be able to have that closeness with God which would give them peace.

Between the two 'best friends' put up a very large piece of cardboard with the word 'Sin' on it. Sin shuts us off from God and from one another. It makes us think of God as our enemy instead of our friend.

We know that Jesus went on to die for love of us all, which knocked that block of sin away between us and God. (Knock the cardboard away.) So now we can all know that lovely closeness to God which gives us real peace and hope, not just when everything is going well for us, but also through the times of suffering.

All-age ideas

- Try this sketch to draw attention to the right attitude of those sent out to proclaim the good news of the Gospel of Peace.

    Make a 'Take 1' clapper-board using card and a split pin. An assistant shows 'Take 1'. They will also need a carton full of the various items to be given out.

    A new recruit is being prepared for a mission by a couple of people holding clipboards and ticking off items as they are given out. (Their lines can also be on the clipboard.)

Tony   OK. We've got the necessary info and equipment for you ready now.

Let's see . . . ah yes, overnight bag, complete with nightwear, toiletries (mouthwash included) and towel; mosquito net, insect repellent (this is the one with the unclogging nozzle), and lightweight complete Bible (with matching magnifying glass).

Margaret Yes, and here's your fully comprehensive insurance policy (it includes return of body to country of origin, if necessary), travellers' cheques, ID card, small change in each currency in case of emergencies, first aid kit and manual, visa card and PIN number – that's sealed, of course.

Tony Now you'll need these letters of introduction, all on headed notepaper, naturally, and our emergency number should you have any difficulties. Oh, and rations . . . dehydrated lasagne and chips, cranberry ice cream, and plenty of soya mince to keep you going if you're not offered anything better.

Margaret Right, there you are! And good luck!

Assistant Cut! *(She comes on with the 'Take 2' clapper-board.)* Take two!

Tony I say, you've got an awful lot of stuff there – it looks as if you're more interested in keeping yourself safe and comfortable at all costs than telling them the good news. How about getting rid of some of it? *(Takes bag away.)* Better to travel light, I think. Then they'll be able to see that you don't mind too much about personal comforts,

	and you'll have your hands free for healing and comforting other people instead of being weighed down with your own possessions all the time.
Margaret	All this paperwork is a bit OTT, don't you think? You're supposed to be ready to go wherever God leads you, and if you've planned every detail of your life already how are you going to stay available? *(Takes the paperwork.)*
Tony	Ah, that's better – there's only one thing you really need, you know, and it's this. *(Places a simple cross round neck.)*
Both	So go in peace, to love and serve the Lord!
Missionary	In the name of Christ. Amen!

• By the entrance door place the following notice: 'Labourers needed for the harvest – attractive rates. No charge for equipment or training – corresponding salary.'

TWELFTH SUNDAY OF THE YEAR

Jeremiah 20:10-13
Psalm 68:8-10, 14, 17,
   33-35
Romans 5:12-15
Matthew 10:26-33

When we are willing to take up our cross with Jesus we will also know his risen life.

All-age talk

Bring along a kitchen knife, a pen or pencil, a can of paint spray and a £10 or £20 note. You will also need two signs, one saying 'Good' and the other 'Evil'.

Begin by observing that lots of things we handle every day can be used either for good or for evil. Ask for two volunteers to hold the signs, some distance apart, and go through each of the objects in turn, gathering from different people how each can be used. Take the objects to the appropriate notice for each suggestion.

Now ask a person to stand up. It's not only *things* which can be used for good or for evil; it's people as well. Stand the person beside the 'Evil' sign. In what ways can a person use themselves for evil? (Collect suggestions from people of all ages.) Stand the person by the 'Good' sign. In what ways can a person use themselves for good? (Collect suggestions.)

In our readings today we heard about how the false prophet Hananiah used his voice to encourage God's people to believe lies, and how Jeremiah wanted to use his voice differently – to build up God's people. We need to try and use our voices to encourage one another and help one another. We need to use our voices to tell out the truth, to proclaim from the housetops, but not to use the voices God has given to spread unkind gossip, or lies, or to be rude and unkind.

It is not just with our voices that we can proclaim the Gospel. What about our hands? Our minds? Our maleness or our femaleness? Our feet? Our ears?

Suggest that during this week they make a point of checking how they are using all the parts of their body, and seeing if they offer all those parts of themselves to God for good.

All-age ideas

- Have little posies of flowers scattered in various corners of the church. At one point, perhaps during a hymn, the children can be sent off to find these 'little acts of kindness', and everyone can say together, 'No act of kindness, however small, goes unnoticed by the God of love.'

- Display the objects used in the All-age Talk with the 'Good' and 'Evil' signs and a large question mark shape in the middle, so that people are reminded as they go out of church. This could be on display for people to see next week as well, so they can check up on their week's focus and keep the teaching in mind.

THIRTEENTH SUNDAY OF THE YEAR

2 Kings 4:8-11, 14-16
Psalm 88:2-3, 16-19
Romans 6:3-4, 8-11
Matthew 10:37-42

As Christ's people we are no longer slaves to sin, but available for righteousness.

All-age talk

Today we have heard in the reading from Romans that we are to think of ourselves as dead to sin and alive to God through Christ Jesus. What does that mean?

Well, perhaps a few sleeping lions can help. Ask for a few volunteers to play 'sleeping lions', while you and some others try to get them to move. They have to remain as still as they possibly can. Point out that they have to think of themselves as 'asleep' to all those temptations to move which are going on around them. That is rather like us thinking of ourselves being dead to sin. We have to remind ourselves that sin is something which no longer concerns us or has any hold on us.

Ask a few people to say what noises there are in their home at night – any creaks or tickings or chimes. Then draw people's attention to the way we have no difficulty sleeping through these noises, because we know we don't have to worry about them. Some parents will have found that if it isn't your turn to get up and feed the baby you're quite likely to sleep through the crying. You are 'dead' to that sound because you know it isn't anything to do with you. And we are told that we are to think of ourselves as dead to sin.

But it isn't just being dead to sin – it's also being alive to God. What does that mean? Perhaps some people who like chocolate can help us here. Choose a few volunteers and tell them to stand with their backs to you and the congregation. When they think they can detect the presence of chocolate, tell them to raise their hand. Now, as you talk about

91

the way we can always hear what we want to hear, start to open a bar of chocolate, and even though there isn't much sound, and they have their backs to you, it probably won't be very long before they notice, either by hearing or smelling, or both.

That's like us being 'alive' to God. We are going to live as dead to sin, but expectant and interested as far as God is concerned. We will be so tuned in to God that we notice his still, small voice, recognise him in all we see and in those we meet, and live with our hearts and ears and wills turned in his direction all through every day, whatever is going on around us.

All-age ideas

• While the choir or congregation are singing a hymn related to the Cross, have two people at the front of the church holding upright a large wooden cross. In the first verse, three people walk slowly up to the front and kneel at the foot of the cross. In the next verse one of these people is given the cross and carries it, with some difficulty, around the church. By the next verse they come back to the front and return the cross to those who were holding it. They now stand with these people while the cross is given to the next person during the following verses. With the last verse all five are standing facing the cross, holding it with both hands. They all carry the cross high down the centre aisle.

FOURTEENTH SUNDAY OF THE YEAR

Zechariah 9:9-10
Psalm 144:1-2, 8-11,
    13-14
Romans 8:9, 11-13
Matthew 11:25-30

To all who are weary with carrying heavy burdens in life, Jesus offers rest for our souls and unthreatening relief.

All-age talk

Bring along four bags or cases, labelled 'Worries', 'Guilt', 'Duty' and 'Wants'. Inside each wrap up heavy bundles, labelled appropriately. Here are some ideas:

Worries

- What if it rains?
- They might crash.
- She hasn't got enough money for that bill.
- He's in with a bad lot of friends.
- I might get it wrong and look silly.
- What if we get broken into?

Guilt

- I'm so ashamed
- God can never forgive me for that.
- I'll never be able to put that right.
- It haunts me every day.
- I'll never forgive myself.

Duty

- I should drive myself even harder.
- I just grit my teeth and wait for life to be over.
- I'll do my duty even if it kills me.
- Day off? That would be lazy!

Wants

- They've got one – I want it too.
- I wish I was rich and could buy whatever I liked.

93

- I want more freedom.
- I want to look like . . .
- I'd be happy if only I had a . . .

Talk about how hard it is to struggle along carrying heavy shopping bags, or loads of kit and books for school, or a delivery of newspapers, or a supposedly portable laptop computer and printer. Who has ever found their load after school too heavy and given it to someone else (like Mum or Dad!) to carry home, so they can be free to run and play? We all find that carrying heavy loads makes our arms ache, and slows us down. We all enjoy it when we can put that heavy load down, and our arms start lifting up into the air, because they suddenly feel so light!

Today we heard Jesus giving us a wonderful offer. He said, 'Come to me all you who carry heavy loads and I will refresh you. Take my yoke upon you and learn from me, for I am gentle and humble in heart, and you will find rest for your souls. For my yoke is easy and my burden is light.' They are such lovely words to hear for any one of you who feels that you are lugging along heavy loads in your life. Let's look at some of the heavy loads we carry.

Struggle along with the four bags, and read their labels. These are some of the most common heavy loads we carry. What is inside them to make them so heavy? With the help of some volunteers open up each bag in turn. Different people can read out the kind of things that weigh us down so much. It's strange that even wanting things can weigh us down, but it's true. Whenever we are not at peace, we are carrying heavy loads. The good news is that Jesus says we can give those loads to him, so that we are free to play; free to live at peace; free to enjoy life again. (If there is space by a cross, or by the altar, have the bags placed there as you speak.)

When we are yoked, or joined up with Jesus, it is going to be much easier to carry the loads we need, and unnecessary to carry the ones that weigh us down so much.

All-age ideas

- If you have young people present, or the young at heart, play 'Sanctify' – one of the songs from the Delirious? album *King of Fools*, as it deals with the problem of wanting one thing and doing another.

- Before or after the service have someone with a broom-handle who can let some of the children and young people try out being yoked up with them, to see how the yoke helps them do exactly what the partner is doing, without effort.

FIFTEENTH SUNDAY OF THE YEAR

Isaiah 55:10-11
Psalm 64:10-14
Romans 8:18-23
Matthew 13:1-23

Seed of God's word, sown in good soil, watered by his rain and warmed by his sunlight, produces a good crop of spiritual fruit.

All-age talk

You will need a seed tray filled with seed compost, some large-sized seeds, a dibber (to poke holes for the seeds) and a cloth bag of pearl barley. You will also need to arrange for a broom to sweep up the scattered barley after the talk. Lay down one large piece of paper to represent a rocky patch, and a few footprints to represent a stony path.

You might like to play a snatch of the *Gardeners' World* theme tune at the beginning, as you set out the seed tray and compost on a table and invite a couple of keen gardeners to demonstrate planting. As the gardeners work, talk with them about why the seed planted like this is more likely to be successful than if we just shake the seeds outside.

Today we heard a story, or parable, that Jesus told, which was all about seeds being sown, and the best growing conditions. Of course, it wasn't just about seeds being planted and growing. Parables are stories with secrets inside, and the secret of this story is that it was really all about us, and how we respond to God's word when we hear it. This is how it works.

Where Jesus lived, it was very rocky, and the farmers had fields with bare rock showing here and there (put down the paper), and stony roads that went right through the middle (put down the footprints). They ploughed the earth in long furrows, like we did here in the seed tray, only much bigger of course, and then the person sowing the seed walked up and down the furrows sowing the seed like this. (Demonstrate with your bag of pearl barley, scattering the seed to left and right.) The problem is that not all the seed goes in the nice soil you have prepared. When God's word is spoken, we are not always ready to accept it. Let's look at where some of those seeds have landed.

Involve a volunteer to look at the stony path and stand over any seeds they find there. Sometimes we read or hear God's teaching and we're more like a stony path than good soil. It just goes in one ear and out of the other, and we hardly notice what we've heard. We might sit here for the readings and our thoughts fly in, like birds, and take away God's message so we don't even remember what was said.

What about the rocky ground? (Send a volunteer there.) Sometimes we hear God's message and get really keen, and take on far too much far too early, so, like plants growing up on rocky soil, we haven't got good roots. We burn ourselves out and drop away.

What about the soil next to the rock? (Send a volunteer there.) Lots of weeds grow here, so there's a lot of competition for the seeds. Sometimes we hear God's message, but there are so many other things going on in our lives, which we consider important, that the really important message of God gets choked and crowded out.

But all the rest is in good soil. We are like good soil when we listen to God's teaching carefully, think about it and what it means, and then live with it. That way we shall certainly grow and produce a good harvest. Let's check this week that we are taking good notice of God's words to us, and giving him proper space and time, so that we grow in his love.

All-age ideas

- For one of the flower arrangements today include plenty of wheat, a bowl of seed and a loaf of bread. Entitle it with Matthew 13:23.

- Invite a group of people to write Bible references

on small pieces of paper, and for people to hand these out from baskets, as if they are sowing the word of God. Everyone can be encouraged to look up and read their text each day during the week. Here are some suggestions for texts: Matthew 11:28-30; Matthew 10:29-31; Matthew 10:39; Matthew 11:4-6; Matthew 9:36-38; Matthew 9:28; Matthew 7:7-8; Matthew 7:24.

Sixteenth Sunday of the Year

Wisdom of Solomon
  12:13, 16-19
Psalm 85:5-6, 9-10,
  15-16
Romans 8:26-27
Matthew 13:24-43

God's justice is always blended with mercy and loving kindness, so that we have real hope.

All-age talk

Borrow and bring along one of those toys (Polly Pocket or Mighty Max) which look like a plain box and hold inside a whole miniature world.

Show everyone the toy, and explain that today we heard another of those parables which Jesus told. Parables are a bit like these toys, because they are stories which have secret meanings inside. You need to open up the story to find the meaning. (Open the toy.) First of all, let's look at the story Jesus told.

If you have an OHP you can illustrate the story using cut-outs of weeds and wheat, and the evil enemy based on the pictures below, as these will show up in silhouette on the screen.

Remind everyone of the story, using volunteers to be the farmer sowing his seed (accompanied by music from *The Archers*), and the evil enemy creeping into the field at night to sow the weeds (accompanied by everyone doing a pantomime hiss). When the farmer finds that his field is sprouting loads of weeds as well as wheat, he is faced with a choice (hold a question mark in a thought bubble over his head).

All the servants say, 'Shall we pull the weeds out for you?' (Have this written on a speech bubble so everyone, or a small group, can say it together.)

99

The farmer shakes his head. (He does.) He knows that if he pulls all the weeds up now he might pull out some of the wheat as well, and he certainly doesn't want to lose any of his wheat. So instead he decides to let both the wheat and the weeds grow together until harvest time, when the weeds can be gathered up and burnt, and the wheat harvested and put in the barn.

That's the parable Jesus told. What's the secret meaning of it?

Here's a clue. The field is the world, and we can all see that in our world there is a lot of good, but also a lot of evil. Why doesn't God burst out of heaven and stop all the evil in the world straightaway, and punish the people who get away with doing cruel and terrible things?

The parable gives us the answer.

If he did that while life is still going on – while the wheat and weeds are still growing – some good might get lost or damaged. It is because God cares about us so much that he won't risk anything that would cause us lasting harm. There's time enough for punishment when the world comes to an end. Then all that is good and honest and kind and thoughtful will be gathered up safely for ever. All that is mean and selfish, cruel and greedy will be completely destroyed for ever. We can trust our God to know the right time to punish and the right time to hold back, because he always acts with love and mercy as well as justice.

All-age ideas

- Make a flower arrangement with wheat and weeds.

- The speech on mercy from Shakespeare's *The Merchant of Venice* has relevance for today's theme, if you have someone with the gift of reading it well. If the reader is appropriately dressed in legal costume, the significance of merciful justice, compared with condemnatory judgement, is highlighted.

SEVENTEENTH SUNDAY OF THE YEAR

1 Kings 3:5, 7-12
Psalm 118:57, 72,
  76-77, 127-130
Romans 8:28-30
Matthew 13:44-52

Jesus, the teacher, enables the ordinary, unlearned people to understand God's wisdom – the eternal laws of his Father's kingdom.

All-age talk

Bring along something that is precious and old, and something that is precious and new. Choose items which your congregation are likely to relate to. (It could be a well-worn teddy and a new Teletubby for a baby, for instance, or an old stained-glass window in the church and someone's new engagement ring.)

First introduce everyone to the old thing, pointing out why it is so treasured and important and valuable. In our faith there are also ancient things which we as Christians value and treasure, such as the stories in the Old Testament which teach us about our God (for example, creation, Noah's flood, the great escape from Egypt, and the teaching of the prophets), and God's law, the ten commandments given through Moses to the people to help them live well and in line with God's will. Although these are old, ancient things, they are precious to us because they help us get to know God and live as his friends. We don't just throw them out because Jesus has come. Jesus valued them himself, and told his followers to go on valuing them.

Now introduce the new thing, explaining why it is treasured, important and valuable. In our faith there are also new things which we as Christians value and treasure. With the coming of Jesus, we are able to have a completely new kind of friendship with God that had never before been possible. Through Jesus dying, rising and returning to heaven, we are able to have the gift of God's life breathed into our own lives. That means that every new

101

morning of our lives there are new possibilities in our daily friendship with the living God!

Not only are we looking forward to the coming of God's kingdom at the end of all time – we can also enjoy living in it now. In our Gospel today Jesus gave us some ideas of what the kingdom of God is like. Here is just one of them.

It's like some treasure you might find in a field. (You could have an exciting-looking treasure box there.) You're so excited about this precious treasure that you go and sell everything else you have, just so you can buy the field and own the treasure. Let's think about that. If you found a diamond ring, would you go and sell your house and car and World Cup coin collection to get hold of it? Probably not. You'd only bother to sell your house and car and cherished possessions if the treasure you had found was worth far, far more than all the things you already had. Jesus is saying that knowing God in a loving friendship and living in him each day is actually worth far, far more than anything else you own.

I don't think many of us realise that yet. It's as if we dig up a treasure box, look at it and think, 'Oh, that's interesting – a box of treasure. I'll pop over and look at it sometimes.' Then we bury it again and go home to carry on living in the same old way without realising what we're missing out on. Next time you catch a glimpse of what God is really like, and how incredibly wonderful he really is, commit yourself to doing something about it, so you can enjoy that treasure of living in peace and love with him every day of the rest of your life.

All-age ideas

- Have an arrangement of a treasure box, spade and a sign against it which says, 'What is God worth to you?'

- Have an arrangement of advertisements for jewellery and property taken from magazines with the caption, 'Value: £???'.

Eighteenth Sunday of the Year

Isaiah 55:1-3
Psalm 144:8-9, 15-18
Romans 8:35, 37-39
Matthew 14:13-21

God feeds all who come to him hungry, and we, as the Church, are expected to share in that work.

All-age talk

Begin by asking people how they like to spend their pocket money. Invite representatives of all ages to join in this. Has anyone ever spent their money on something which has let them down, or been disappointing, so that they end up wishing they had saved their money? Ask a few people to share their experiences.

It may be that you have had to watch as someone you are fond of wastes their money. You can see that it's all going to end in disappointment, or even tragedy, but they won't listen to you, and all you can do is stand by and wait to pick up the pieces when it all goes wrong, without saying, 'I told you so'! It's our love for the other person that makes us ache to see them wasting their money like that; because we love them we want better for them than to be sad and disappointed by things that aren't worth buying.

That's how it is with our parent God, who loves us to bits, and aches as he watches as we spend not just our money but our time and our love on things which are not going to be good for us, or satisfying or rewarding. He wants better for us than that. God wants us to be aware of our need for his love and power in our lives, and to come to him for it, because he is happy to give it to us free.

Look at all those people in the Gospel story today. Why had they bothered to leave their towns and villages and walk miles out into the country? They bothered because they knew their need of Jesus and were prepared to 'spend' their whole day

103

looking for him and listening to him, hanging on his words. What did Jesus do? Did he let them down or disappoint them? No! He was there for them, ready to heal the sick friends and relations they had brought, ready to reassure them that God loved them, and teach them about how they could best please God in their lives.

And when their tummies started rumbling, and they knew physical hunger as well as spiritual hunger, what did Jesus do? He fed them! All he used was what they had. That's what he always uses. Are you a three- or four-year-old, ready for Jesus to use your life? Then that's what he'll use to make lots of other people really happy. Are you a seventy- or eighty-year-old, ready for Jesus to use your life? Then that's what he'll use to bring blessing and hope to lots of other people. And it's the same with all the rest of us in between.

What about our church? Are we ready to be used by Jesus? If we are, he will use us, and lots of people in this area will be blessed and given hope; if we aren't, and can't be bothered to go and spend time seeking Jesus out and listening to him, then he won't be using us and the people in our area will lose out.

Let's make sure that doesn't happen. Our job is to make ourselves available, and help give out to the people the gifts of God, so that all are properly fed.

All-age ideas

- Incorporate a lunch box of bread and 'fish' in a flower arrangement of water and harvest colours.

- Have a display which on one side has an extravagant restaurant menu with high prices. On the other side have a menu with such 'dishes' as forgiveness, healing, justice, compassion, love, and against each have the price '£ NO COST'.

NINETEENTH SUNDAY OF THE YEAR

1 Kings 19:9, 11-13
Psalm 84:9-14
Romans 9:1-5
Matthew 14:22-33

God is faithful to us through all the storms of life, yet our faith in God is so very small.

All-age talk

If you know a juggler, invite them to come and juggle. Failing this, give out some balloons to a group of older children and ask them to keep them in the air, in as controlled a way as possible, using hands, head, knees and feet.

As the juggler or children perform, draw attention to the way they need to concentrate and keep their eyes on the balls or balloons if they are to be sure of catching them under control. Notice how the moment they lose concentration, or lose balance, things go wrong.

Today we heard in the Gospel about some people in a boat, weathering a terrible storm. It was the disciples, and Jesus had sent them off home while he himself went off to pray on his own after he had fed all those five thousand people. He needed to be alone with his heavenly Father to talk that over, and give special thanks for all that had happened. The waves were churning, and the boat was rocking and the disciples were frightened – especially when they saw Jesus walking across to them. This was water, and you can't walk on that! We are told they thought Jesus must be a ghost, and they got more scared than ever.

Let's look at what Peter did next. He called out to Jesus, 'If it really is you, then tell me to come to you over the water.' Why did he say that? What was he doing? It sounds as if he was testing whether Jesus was real or not, like us saying to a friend, 'If you've really been up in space, show me a photograph to prove it', or 'If you really love me, how about helping with this washing-up'.

Jesus knows he isn't a ghost, and he takes Peter up on what he's asked. 'Come on, then!' he says. There's no way out now! Peter concentrates on Jesus, like the juggler concentrated on the balls. He gets as far as climbing out of the boat, and he starts to walk towards Jesus, still concentrating on him, and then suddenly it all hits him. 'This is crazy! This is impossible! The water can't possibly be holding my weight! Rationally I know I ought to be sinking!' And as those doubts make him panic and lose his sight of Jesus, he does just that – he starts to sink and has to shout out in terror to Jesus to save him. And, of course, Jesus reaches out to him and gets him to safety straightaway.

Trusting Jesus is keeping ourselves concentrating on him and his love, underneath everything else that we do. Suppose you're buying some sweets. At the same time you're aware of Jesus and his love. What difference does that make? You will probably buy without being greedy, and you'll probably end up sharing what you get. Suppose you are travelling to work, and you've also got your eyes on Jesus. That will affect the way you drive, and the way you treat other commuters.

Today Jesus is saying to each of us, 'Yes, it is OK for you to put your total trust in me. Just keep that in mind and all the things which make you feel frightened and insecure will not let you sink – you can walk straight over them, confident in my love and power.'

All-age ideas

- Involve a group to make some sound effects as a background to the reading about Elijah. Having read the passage through together, good ideas may well be suggested, but here are a few to start you off:

  Wind – breathing and shakers, getting louder and then softer.

  Earthquake – Drums, shaken tray or hardboard, large cartons being banged with wooden spoons.

Fire – Crunching up cellophane, and plastic bags, and shakers.

Still, small voice – Very quiet triangle or shaker fading into silence.

• Using music such as the storm in *Noye's Fludde*, have a group of dancers to whirl and leap around like a raging sea in a storm, and gradually calm to gentle movements and stillness. You could dress them in sea-coloured tabards, on the shoulders of which are sewn thin strips of blue and green. These will then fly out as they move. Otherwise they could wave large flags and long streamers of sea-coloured fabric.

TWENTIETH SUNDAY OF THE YEAR

Isaiah 56:1, 6-7
Psalm 66:2-3, 5-6, 8
Romans 11:13-15,
  29-32
Matthew 15:21-28

The good news of salvation is not limited to a particular group or nation but available for the whole world.

All-age talk

Ask everyone who is a Brownie to stand up. That means that everyone left sitting down is a non-Brownie. Do the same with various other groupings, such as Scouts, servers, the short-sighted or cocopops-eaters. Each time we become a member of a group, there are lots of others who are not included.

Remind everyone of the promise God first made to his friend Abraham, whose family the Bible traces right back to Noah. What was it that God promised to Abraham? God promised that (1) he would make his family into a great nation, and (2) all the people on earth would be blessed by this nation which was starting with Abraham. That's quite a promise! And because God always keeps his promises, it came true. Abraham's grandchildren and great-grandchildren and great-great-great-grandchildren did grow into a great nation of God's chosen people.

The people of Israel (as the nation came to be called) were rightly proud of being God's chosen people. Like the groups we had standing up, they thought of themselves as God's chosen, and everyone else was outside and not included. They called all the outsiders 'gentiles'. Probably most of us here are gentiles.

So much for the first part of that promise to Abraham: 'I will make you into a great nation.' But there was a second part, wasn't there? What was that? It was that *all the people on earth* would be blessed by the nation which God had started with Abraham. All through the Old Testament there were prophets like Isaiah who reminded the people of this bit of the promise. 'This is not just for you, remember,' they'd say. 'We are called to bring blessing to all the other people on earth eventually!'

It was true. Starting with the chosen nation, God wanted all the people on earth to have that special friendship with God which Abraham had. It isn't just for a few people, or for one particular nation, but for people of every age, country and time. It's for all the Brownies and the Scouts and the short-sighted and the servers and everybody else, because with God not one person is left 'on the outside'. God's loving is for everybody, everywhere, every time.

If that's how it is for God, then that's how it must be for us as well. We must make sure that in all our loving we don't leave people out. Think about that when you are playing or working in a team, or chatting in a group. Check whether there are people we deliberately avoid. Do we assume some people are not worth telling about Jesus? Would we rather some types of people didn't come to our church?

If God had thought that about us, most of us wouldn't be here. It's his love for us that brought us, and he has love for lots of others who need us to show it to them, and love them into the kingdom.

All-age ideas

- Give the church an international flavour today, with banners and flags representing different countries, and a globe or world map surrounded or dotted with candles.

- Have a display with 'Jesus is Lord' written in as many different languages as possible.

Twenty-First Sunday of the Year

Isaiah 22:19-23
Psalm 137:1-3, 6, 8
Romans 11:33-36
Matthew 16:13-20

The Church is the Body of Christ, built on strong rock of faith and energised by the living Breath of God.

All-age talk

Beforehand, ask a few people of different ages to provide you with a photograph of them when they were very young, and have these pictures duplicated, or shown on an OHP. Don't identify them, but say they are all members of the church community. When people have had a go at guessing the identities, ask the people to come to the front. This narrows the choice, and makes it easier to see who's who. We might have a hunch about someone, and can ask them directly. They will tell us whether or not we are right, and then we'll know for certain. (Invite people to do this.) Once we know the true identity, it's often easier to see the likeness!

In today's Gospel, Jesus knew that people had all sorts of ideas about who he was. Some ideas were close to the truth, some were wide of the mark, and Jesus always wanted his followers to make the discovery for themselves. Discovering something for ourselves means that we always remember it far better than when we have simply been told things. (People may remember discovering for themselves that fire burns, for instance, that cement hardens into a solid lump, or that overloading a computer can cause it to crash.)

No doubt Jesus sensed that the disciples had almost got to the point of discovering that he was not just their friend and teacher, but also the promised Messiah, the Son of God. This conversation, starting with what other people think, will help them tip over into that 'Aha!' of learning, that point when

110

you suddenly know something and everything falls clearly into place.

It is Simon, the fisherman, who comes out with it for the first time. 'You are the Christ,' he says, 'the Son of the living God.' It must have been a bit like when you first say the words 'I love you' or 'I'm three'. It's the first time you have ever said it and as you say it, you know it is really true, and your life will never be quite the same again.

All-age ideas

- Have a display with unfamiliar or disguised pictures of well-known people with the caption, 'Who am I?' Have also a large picture of Jesus with the caption, 'Who do you say I am?'

TWENTY-SECOND SUNDAY OF THE YEAR

Jeremiah 20:7-9
Psalm 62:2-6, 8-9
Romans 12:1-2
Matthew 16:21-27

As Jesus prepares for the necessary suffering of the cross, he is tempted, through well-meaning friendship, to avoid it.

All-age talk

You will need two lengths of bramble, and gardening gloves to handle them. If you can get hold of a length of chain as well, this would be excellent; otherwise, rope, or a paper chain will do fine.

Lay the two lengths of bramble to form a cross on the floor, explaining what you are doing for the benefit of those who will not be able to see this. Make the point that you are wearing protective gloves as the brambles are painful. Explain that the brambles represent all the suffering and pain of the cross. Ask for a volunteer to stand at the top end of the cross. This person represents all of us humans, chained up in all the sin and selfishness that stops us from living freely. (Chain their hands together.) Ask another volunteer to stand at the foot end of the cross, some distance from it. This person represents Jesus at the point of today's Gospel.

Last week we heard how Simon Peter was ready to speak out the truth he had realised about Jesus – that Jesus was the Christ, the Son of the living God. Jesus knew his friends had to be sure of this before they could cope with the next stage of the plan. Now that was in place, and it was time for Jesus to get his friends ready for what had to happen next.

Jesus couldn't just go on working in one part of our world, because he had come into the world to save all of us. That would mean walking a very painful road – the way of the cross. The pain of

112

giving his life on the cross was the only way for Jesus to be able to reach us and set us free. He couldn't get round it; he had to go through with it, even though he knew it would hurt.

Ask the person who is representing Jesus to take their shoes off and start walking towards the cross. Before they get there, stop them as you remind people how Simon Peter couldn't bear to think of his friend going through all that pain, and said, 'Never, Lord! This shall not happen to you!' But if Jesus had listened to him (walk round to the representative human in chains), we would never have been set free from the sin that imprisons us. Never. There would have been no hope for us any more.

(Go back to 'Jesus'.) The good and wonderful news is that Jesus loved us far too much to let his own suffering stop him from saving us. Today we won't make (Lawrence) walk barefoot over those brambles, but as we think of Jesus gladly stepping out to Jerusalem, where he knew he would meet terrible pain and suffering, let's thank him in our hearts for loving us so much that he was prepared to do it anyway (walk round to the human in chains) so that we could all be set free. (Set the person free.)

All-age ideas

- Have a photo/picture display, taken from newspapers and magazines, under the caption 'Take up your cross', of people who are carrying substantial burdens in their lives.

- Have the bramble cross placed on the floor near the altar so that people see it and are reminded of its meaning as they receive communion.

TWENTY-THIRD SUNDAY OF THE YEAR

Ezekiel 33:7-9
Psalm 94:1-2, 6-9
Romans 13:8-10
Matthew 18:15-20

It is our responsibility to encourage and uphold one another in living by the standard of real love.

All-age talk

Ask a number of volunteers to get themselves into a line in order of size. When they have achieved it they can be applauded. Draw attention to the way they helped each other in the task, and showed one another if they were in the wrong place, whenever that was noticed. Because they were working on the task as a team, no one got terribly upset by seeing they were in the wrong place – they just moved into the right place.

Today's Gospel gives us all some teaching about helping one another to keep in order as we live as Christians. The good thing about being a Church is that we are all in the same team, God's team, and we can help one another along. But we're not always very happy to do this. The truth is that we are all going to make mistakes and be in the wrong place with God sometimes, so we need to get used to reminding one another and being reminded without getting too upset about it.

Let's look at what we mean by being in the wrong place with God. (Ask some volunteers to stand facing the cross.) Explain that when we are facing God we are living in his love, and whenever we don't live lovingly, we are turning our backs on God. (Ask the volunteers to turn and face the cross when you say something which is loving, or turn their backs on it when you say something which is unloving.) Here are some suggestions: telling lies, telling the truth, looking after someone, being friendly,

114

grumbling about everything, making sure you get your own way, being generous in your giving, telling dirty or unkind jokes, being bossy and pompous, listening carefully, cheering someone up.

And this is the way we want to be as the Church, with all of us facing God's way. It's our job to help one another keep facing that way, and to help them turn round if they are facing the wrong way.

Supposing we are behaving in an unloving way, then, turning our backs on God? (Turn one of the volunteers around and make up the wrong behaviour they are involved in.) How can the rest of the church help?

In today's Gospel we heard what Jesus said: 'Go and take him to one side and talk it over with him.' (Let one of the volunteers tap him on the shoulder and lead him off a short way from the others, pretending to talk with him.) The point is that we don't always realise that we're in the wrong place, and it is kind to let one another know, so that we can do something about it.

We actually ought to be grateful if someone takes us aside and says, 'Look, I've noticed that you've got really snappy lately. Is anything the matter?' We may have thought we were hiding our worry very nobly, and it will help us to talk it over and recognise that we've been taking our problems out on other people. Or perhaps someone is kind enough to take us aside and say, 'I don't suppose you realise, but you never actually look at people when you are saying hello, and it makes them think you aren't interested in them.' Or 'Have you noticed that every time I say anything at all you contradict me? Have I offended you in some way?' Or 'I've noticed you are always nasty to Paul whenever Steven and you are playing, and that's not very kind. What do you think you could do to stop that happening?'

It may not be a wonderful feeling to know that our faults and failings are noticed, but if it's going to help us put things right, then let's practise being thankful instead of offended, and be ready to help one another up whenever we fall down.

All-age ideas

- Make the Penitential Rite, or a penance service, a chance for a real checking of any selfish or unloving habits we may have slipped into. Here is a possible form for this:

Leader How is it that we are called to live?

All We are called to love God and to love one another.

Leader In that case, let us think about the times we would prefer God to be closing his eyes or blocking his ears.

What would we prefer God not to see us doing?

(Silence for reflection)

What would we prefer God not to hear us saying?

(Silence for reflection)

What would we prefer God not to know us thinking?

(Silence for reflection)

God desires not the death of a sinner but rather that he may turn and live.

All O God, you see all things, hear all things, know all things, and we are ashamed of the unloving way we sometimes act, speak and think. Have mercy on us and forgive us, and enable us to put things right.

- Display three large signs or posters with an eye, an ear, and a thought bubble, and the words: *'Does God hear you speaking with love?' 'Does God see you acting with love?'* and *'Does God find you thinking with love?'*

TWENTY-FOURTH SUNDAY OF THE YEAR

Ecclesiasticus
    27:30-28:7
Psalm 102:1-4, 9-12
Romans 14:7-9
Matthew 18:21-35

Forgiving is a natural result of loving, so it is not an option for us but a command.

All-age talk

First ask anyone who has never done anything wrong, *ever*, to raise their hand. Make it quite clear that doing wrong doesn't stop when you grow up, and it's a problem that we all have to deal with. In which case there's going to be another problem we need to deal with. What about when people do things wrong which hurt and upset us? It's bound to happen, and today we are given some very useful teaching from our Lord Jesus to help us with it.

Suppose someone lets you down, cheats on you, loses their temper with you and says some cruel unkind things, lets you down again, steals from you, makes you look stupid, and breaks something you've let them borrow. (Count on your fingers seven typical offences.) Peter goes to Jesus and says, 'Is seven times about the limit for forgiving someone? It seems fairly generous to me. You might as well give up on them after that, don't you agree? Or am I being a bit over-generous – more forgiving than is good for me?'

Jesus says, 'Actually, seven times isn't nearly enough! You need to keep on forgiving until you've lost count and just do it anyway.' And then he tells one of his stories to explain what he means.

Give a volunteer a sign to hold which says 'IOU millions'. The story is about a servant who owes loads and loads of money. He has a wife and children, and he's borrowed so much and has been using his plastic money facility so much that he's stacked up a huge debt to his master, which he can't pay off. The master calls for him (use another

117

volunteer and give him a mobile phone or a smart jacket) and demands the money. The servant kneels down and begs (he does this) to be given more time to pay. The master feels sorry for the servant and lets him off the whole debt! Just like that! (Master draws a thick black line through the IOU.) How do you think the servant feels? (Collect ideas.)

Now that is what God has done for each of us. Ask them to think of all the things they've done wrong, perhaps which no one else knows about except them and God. Think of all the meanness, selfishness, pride, hypocrisy and so on that we have been forgiven completely by God. It's just as if we owed God millions of pounds (hold up the IOU) and God has drawn that line through it, setting us free from the debt.

So here is this happy, free servant, who finds a fellow servant owes him a few pounds. (Give another volunteer a sign with 'IOU a few pounds' on it.) And the same thing happens. The servant goes on his knees and begs (he does this) to be allowed more time to pay. But what does the servant do? He grabs him by the neck and shakes him (not too realistically) and has him thrown into prison until he pays up. What Jesus wants us to ask ourselves is this: Is it fair or right for the servant to behave like this? What do we think?

Next time we are not wanting to forgive someone, let's remember how God has treated us, and pass on that loving forgiveness time and time and time again.

All-age ideas

- In a discussion group, or with children, the Gospel could be acted out, either by miming while it is narrated or by different people taking the parts and saying their words.

- Place the cancelled 'IOU millions' sign in a place where it can be seen as a reminder of what God has done for us in releasing us from our sins.

TWENTY-FIFTH SUNDAY OF THE YEAR

Isaiah 55:6-9
Psalm 144:2-3, 8-9,
   17-18
Philippians 1:20-24,
   27
Matthew 20:1-16

We have no right to be envious at the generosity and mercy God shows to others.

All-age talk

Today we might usefully think about being grumpy and sulking, something most of us do from time to time. (Have one or two volunteers to give a really sulky, grumpy face.) Did they notice how sulky and cross Jonah was in our first reading? Do we do this if we have a row? – remembering things that were said at other times and throwing them back at the person we want to upset, and saying, 'I knew it would end up like this! If you'd listened to what I said, this would never have happened!' We feel quite at home here! And if we're a loving parent on the receiving end of all the anger and resentment, which we know comes from a lack of understanding or experience, perhaps we can sense something of how God feels, loving this very hot-headed, angry person shouting at us, and knowing that our job is to stay calm, stay loving, and pick up the pieces once they've got over it.

What is it that makes us sulk, usually? (Collect answers.) Usually it's when we feel hard done by, as if we have been unfairly treated and been given a raw deal, or when we see others get off lightly.

Jesus told a story about some sulking workmen, which we heard today. The ones who worked all day agreed their wage, and at the end of the day they got it in full. Why were they sulking? Because some other workmen, taken on much later in the day, were paid the same wage. So they sulked. And we often behave in the same way. (Sulky faces.) In

119

Jesus' story the owner helps the workmen to understand why they are sulking. He asks them, 'Are you jealous because I am good to these people as well?'

We all need to understand that God doesn't split us up into some who are OK to be saved and some who aren't worth bothering with. We shouldn't get jealous or angry if Christians of another church or tradition seem to be having God's blessing as well as us, or if people who have made bad mistakes in the past are allowed to be part of our fellowship. If we are loving, like God loves, this will make us not sulky (sulky faces) but happy (happy faces).

All-age ideas

- On large notices or posters, stuck on the walls or pillars, display the qualities of our God which today's readings emphasise: gracious; full of compassion; slow to anger; of great goodness; rich in love.

- Mime the parable of the workmen while it is being narrated, or have a group act it, expressing the dialogue in their own words.

Twenty-sixth Sunday of the Year

Ezekiel 18:25-28
Psalm 24:4-9
Philippians 2:1-11
Matthew 21:28-32

God longs for us to die to sin and live, but it has to be our choice, too.

All-age talk

Bring along the details of a children's colouring competition, and also one of those junk mail promotional letters which tell you that you have already been selected as a winner.

Begin by sharing this exciting letter with everyone, reading out some of the blurb, and getting a volunteer to scratch any secret messages included. No doubt many of us receive these kinds of letters. When we do so, we have a choice: are we going to bin it (or preferably recycle it), or will we take them up on their wonderful offer and claim our prize? What we decide will depend on all kinds of factors, such as how busy we are, how desperate for winnings we are, how many previous disappointments we have experienced, and whether we actually believe them.

But one thing is certain. Unless we decide to return our reply slip, we have no chance of winning anything at all. It's the same with colouring competitions. A prize is offered and anyone has a chance of winning. But if you don't get your felt-tips or paints out and do the colouring, and send it off in time, you will have no chance of winning a prize, however good you are at colouring.

Today we are being reminded by God that he has great prizes and gifts for us, which he longs for us to enjoy. He wants to see us all as winners, happily receiving the gift that has been reserved specially for us. But . . . and it is a big 'but' . . . unless we choose to turn to God and take him up on his offer, we will have no chance at all of winning. If we

121

choose wrong instead of right, evil instead of good, and self instead of God, we cannot have the joy and peace and life that God longs to give us. We don't just get it anyway, however we live. Lots of people think that is what happens, but it isn't because God isn't like that. He is a God of goodness and love, truth and kindness. Do we want to go along with that? We have to choose it, then, and start doing something about it.

As soon as we choose it, God can give us all the help we need, and he will, because all he wants is for us to know complete and lasting happiness with him.

All-age ideas

- As people come into church give everyone a copy of the form shown below, and provide time for them to fill it in. Actually ticking the boxes emphasises their commitment, and the forms can be given with the offering and presented for God's work.

	YES	NO
Do you turn to Christ?	☐	☐
Do you turn your back on evil?	☐	☐

- Everyone can say these words from Philippians to one another, as words of encouragement:

It is God who works in you to will and act according to his good purpose.

It is God who works in you to will and act according to his good purpose.

TWENTY-SEVENTH SUNDAY OF THE YEAR

Isaiah 5:1-7
Psalm 79:9, 12-16,
    19-20
Philippians 4:6-9
Matthew 21:33-43

God does everything possible for our spiritual growth and well-being, but still we can choose hostility and rejection.

All-age talk

Bring along a watering can, secateurs, a gardening fork and some slug pellets. Show everyone these things and have any gardeners in the group (both young and old) explain to you what they are all for. Ask if anyone has been using these this year, and what has been grown and eaten.

All gardeners can feel in good company, because one of the often-used pictures of our God is as a gardener. In our reading from Isaiah, God is imagined as a gardener planting vines in a vineyard – digging the ground, and getting it all ready, planting carefully, weeding and watering regularly, supporting the branches and pruning, and really caring for this vine so that it may bear a wonderful juicy crop of grapes. Gardeners are always fond of what they grow – that's why they'll go to any lengths to protect their plants from things like slugs and greenfly. We can imagine God caring like that (only more so) for his people, and wanting desperately to protect them from evil and sin.

But when this gardener comes to pick the crop of grapes which he has grown so carefully, he finds they are not delicious and sweet but bad and sour, and the lovely vineyard ends up all overgrown and wild. Like a gardener, God has looked for the good fruit of justice in his people but found only bloodshed; he has looked for the good fruit of righteousness and found only the cries of those who are treated badly. What kind of fruit does God the gardener find in us, in his Church, or in our society?

123

Does what he finds in this church and this world put a smile on his face, or does he find instead sour fruit which makes him sad?

We all know the kind of thing that delights God. He loves to find such fruits as love, joy, peace, patience, kindness, goodness, gentleness and self-control. He loves to see justice, mercy, right living, purity and honesty. May this garden grow a bumper crop of such fruits, that will gladden the heart of God and bring blessing and healing to our town.

All-age ideas

- Incorporate grapes and secateurs in one of the flower arrangements.

- Have the parable section of the Gospel mimed as it is read. Use clear, unfussy and stylised movements. Have the owner at the back of the action, facing the congregation, with his hands on the shoulders of the son until he sends him off. As two farmers grab the son and throw him out of the vineyard, they both pull his arms so that for a moment the son is stretched as if on a cross, and at the back the owner assumes the same position. At verse 40 the group freezes in attitudes of hatred and rejection. As the owner approaches, arms by his sides, they turn and see him, cover or avert their eyes, and creep away.

TWENTY-EIGHTH SUNDAY OF THE YEAR

Isaiah 25:6-10
Psalm 22
Philippians 4:12-14,
    19-20
Matthew 22:1-14

We are all invited to God's wedding banquet, but in accepting we must allow the rags of our old life to be exchanged for the freely given robes of holiness and right living.

All-age talk

As people come into church make sure that everyone is given a small picture or cut-out paper shape of a robe of righteousness, with this title on it:

Probably we have sometimes looked into our wardrobes before a party and decided that we have nothing suitable to wear. However jam-packed the wardrobe is, with all that extra junk stuffed in to keep it out of sight, we can't find anything we want to wear! Prepare to be impressed: the wardrobe space of today's teaching is quite something.

Mention the piece of paper they were all given when they came in, checking for any who have been missed and providing for them now. Everyone has been given a beautiful wedding garment! That's what used to happen when guests were invited to palaces. It was the practice for kings to provide thousands of guests with a suitable robe each from their vast wardrobes in which thousands of garments were kept ready specially for such occasions. (Dress a volunteer up in a clean white robe – a surplice is fine.) They had special servants to be in charge of those huge wardrobes.

In Jesus' parable of the wedding feast we can imagine all the poor and the dirty straggling along to the palace in their smelly rags, and the people in charge of the king's wardrobes fitting up everyone with a clean, beautiful robe to wear, before ushering them into the grand dining hall. No doubt they felt different dressed like this – perhaps they even walked taller and were more polite to each other than usual! Then the king comes in to inspect his guests. (Perhaps everyone sits up straighter, like you do when someone important walks into assembly.) He is glad to see the palace full of guests who have accepted his invitation, because the original guests had refused to come. Everything is light and warm and happy.

Suddenly the king finds a guest who has accepted his invitation but rudely refused to wear the proper clothes provided. He's still in the filthy rags he came in, and the king has him put outside in the darkness with those who had chosen to turn down his invitation.

What is Jesus teaching us in this parable? One thing is that God is very happy to invite all of us to the Church of Christ and feed us here with love and rejoicing. So we can be happy together in God's company and enjoy ourselves in our worship. The other thing is that if we say yes to God, we do need to let him reclothe us, and not expect to go on wearing the rags of bickering and fighting, lying and cheating, self-indulgence and lack of self-control which we came in. That's why we always start our worship by saying sorry to God, and hearing his forgiveness, letting him clothe us with robes of righteousness.

All-age ideas

- Have an arrangement of golden flowers set inside a treasure chest labelled 'Holiness'.

- Try this sketch in which a reporter is interviewing some of the guests.

Reporter Well, I'm standing here in the great hall; it's filled with the warm glow of candle light, the smells of delicious food and the sound of crowds of people enjoying themselves. Quite a wedding feast! Excuse me, sir, may I interrupt your meal a moment and ask how you came to be invited to this banquet?

Guest 1 Yes, sure. I was trimming my hedge.

Reporter Trimming your hedge?

Guest 1 That's right – crazy isn't it! One minute I was trimming my hedge, feeling hungry, and the next this servant from the palace comes along and says I'm invited to the king's banquet! It seems the original guests had turned it down. So I'm here with the wife and kids, and we've never enjoyed ourselves so much, isn't that right, dear? I've never been to a banquet before, but I tell you, I could get used to it!

Reporter And here's a very senior citizen. Good evening, madam.

Guest 2 Eh?

Reporter (*Shouts*) Good evening, madam! how are you liking the banquet?

Guest 2 Oh, it's wonderful, dear! Just wonderful! We're being so well looked after – and I've never felt so loved and honoured in all my life. Just think – me being treated like this! It makes me feel young and beautiful again.

127

Grandchild You are beautiful, Gran!

Guest 2 What's that, my chicken?

Reporter Well, as you can see, the atmosphere here is amazing – so much joy and happiness for so many people! And none of them bought a ticket. When the original guests turned it down, the king just had all these ordinary, poor folk invited and brought in from the streets and farms, and gave them each a wedding garment to wear so he'd have a full gathering to celebrate his son's wedding. And I must say, it's the most happy and extraordinary wedding celebration ever. I'm going outside now . . . it's dark and cold out there, and there's a whole lot of people who sadly don't realise what they're missing.

Twenty-ninth Sunday of the Year

Isaiah 45:1, 4-6
Psalm 95:1, 3-5, 7-10
1 Thessalonians 1:1-5
Matthew 22:15-21

All leaders and rulers are subject to the ultimate authority and power of God, the living truth.

All-age talk

Unless the size of your congregation makes it far too expensive, give everyone a penny. Invite everyone to look at their coin. On one side there is a picture of someone's head. Whose head is it? It belongs to Queen Elizabeth II. She is there, just as Caesar's picture was on the coin Jesus looked at, because she is the Head of State and we are her subjects. In our country there are taxes to pay to make sure that everyone, both rich and poor, can have schools, roads and hospitals. There are laws to keep, so that we can all live safely and peacefully, and there are police to check that we keep the laws. Those who break them are sent to prison or charged a fine.

Each country works out its own way of organising all this, and some are fairer than others. Each country has leaders – people who are in charge – and the country Jesus lived in was ruled by the Romans.

Now invite everyone to hold their coin in the palm of one hand. This penny is not very big. It won't buy very much. It sits here in your hand, and your hand is here in this church building. It's only a very little part of all the space in here. As you hold your penny, your hand is surrounded not just by the space of this building but by the whole universe. Now God is greater than the universe, because he is the One who thought and loved our universe into being.

There's a huge, huge difference between the kind of power and authority human leaders have, and the kind of power and authority God has. We are to give to God what is God's. What is God's? Is

129

there anything God doesn't know? No. Is there anywhere God can't reach? No. Is there anything or anyone God doesn't care about? No. God is much greater and more wonderful than we can imagine, and he holds all creation in the palm of his hand, like you are holding the little penny in the palm of your hand.

No wonder we've all chosen to come and spend some time praising him this morning! God is worth everything we can ever give him.

Of course, we are to respect our leaders, and keep the laws. We are to be good citizens, just as our Christian rule of love tells us. But we also need to remember who is ultimately in charge, and put God first. We need to be prepared to make a fuss if any laws are passed which are against God's law, and we need to do what we can to help our leaders uphold the authority of the God who made us all.

All-age ideas

- Use the coins as a focus for prayer, praying for all leaders and rulers as we look at the monarch's head; for the world, as we see the roundness; for the blind and spiritually blind as we feel its edge; for the imprisoned as we see the portcullis; and for the rich and the poor.

THIRTIETH SUNDAY OF THE YEAR

Exodus 22:20-26
Psalm 17:2-4, 47, 51
1 Thessalonians 1:5-10
Matthew 22:34-40

We are to love God with our whole being, and love others as much as we love ourselves.

All-age talk

Hold a large edition of the Bible, and tell everyone that today we are all going to read the whole lot as part of our talk!

Explain that today we heard Jesus giving us a summary of the whole of the Bible, in a couple of sentences. (Reader's Digest can eat their heart out!) He was saying that everything in all the law and the prophets was an exploring and working out of this. (Have Matthew 22:37-39 written out large, and invite everyone to join you in reading it out.) There – we've read the Bible! Or, to be more precise, we have read the subject matter of the whole Bible, because everything in it is to do with what we just read – people learning to love God with their whole being, and their neighbours as themselves. It's the story of their learning, their mistakes and failures, and of God's great love helping us make the impossible possible. (Well worth reading the full-length version!)

Let's look at what it means to love others as we love ourselves. How do we love ourselves? Invite a couple of friends to come and help show us. Get one to stand behind the other, with the front person putting their hands behind their back, and the back person providing them with substitute arms by pushing their own arms through the front person's. Have someone offering them a wrapped chocolate which they eat, and give them a brush so they can do their hair.

All day long we look after ourselves like this, feeding and washing and scratching ourselves whenever the needs arise. Even if we don't admit to loving ourselves our actions show that we do. If we start getting too hot, our body kindly makes us sweat to cool us down. If we're threatened by the cold, our helpful body sets us shivering and raises our hairs to warm us up again. And if there's a real emergency (the children can make an ambulance siren sound), the body shuts down some systems and kicks in with others to keep us alive as long as possible. That's love for you!

So if we are to love others like that, we'll be attentive, looking out for one another's well-being and ready to help when we see someone in need. We'll be doing what we can to feed the hungry and look after those with problems. We'll scratch where it itches but not where it doesn't. We'll be ready to drop everything and be there for people if there's an emergency and they need us. We'll do everything we can to help them feel better and get through the difficult times.

And where does all this love come from? From our wonderful God, who made us all in the first place, and loves to see all his children caring for one another like this.

All-age ideas

- Sing this summary of the law to the tune of *London's burning* in a round with actions. Then the whole of the law is being celebrated in voice and action, just as people are doing in real life twenty-four hours a day around our planet earth.

  You shall love the
    (hands on heart)
  Lord your God with
    (arms raised)
  all your heart and
    (hands on heart)
  all your mind and
    (hands hold head)
  all your strength! All your strength!
    (show muscles in arms)

And love your neighbour,
(arm round neighbour on one side)
and love your neighbour.
(arm round neighbour on other side)

- Make decorated banners or posters, proclaiming the summary of the law.

THIRTY-FIRST SUNDAY OF THE YEAR

Malachi 1:14-2:2, 8-10
Psalm 130
1 Thessalonians 2:7-9, 13
Matthew 23:1-12

Our lives need to reflect our faith; we are not just called to tell the good news but to live it as well.

All-age talk

Bring in an ordinary mirror. Also make a distorting mirror using a sheet of the very shiny wrapping paper or cooking foil. It can either be stuck on bent card or simply held by two volunteers. Invite a few people to see themselves in both mirrors, or walk the mirrors round the church reflecting people here and there. Which reflection looks most like them?

Sometimes we are like good mirrors, when we reflect God's loving by being loving to others. Or we may reflect God's forgiving nature when we forgive someone who has been unkind to us. Or we may reflect God's faithfulness when we are trustworthy and faithful ourselves.

But sometimes we are like bad mirrors. We distort God's loving into possessiveness of other people; we distort relaxing into laziness; we distort honesty into critical gossip, or pleasure into greed. Worst of all, we distort trust. We are designed to trust God and depend on him, and when we start trusting things or our own image instead of God, our lives get twisted and misshapen, and we can no longer reflect to other people the truth of our God. We may tell others about God but our lives will only reflect a distorted picture of it, so they end up thinking God is a slave driver, or without any compassion and forgiveness.

How terrible if even one person has been stopped from putting faith in the living God because they have been put off by the distorted image of God they see in our lives! We need to be like mirrors

134

that are straight and true, with our lives reflecting the true loving God we say we worship.

All-age ideas

- This dance expresses getting our lives sorted out and our agendas untangled so that we can be open to God. While the choir or congregation sing *O Lord, your tenderness* quietly and prayerfully, a group of about six people of all ages get completely tangled up together. Slowly they get untangled, raising their arms upwards in thanks and praise as they do so, and then helping to free those who are still 'knotted'. During the repeated 'O Lord, I receive your love', they slowly form first a circle facing inwards with their arms raised to God, and then a circle with their arms extended to one another and out to the congregation, expressing the truth that when God fills us with his love it enables us to reach out in love to other people.

THIRTY-SECOND SUNDAY OF THE YEAR

Wisdom of Solomon
  6:12-16
Psalm 62:2-8
1 Thessalonians
  4:13-18
Matthew 25:1-13

We need to keep ourselves awake and prepared so that the Day of the Lord does not come to us as darkness rather than light.

All-age talk

Beforehand prepare some sticks with red paper flames stuck on the end.

Begin by asking who has ever been a bridesmaid or a page-boy at a wedding. Were any of them late for the wedding? Today we heard a parable Jesus told about some bridesmaids. Some were ready when they were needed, but some weren't.

Show the 'torches' which were used at that time. Material was soaked in oil and tied on to the end of sticks. When you set light to them they would burn well, so the bride and bridegroom, coming from the bridegroom's house in the evening of the wedding, could have their way lit by the bridesmaids' torches. (Have a bride and groom and some bridesmaids to show this, holding their torch sticks.) At least, they could if the bridesmaids had their oil with them.

The problem in Jesus' story was that half the bridesmaids hadn't checked their oil supplies, so when the bridegroom needed their torchlight, they were rushing off to buy more oil, and ended up being shut out of the wedding feast.

What is the hidden message in this parable? What is Jesus wanting us to understand?

He wants us to be ready, and have our oil supplies topped up, so that whenever the bridegroom returns, even if he takes longer to arrive than we were expecting, we will be there waiting, shining brightly in the darkness. Then the bridegroom can lead us all into the celebrations and the feast.

Fill the oil lamp and light it. God's Spirit is like the oil we need to keep us burning brightly with God's love. If we stop keeping ourselves 'topped up' by forgetting to pray and read the Bible each day, our lives will stop shining, just as the girls' torches went out. Then, if Jesus suddenly returns, unexpectedly, either at the end of time or in a situation where our bright Christian love is badly needed, we won't be able to help.

So Jesus is telling us to keep praying, keep listening and keep loving. That way, we'll be all ready whenever he needs us.

All-age ideas

- Have an oil lamp and bottle of oil with some bridal flowers and a veil as one of the flower arrangements today.

- Give out small squares of foil or shiny paper to everyone as they come in. Invite everyone to look at their 'mirrors' and imagine them reflecting back their spiritual rather than physical state. Allow everyone space and time to recognise any areas which need bringing to God's love for forgiveness and healing.

- Invite a group of people to mime the parable in the Gospel as it is read.

THIRTY-THIRD SUNDAY OF THE YEAR

Proverbs 31:10-13,
  19-20, 30-31
Psalm 127:1-5
1 Thessalonians 5:1-6
Matthew 25:14-30

The Day of the Lord will hold terror for the wicked and unprepared, but rejoicing for those living in God's light.

All-age talk

Beforehand place three boxes of different colours around the church. In the red box put five one-pound coins (cardboard ones are fine!), in the blue box put two one-pound coins and leave the yellow box empty.

We know that one day the world as we know it will come to an end. We know that life as we know it will finish. All the prophets and Jesus teach us in the Bible that there is going to be a Day of the Lord, when we will see Jesus in all God's glory, and all that is evil will not survive. That includes people. How we live now in our lives will affect what happens to us that day. We do need to know that.

When will it happen? We don't know the time or date; in fact, what we do know is that it will happen suddenly, without us having loads of time to change. That's why we need to live every day as if it were our last.

But God doesn't want us so scared of the last day that we can't enjoy life here. Jesus came to set us free from that fear, and, if we are walking through life as Jesus' friends, there is nothing to be frightened of, because it's only the evil and bad and selfish that will be destroyed; everything that is good and loving and honest will be gathered up safely for ever.

Jesus told one of his stories with secrets – parables – about making the most of all the gifts God has given us, and we need three people to help us with it. (Make sure that the third servant chosen has been warned beforehand that she will be told off in the

138

story, and is confident enough to cope with that.)

In Jesus' story, a man is going on a long journey and, before he goes, he gathers his servants together and entrusts his property to them to look after. (Give five coins to one servant and send her off to find the red box. Give two coins to another servant and send him off to find the blue box. Give one coin to the last servant, and send her off to find the yellow box.) The man went off on his travels, and after a long time came back home. He called the servants to him to settle accounts with them. (Call the volunteers together with the boxes.) Let's see how the first servant has got on. (She opens the box and counts out to the owner ten coins. Be very pleased. Everyone can clap.) What about the second servant? (He opens the box and counts out four coins. Praise and applause.) What about the third servant? Tell everyone how this servant told the owner she was too scared to do anything with her gift, so she just hid it as it was. (She gives it back.) The owner was not pleased at all because the servant had not made good use of the gift she had been given. (Tell the servant off, and thank all the actors for their help.)

We all have gifts God has enjoyed giving us. Some of us are good at being friendly and welcoming, some good at looking after animals, working out money, ironing, or thinking out solutions to difficult problems. Whatever our gift is, we need to enjoy using it and making the most of it for the good of everyone.

All-age ideas

- Have a display of paintings and photographs which show people in ordinary situations, with the title: 'Flower where God plants you.'

- As well as an offering of money, suggest people give an offering of time. They can be given circles of paper as they come in, and commit themselves to a daily prayer time. The circles are then collected and offered to God.

CHRIST THE KING

Ezekiel 34:11-12, 15-17
Psalm 22
1 Corinthians
  15:20-26, 28
Matthew 25:31-46

In total humility, at one with the least of his people, Jesus, the Messiah or Christ, reigns as King, with full authority and honour for eternity.

All-age talk

Bring along a crown and robe, some pretend bags of money, a dish of fruit and two fans on sticks as shown below. Drape some cloth over a chair.

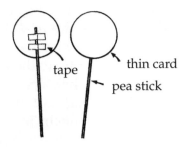

tape

thin card

pea stick

Tell everyone that today we are celebrating that Jesus Christ is King for ever. Ask a volunteer to come out and dress them up in the grand robe of very costly material, hand-embroidered by expert craftsmen, and the solid gold crown, studded with real diamonds and rubies. Sit the king on a grand throne covered in pure silk and made from finest marble, and provide him with some servants to stand around and wave him with fans, bowing before him. Give him bags of money on a table nearby, and provide a dish of fresh fruits for him to snack on between banquets.

Is this right? Is this what King Jesus is really like? No, it's all wrong! Although Jesus has been given all power and majesty and honour, and is King of all time and space, he is a very different sort of king. He lays aside his majesty (help the king up from his throne), lays aside his robe and his crown (take them from him), lays aside all wealth

140

and comfort (the servants move the table), so that he can be one with us (he shakes hands with the servants) and live among us, caring for us, searching for the lost, and binding up the injured. (Thank the servant and the king for their help.)

Now if that's how our king behaves, then that's how we are to behave as well. If we worship and honour a Servant King, who doesn't greedily look after his own needs all the time but makes a point of looking after other people's needs, then that's what we have to do! Our wealth and treasure will be in loving service, wherever we're needed. That's how Jesus will recognise us as his people, when we get to the gate of heaven.

All-age ideas

- Have the crown and robe and the other props near the altar as people come up to communion, with the title 'The Servant King'.

- Have the parable mimed during the Gospel. To help everyone understand that the sorting is checking existing citizenship of the kingdom, give all the 'sheep' a cross on their foreheads, which the king looks for as they are chosen and welcomed.

YEAR B

FIRST SUNDAY OF ADVENT

Isaiah 63:16-17, 64:1,
  3-8
Psalm 79
1 Corinthians 1:3-9
Mark 13:33-37

Be alert and watchful; keep yourselves ready.

All-age talk

Beforehand prepare a large sun shape from yellow paper and a large cloud from grey paper. First show everyone the sun. If this is showing in the sky during the summer, what can we tell about the best clothes to wear? Now slide the large grey cloud over the sun, so that the sun is hidden. What might it be wise to take with us if we are going out in this weather? We are very good at reading the signs in the weather to help us keep comfortable.

We read lots of other signs as well. At traffic lights, or at the top of scary water chutes, we know that red means stop and green means go. We know by the special music when *The Simpsons* or the news is about to come on. We know by the smell of cooking that dinner is nearly ready.

In today's Gospel, Jesus tells us to keep alert and check the signs which will tell us when he is going to come to earth again. This time he won't be coming as a tiny baby, but full of God's glory and in great power, riding on the clouds of heaven. It will be such an amazing event that it will rock the whole cosmos – the whole of nature will be shaken. Jesus told his disciples that the sun will be darkened, and the moon will lose its light, and stars will fall from heaven. This is something that every being will notice, both those who are alive on earth at the time and those who will have already died. Jesus tells us that even he doesn't know exactly when it will happen, but it certainly will take place, and we will all need to be ready for it, whether we are still alive here or already dead.

So how can we make sure we are ready? How can we read the signs?

The best way of making sure we stay ready is by keeping our eyes open – our spiritual eyes. That means keeping in touch with God on a daily basis. We need to get into a habit of praying, not just once a week on Sundays, but all times of every day. A good way of remembering, and getting ourselves into such a habit, is to get in touch with God every time we check our watches, or every time we put something to eat in our mouths.

Sensible sailors or hill walkers will check the weather forecast every time before they set out, so they are prepared. We need to check with God his will and guidance every time before we make decisions or spend money. Then our faith will be living and active, growing as we grow, and keeping us alert and available, so that whenever Jesus comes again in glory we shall be ready to welcome him with joy.

All-age ideas

- This response can be used at the Penitential Rite:

  Lord, we are sorry for the days we hardly speak with you at all.

  Lord have mercy.
  Lord have mercy.

  Lord, we are sorry for the times we refuse to follow in your way.

  Christ have mercy.
  Christ have mercy.

  Lord, we are sorry for the opportunities we miss for serving you in others.

  Lord have mercy.
  Lord have mercy.

- Direct people to look at the cross as a sign of God's generous, self-giving love, and think about a spiritual 'new year' resolution at this beginning of the Church's year. This can be done either in a time of silence or accompanied by quiet music.

145

SECOND SUNDAY OF ADVENT

Isaiah 40:1-5, 9-11
Psalm 84
2 Peter 3:8-14
Mark 1:1-8

John the Baptist prepares the way for the coming of the Messiah by helping the people to realign their lives.

All-age talk

Bring in a washing-up bowl with some water in it and a mop. Produce a mug or two which you were using earlier and explain how these are dirty and need washing up. You hope the mugs won't be too embarrassed by being shown dirty like this in full view of everyone. They are very particular mugs and prefer people to see them clean.

We are often a bit like that. We like people to see us when we're proud of what we are like and what we are doing. We don't like it much if someone catches us screaming at the dog, telling or living a lie, or being lazy or greedy. Usually we try to cover up the things we do which we aren't proud of. Perhaps we'll make out it's someone else's fault that we're late or grumpy; perhaps we'll think up good excuses for wrong behaviour. We get so good at this that often we believe our cover-up stories and stop noticing that instead of pretending we're clean-living Christians, what we actually need is a good, thorough wash.

The people who came to hear John the Baptist were just like us. There were things in their lives which were wrong and selfish, and they had become used to making excuses for themselves till they were quite content to live with their bad habits and carefully groomed images. But John got them thinking. And as they thought about their real selves and what they were really like, they suddenly started to realise that they were like dirty mugs which needed a good wash. If they were washed clean, they could be free from all the pretending and cover-ups, and just be themselves again.

146

John told them it was quite easy to do – they just needed to name all those big and little sins aloud to God without hiding them, and choose to turn their back on that way of living. He said he would dip them right under the water in the river as a sign that their lives were being washed clean.

(Ask for a volunteer to come and wash up the mugs.) For some of them it must have felt very humiliating to do that in public, especially if they had groomed their images so well that they had kept their sins well hidden. And it must have been such a relief for others, who had worried about their sin for years and years, to have it washed away at last.

When they were all washed clean, like our mugs, without any need to hide from God or each other any more, John told them something very important. This washing was just the beginning; soon someone was coming who would be able to plunge them deep into the depths of the Holy Spirit, so they would be completely surrounded and filled with the loving God. And the person who would make that possible was coming very soon.

During Advent we can get ourselves ready for Jesus' coming to us, just as they did. We can look at what we are really like; how we really behave with others; recognise the parts of us that are real enough but we hope others won't see. Anything we find which needs washing away we need to confess to God, tell him how sorry we are about it, and the way we have made excuses, and choose to turn our backs on that way of living. You can talk to God on your own or go to your priest for the Sacrament of Reconciliation, especially if you feel you need some help with changing. We all need to come to God regularly for thorough washing, and he is the only one who can make us clean and free.

All-age ideas

- Use the Rite of Blessing and Sprinkling Holy Water in place of the Penitential Rite.

- Use today as an opportunity for everyone to renew their baptismal promises.

THIRD SUNDAY OF ADVENT

Isaiah 61:1-2, 10-11
Magnificat:
  Luke 1:46-50, 53-54
1 Thessalonians
  5:16-24
John 1:6-8, 19-28

In Jesus, God will be fulfilling the Messianic prophecies about the promised Saviour.

All-age talk

Talk about the buying of Christmas presents and take out a list you've been making of all the Christmas jobs and how far you have all got with them. At this stage of Advent some people have probably got all their presents bought, wrapped and hidden, while others have hardly begun.

Before Jesus had been born, the people of Israel had been waiting ages and ages for God's Saviour to come and save them. Every young woman would pray that her baby might be the Messiah, just as her grandmother had done before her. Through all the terrible crises of national life, the prophets had kept alive in the people of Israel their calling to be God's people. One day, the prophets all said, God would actually come in some way to be really 'with them' personally. They were to keep themselves ready and watchful for when that happened.

(Take out another 'list', and unroll it. On this are written the checkpoints from today's Isaiah reading.) The prophets even gave them a kind of 'Christmas' or 'Messiah' list of things to look out for in God's chosen one, the Messiah, or Christ. They would be able to recognise the Messiah when he came because these are the things he would do:

- tell the good news to the poor
- comfort the broken-hearted
- set free those feeling imprisoned
- announce the time when God would show his merciful judgement
- give people clothes of praise and joy to replace their sadness

148

- be fair to everyone
- make what is right grow strong
- put wrong things right

Now who do we know who did come and do those things, and is still doing them now? Jesus! And when was it that Jesus came into our world? At Christmas. So all their waiting and hoping was worth it. And anyone who wasn't sure could check with the Christmas (or 'Messiahmas') list and see for themselves. And so can we.

All-age ideas

- Have the Isaiah passage read with a group of voices, people of different voice tones speaking different sections. Work the best way out for your group by gathering to read through the whole passage and talking about it first, so their understanding will be reflected in the reading. Try out suggestions and be prepared to adjust them if they don't sound right. Each person can mark their parts on a copy of the passage.

- Mime the Gospel reading, but have the conversation section learnt so the actors say their own words.

FOURTH SUNDAY OF ADVENT

2 Samuel 7:1-5, 8-11, 16
Psalm 88
Romans 16:25-27
Luke 1:26-38

God's promised kingdom, announced both to King David in ancient times and to Mary by the angel Gabriel, will go on for ever.

All-age talk

Bring in something to show which you thought would last you a long time, but hasn't (like a pair of shoes or a felt-tip pen), and something else which you didn't think would last at all and it has (like a paper bookmark or a jar of Marmite). Talk about these and the way some things, like great cathedrals, are built to last for hundreds and hundreds of years, while other things, like newspapers or toilet paper, are not designed to last very long at all.

King David was wanting to build a temple for the glory of God which was a strong, permanent structure, rather than a temporary tent. And God told David that his ideas for the kingdom were far more long-lasting even than a strong building; God's idea was for a kingdom of love and peace that lasts not just for a long time but for ever and ever and ever. And Jesus would be the king. The angel Gabriel was sent to Mary to tell her all about it.

'You are going to have a child, Mary,' said Gabriel, 'and he's going to be the king of a kingdom that will last for ever.' The angel even told Mary what to call her child when he was born. (Show a large notice with the word 'Jesus' on one side of it.) He was to be called Jesus.

Names are important, and they often have a special meaning. Pick out some of the names in the congregation and look up what they mean in one of those 'your baby's name' books. The name Jesus has a meaning as well. It means 'Saviour: the one who saves' (show this written on the other side of the Jesus sign). Through King Jesus, God was coming to save his people.

When Jesus, the Saviour King, was born at the first Christmas, that was just the beginning! God's kingdom is still here today, and it's still growing.

All-age ideas

- Set out the passage from Romans on a sheet for everyone to read, like this:

  Men/boys   Now to him who is able to establish you, by my Gospel and the proclamation of Jesus Christ,

  Women/girls   according to the revelation of the mystery hidden for long ages past,

  Men/boys   but now revealed and made known

  Women/girls   through the prophetic writings by the command of the eternal God,

  Men/boys   so that all nations might believe and obey him –

  All   to the only wise God be glory for ever through Jesus Christ! Amen.

- Place a globe or a world map near the Advent candle wreath.

CHRISTMAS DAY

Isaiah 62:11-12
Psalm 97
Titus 3:4-7
Luke 2:15-20

Jesus Christ, the world's Saviour, is here with us, born as a human baby.

All-age talk

Ask a few volunteers to take the microphone (or shout) and wish everyone a happy Christmas. We've all spent the last month preparing everything – the food and drink, the surprises, the gifts, the decorations – so that we can make a good job of wishing our loved ones a really happy Christmas.

What are we wishing them when we say 'Happy Christmas!' to them? Collect some ideas of what we want for them. They will probably include lots of good wishes directly linked with partying and family celebration. We choose this particular day to wish people those good things we might want for them every day of the year.

Why is the festival of Christmas such a good time to wish people wonderful things in their life? (Arrange for someone to be given a lighted candle at the back of the church at this point, which they carry up to you.) All those things we wish those we love are to do with wanting their lives to be bright and shining, well lit and beautiful in every way. And today, Christmas Day, we are celebrating a life shining with God's glory, which has come right among us. Jesus, the promised Christ, has been born.

So we are right to wish everyone a happy Christmas. What better way to celebrate God's great love for us all than by wishing everyone we meet the light of loving in their lives! Don't let it stop at the ones in your family or circle of friends. Wish it (and mean it) even to those you don't always get on with; wish it to those you hardly know, like the bus conductor, the toll collector at the road tunnel, the other people walking their dogs this afternoon and anyone else you should meet.

152

Pray for them and wish them the light of God's blessing in their lives as you spread the message – Happy Christmas!

All-age ideas

- Have lots of candles around the church today, ensuring that they are really safe. Try nightlights on window ledges and/or along the front edge of the altar. Have some of the children holding candles around the altar at the Eucharistic Prayer. Or give every family a candle, which has been alight during worship, to burn at home each day of the twelve days of Christmas.

- Dress the children up to mime the Gospel, in a series of 'stills'.

- Give out bells, shakers and streamers to be shaken and waved all over the church during the Gloria.

FIRST SUNDAY OF CHRISTMAS: THE HOLY FAMILY

Ecclesiasticus 3:2-6,
  12-14
Psalm 127
Colossians 3:12-21
Luke 2:22-40

The Saviour of the world is born as a fully human baby into a real human family.

All-age talk

If possible play a snatch of the music from one of the 'pet rescue' type of programmes currently showing. One of the popular sections of such programmes is when various creatures are shown who need a good home, and people can phone in to offer that 'home' care which the animals so badly need. So many people phone in that they have to limit the response to those living in the area, and remind all the generous, loving children that they must check with their parents before the family home is offered!

Produce a realistic-looking toy dog or rabbit, and invite everyone to choose an ideal home for such an animal. Work out a short history of the animal, such as its age and background, expected full-grown size and eating requirements, together with any particular problem it may have (such as being scared of cats, or needing lots of company). Gather ideas about a suitable home for this animal.

When Jesus was born into our world as a human baby, it was very important that he was born into a suitable home to grow up in. Let's forget what we know about Jesus' family for a minute and imagine that we are in God the Father's place – looking for a good home for Jesus to be born into. What sort of home might God have thought it had to be? Collect ideas of a good home for Jesus, the Saviour of the world, and write these up, either on an OHP or on large sheets of paper which volunteers can hold up and show everyone.

Now look at how these can be seen to fit in with

the home that Mary and Joseph provided. It wasn't a rich home with lots of money to spend on Jesus, but there was lots of love in it, both for God and for one another. In many ways it was very ordinary, so that Jesus grew up knowing what ordinary family life was like for everyone else. It was a home where the parents really believed in God and lived that out in their everyday lives.

If we invite Jesus to live with us in our homes, then every home we represent can become a holy family, where Jesus shares our ordinary living, our tears of laughter and of sadness, and our dependence on God for everything.

All-age ideas

- This week's Gospel could be mimed, using nativity play costumes if available.

- Consider having a collection today, either of money or basic toiletries, to be taken to a local organisation which provides practical help for families in need or in crisis.

- Involve extended families (including singles and 'adopted' grandparents, aunts and uncles) in readings, prayers and welcoming ministries.

SECOND SUNDAY OF CHRISTMAS

Ecclesiasticus (Sirach)
 24:1-4, 12-16
Psalm 147
Ephesians 1:3-6, 15-18
John 1:1-18

The Word made flesh at Christmas was always with God, always expressing his creative love.

All-age talk

Start by giving everyone one minute to find out from and share with someone else something that went really well, or was really funny, or was a complete disaster over this Christmas. One thing all humans have always loved doing is talking together! Toddlers, children, young people, middle-aged and old people all love a chat. Even babies talk, in their own way. What would we do without the telephone, especially if we can't get out like we used to. With e-mail we can chat to people all over the world, and with television, radio, magazines and newspapers people can chat to us about anything and everything. Ground control can direct astronauts in space, pilots can be talked down to a safe landing, and surgeons can talk their students through complicated heart operations. Politicians can shout their ideas to crowds of people, and friends can whisper their secrets. All of this is the magic of words.

Why do we talk about Jesus as the Word of God?

Whenever we use words we express ourselves. Jesus expresses God, not in a speech bubble but as a human being like us, so that we can understand God in a better way than ever. God has always expressed himself, of course, so the Word of God has been there as long as God has – for ever. God *said*, 'Let there be light!' God *said*, 'Let there be stars and plants and animals, fish and birds.' God *said*, 'Let there be people in our likeness to look after the earth.' So it was the Word of God which spoke those things into being through love.

Then, at Christmas, the Word of God actually

156

took shape itself – human shape. And his name was Jesus, which means 'the one who saves us'.

All-age ideas

- For the Penitential Rite:

  The shape of God's Word is a loving Saviour;
  how loving are the words we speak?

  Lord, have mercy.
  Lord, have mercy.

  The Word of God is willing to be vulnerable and accessible;
  how high are the walls we build?

  Christ, have mercy.
  Christ, have mercy.

  In humility, the Word of God lays aside his glory;
  what importance have we given to the things we possess and desire?

  Lord, have mercy.
  Lord, have mercy.

- On the walls or pillars, have speech bubbles with the following sentences in:

  Let there be light.

  Let the earth produce growing things.

  Let us make human beings in our image.

  In one speech bubble have a picture of the infant Jesus.

THE EPIPHANY OF THE LORD

Isaiah 60:1-6
Psalm 71
Ephesians 3:2-3a, 5-6
Matthew 2:1-12

Jesus, the promised Messiah, is shown to the Gentile world.

All-age talk

Consider using the suggested sketch in the All-age Ideas just before the talk. Have a number of masks, based on the pictures below, to put on some volunteers, which alter the way we see them and act towards them.

Vicky

Sidney

With the first volunteer, explain that Vicky is feeling really fed up because her Christmas tokens were stolen before she got round to spending them. (Aah!) Have everyone making a 'ding dong' doorbell noise. It's the football squad coach! Quick, Vicky chooses to put on the bright, happy mask! (Help her on with it.)

With the second volunteer, explain that Sidney's feeling really fed up because his Christmas tokens went through the wash by mistake and are now a hard crusty blob. (Aah!) The doorbell rings again. (Ding dong.) It's someone Sidney doesn't know, and they're wearing the colours of a team Sidney doesn't support! Quick, where's that angry 'What on earth do you think you're doing here?' mask? (Help him on with it.)

We all have lots of masks which we keep by the door. Sometimes it's right to wear them, and helps us get out of a bad mood faster. But sometimes we forget what is mask and what is real, and that's not so good.

For some people we are always on our best behaviour, showing them how kind and friendly we are, how ready to help and forgive them. With others we want to show them that although we're doing our grudging best to be polite, it's a real effort and we'd far rather we didn't have to have anything to do with them. Some people we're happy to welcome to church, some we hope will never come, at least to the same church as us! Sometimes we're not very good at welcoming people who look different, wear different clothes or speak with a different accent from ours. We make it quite clear to them that they are outsiders.

But today we hear that God led these strangers all the way to Bethlehem, specially to show them his baby Son! We hear that King Herod pretended to make them welcome. And we hear that at Jesus' home they really were made welcome. God wanted these 'outsiders' to be among the first to meet his Son because Jesus had come into the world for everybody, and not just for the Jewish people.

As Christians, we need to remember that the good news of the Gospel is for everyone, and not just those like us. So today we ask God to turn us into people who are happy to welcome outsiders, without needing any masks to pretend.

All-age ideas

- This short sketch explores the idea of Jesus coming for the whole world.

  (Joseph, Mary and the baby Jesus are at the front of the church. The wise men walk up the aisle towards them and knock on a 'door'.)

  1st wise man   Excuse me, is anyone there?

  (Joseph comes to the door)

159

Joseph	Bit late for visiting, isn't it? What do you want?
2nd wise man	Our navigation lights only work at night, I'm afraid. *(Points up to the star)* Is there a baby king here at all?
Joseph	You must be joking – does this look like a palace? Go and annoy some of your own lot – we're a respectable Jewish household here. *(Slams door. Wise men shrug, look at their presents and turn away.)*
3rd wise man	I thought it was too good to be true – a Saviour for the whole world. It's not for us, then. We're not included, obviously. *(They walk away)*
Mary	What was all that, Joseph?
Joseph	Oh, a bunch of star-gazing weirdos. You should have seen their ridiculous clothes! I didn't let on about our little Jesus, though. Got to protect him from all those prying Gentiles, haven't we!
Producer	CUT! What's happening? That's not the script! It didn't happen like that at all! *(Turns to wise men)* Come on, you lot! God wouldn't have got you seeking just to have you turned away!
	(The wise men turn and walk back up the aisle. As a narrator reads Matthew 2:10-11, they mime the actions, and Joseph and Mary embrace them.)

- Have gifts of burning frankincense, gold and myrrh brought at the offertory, while the appropriate verses of *We three kings* are sung.

THE BAPTISM OF THE LORD

Isaiah 42:1-4, 6-7
Psalm 28
Acts 10:34-38
Mark 1:7-11

Through the Holy Spirit, Jesus is affirmed at his Baptism as God's beloved Son, and we too are given the Spirit of God which affirms us as God's adopted daughters and sons.

All-age talk

Bring along a pair of wellington boots which fit you, or arrange beforehand for a volunteer to bring their boots and do the actions as you talk.

Stand the boots together where they can be seen, and explain that these boots (being very keen, conscientious boots) want to walk wherever you go. (Walk about and watch the boots, still sitting there and not moving.) They are trying very hard, but they don't seem to be getting anywhere, do they? Perhaps they need a bit of encouragement. (Some of the children can encourage the boots from a distance!)

Poor old boots – they'd love to be walking where you walk, but they just can't manage it. Why not? Because they haven't got you inside them!

Climb into the boots and see the difference. Suddenly they are able to walk around wherever you walk. They can even jump with you, run with you and dance with you! And all because they have you in them.

Now what has a keen pair of boots got to do with our readings for today? Well, we can know lots about Jesus and what he did on earth and what he said, and that can make us very keen to live like him – in a loving, generous, honest way. But unless we ask God to be in us, getting to know him as a person, rather than a set of facts, or a bit of a history lesson, we'll be like the boots on their own, wanting to move with God, but not able to do it on their own. (As you say this, take off the boots and put them on their own while you move around.)

161

As soon as we ask God into our life, his Spirit comes and moves in us (put the boots on again), and that makes it possible for us to go wherever God wants us to go, and act as God wants us to act. The Spirit of God which was seen settling on Jesus when John baptised him in the river Jordan, settles on all of God's children as they put their faith and trust in him.

So let's not waste our time trying hard to do good things *for* God like a pair of boots without any living feet in them. Instead, let's invite the Spirit of God every day to come and fill us, so God's life is *in* us, and can let us dance through life with praise, walk beside those who need our help, and stick to the right path all the way to heaven.

All-age ideas

- Decorate the font with blue and white flowers, shells and stones, and have posters or banners nearby expressing the Spirit of God, with the words: 'Come, Holy Spirit, fill my life!'

- Renew baptismal vows, and recall our own baptism, with everyone marking a cross on their foreheads with their thumb as they say, 'I turn to Christ'.

- Invite everyone to pray silently and fervently for the Holy Spirit to come and fill them and the whole Church with God's life. Encourage everyone to continue that prayer wherever they are each day at midday. If every person did that in every parish using this book, that's a huge crowd of praying people, all focused on asking for more of God in our lives!

FIRST SUNDAY OF LENT

Genesis 9:8-15
Psalm 24
1 Peter 3:18-22
Mark 1:12-15

After his Baptism Jesus is led by the Spirit into the wilderness before returning to proclaim God's kingdom.

All-age talk

Bring with you a compass, and a chart showing that there are six weeks before Easter Day.

Explain that in six weeks' time it will be Good Friday and Easter Day, when we will all be celebrating Jesus rising to new life that lasts for ever, after being put to death on the cross. That's such a very special, important thing to celebrate that the Church decided we all need a few weeks to get ourselves ready for it. Time to think carefully about what it means to be a follower of Jesus. Time to sort our lives out a bit. Draw attention to the change of colour in church – purple is quite a serious, thoughtful colour, to match our serious, thoughtful mood in these next six weeks, which are called Lent.

Why *six* weeks? We are told that when Jesus had gone to the river Jordan and been baptised by John, he went straight off into the desert hills, to spend forty days, getting ready to tell everyone the good news of God's kingdom. He didn't get ready by reading lots of books and doing lots of homework, or talking to lots of people. He got ready by living very simply, even going without food, and letting God lead him into the areas he needed to think about. He wanted to spend time finding out what God really wanted him to do with his life.

So, as the Church, we're going to do the same. Today is the day we all set off into the desert for six weeks. What do you think we'll need to take with us? Produce various items of combat gear, and mountain-walking clothing and equipment. Then kick it all away. We're not going to need any of this. All we need is one thing – a compass. What does a

163

compass do? It helps you walk in the right direction. We need a special compass that always points us in God's direction.

Explain that you happen to have just the compass we need, and produce a cross – a wall-hanging one is about the right size so that people can see it easily. This is a special compass for us to take into the desert of Lent with us. Hold the cross flat. It points us always towards God's love, and at the same time it points back at ourselves. We can't pretend in this desert. We've got to be honest to God about who we are and how we are thinking and feeling. That's the only way the compass will point us in the right direction. Are we ready for the desert of Lent?

The first step on our journey is to agree to live more simply for a while, and go wherever God takes us. We can spend this week doing that, remembering to use our compass every day.

All-age ideas

- Invite everyone to close their fists and think of all the things they would hate to have to give up. Thank God for them all, recognising that we are not owners of anything, but stewards. As they feel ready to, invite everyone to open their hands slowly to God, with all that is in there open to be used in his service of love. As they do so they can say, silently, 'Here I am, Lord. I offer you my life.'

- In place of the Creed consider using the baptismal promises, to remind everyone of their baptism.

- Construct a rainbow of God's promise for people to walk under as they come into church. This might be a paper archway fixed with Blu-Tack above the doorway and painted by the children.

SECOND SUNDAY OF LENT

Genesis 22:1-2, 9-13,
   15-18
Psalm 115
Romans 8:31-34
Mark 9:2-10

Christ's willingness to face suffering and death, in order to save us, proclaims the total sacrificial love of God.

All-age talk

Gather ideas about how to listen well. This may include such things as stopping our own noise, being very still, wanting to find out what's going on, concentrating our minds, and engaging ears, brain and heart all at once. Having talked about it, try it out, by listening to every sound around us (and even inside us!).

Now show a mountain picture on an OHP, or in a few calendar pictures which children walk around the church, while you describe how mountains have long been thought of as very special, holy places. Jesus took three of his disciples up a mountain where they watched Jesus lit up with the glory of God's brightness as he prayed. Part of that amazing experience was hearing the voice of God speaking into their hearts and minds. They heard it and didn't miss it because they were really concentrating and wanting to know what all this was about. They were still and their ears were engaged with their brains and their hearts.

So what did they hear?

Have the words written large (in lower case) for everyone to read in a stage whisper: 'This is my beloved Son – listen to him.'

Out of all the listening we do every day, and out of all the listening we'll do over our whole lifetime, there's one thing which God himself has told us to listen to. And that isn't a particular programme or CD, it isn't a particular political leader or even our best friend. It's Jesus. And God has given us a personal recommendation to listen to Jesus with all our very best listening skills, because God knows that if we really listen to Jesus we shall start to understand the meaning of life, who we are, and how to live this life we've been given.

All-age ideas

- Fill the church with light from candles – in clusters, or held by the congregation.

- For the Penitential Rite:

  We have been possessive
  over what is freely given by you.

  Lord, have mercy.
  Lord, have mercy.

  We have avoided standing up
  for what we know to be right,
  in case it brings suffering.

  Christ, have mercy.
  Christ, have mercy.

  We seek our personal comfort
  more than we seek your kingdom.

  Lord, have mercy.
  Lord, have mercy.

THIRD SUNDAY OF LENT

Exodus 20:1-17
Psalm 18
1 Corinthians 1:22-25
John 2:13-25

God's wisdom may shock us. Jesus, obedient to God's Law and fulfilling it, dies a death which, according to the Law, makes him cursed.

All-age talk

Begin by asking for some volunteers to read the following conversations.

1. **Mum:** David, it's time to stop playing and go to bed now.

   David: Oh, but Mum, I'm much too busy!

2. **Dad:** Turn that music down, Gary!

   Gary: But I like it, and it needs to be loud!

3. **Hilda:** George, it's time you gave up smoking.

   George: But, Hilda, it's my decision, and none of your business.

4. **Fred:** Now, Mother, you need to wear a hearing aid.

   Mother: What's that, Fred?

   Fred: A HEARING AID! YOU NEED TO WEAR ONE, MOTHER.

   Mother: No, I don't – I can hear perfectly when people bother to speak up properly!

All through our lives we're supposed to be obedient, and all through our lives we prefer to do as we like!

Today we're on the third week of our desert journey together through Lent. And we're going to look at what it means to be obedient, and why it's a good thing to work at, even though we all find it so very difficult to do what we're told.

Scatter the ten commandments, written on pieces

167

of card, over the aisle, or stick them with Blu-Tack on to pillars.

In our first reading we heard the ten commandments – ten useful rules to help us live God's way. These rules were given to the people through Moses, the great leader who had led the people out of slavery in Egypt. They've all been in the desert for quite a long time, learning to be God's people, like we are through Lent. And then God gives them the Law, which they are told to obey. They are still good rules, and when Jesus came he didn't say, 'Listen, everyone, now I've come you don't need to bother with all those commandments any more!' Jesus insisted that he had come not to destroy the Law but to fulfil it, to fill it full of God's love.

So Jesus summed all the rules up in two parcels. Produce one bag labelled 'Love God' and another one labelled 'Love one another', and sort out the first four commandments into the first bag and the second six into the second bag. That makes them easier for us to carry around in our heads (hold a bag in each hand), but we need to remember what's inside each bag, and take them out to look at from time to time, like we've done today.

So Jesus thought it was good to be obedient. He was obedient to his heavenly Father, even when that turned out to mean he had to die on the cross! The reason he was obedient was because he really understood why it was important.

If we understand the reason for being obedient, we're much more likely to try and do what we're told. If Fred's mother really understood how difficult it was becoming for the family to talk to her without her hearing aid, she'd *want* to wear it. If Gary really understood how hard it was for his Dad to concentrate on his work with the music so loud, he'd *want* to turn it down a bit.

In other words, obedience is all to do with acting out of love. As we get to understand and love God better, we shall find we are more and more keen to do what he wants us to.

All-age ideas

- Use the first reading as an extended form of penitence, encouraging everyone to get to know the commandments by adding visual clues. (These might be a large number one; a blank piece of paper; a cardboard speech bubble with 'Keep it clean' written on it; a calendar page with Sunday circled in red; a bunch of flowers with a label reading, 'To Mum and Dad'; a gun; a wedding congratulations card; a swag bag; a file clearly labelled 'Lies'; and a thought bubble with 'If only . . .' written on it.)

- Have two voices to read the commandments alternately, with someone holding up a finger as each is read, till all ten fingers are held up. In their places, everyone can follow this counting off process as a focus. After each commandment, pause for reflection before everyone says, 'Lord, have mercy on us'.

- The commandments could be written up and displayed on walls and pillars for today.

Fourth Sunday of Lent

2 Chronicles 36:14-16,
  19-23
Psalm 136
Ephesians 2:4-10
John 3:14-21

God loves us so much that he is generous with his mercy.

All-age talk

Ask if anyone has ever tried to rescue a bird or worm, dog, cat or snail, and invite one of two of these stories to be told. Children, particularly, are ready to rescue small creatures, even if the hope of recovery seems slight. Adults are good at doing such rescues as well. We think it's worth having paramedics to race to where someone has had an accident or a heart attack and try their best to keep them alive and make them better.

Whenever we do this we are behaving like God our Father. It is God's character to want to rescue and save.

We know it feels wrong and sub-human to walk past someone who's suddenly fallen down and hurt themselves. We know it feels right and human to do whatever we can to help them.

In our Gospel today we're listening in on a conversation Jesus is having. He is teaching Nicodemus about how much God loves us. In some ways we are all like people who have collapsed on the pavement and badly need a paramedic to give us the kiss of life. We may be physically fit and healthy, but when we look at the state of our souls, at the secrets we guard and the ways we think, it doesn't look quite such a healthy picture. By the unloving things we think, speak and do, and the loving things we fail to do, we are in dire need of a spiritual kiss of life.

And that's what God gives us, through Jesus coming to live among us, dying for us and rising to new life. He is the one who can give us that spiritual kiss of life we need, breathing his life into us and saving us from being condemned to everlasting death. That's why he came – not to condemn us, but so that we may be saved.

All-age ideas

- Have a group of people to help read the Gospel. All the way through from 'Yes, God loved the world . . .' there are alternating phrases – 'not to . . . but so that . . .' – so that it can almost be read antiphonally, with the main reader reading the introductory verses.

- This mime can be done in silence or while people sit and sing either *Only by grace can we enter* or *Make me a channel of your peace*. Prepare large signs in the shape of arrows, with one of the words on one side and one on the other: Hate/Love; Conflict/Peace; Death/Eternal life; Doubt/Faith; Despair/Joy; Injury/Pardon. All the negatives point the same way. People walk to the centre or front with their arrows clearly showing on the negative side. Someone carrying a processional cross walks slowly along the line of people. As the cross comes close to them each turns direction so that the arrows are all pointing the way the cross is going, and the positives are displayed.

FIFTH SUNDAY OF LENT

Jeremiah 31:31-34
Psalm 50
Hebrews 5:7-9
John 12:20-33

Through Christ's death, full life would come to people of all nations and generations.

All-age talk

Bring with you a box of assorted sweets or chocolates, and invite a couple of volunteers to choose one. Ask them why they chose it (there may be no reason at all) and whether they are happy with the choice they made.

All our life long we are faced with making choices. Sometimes the choice isn't that important; if you make a mistake and choose a chocolate which isn't a favourite, you haven't lost out much. But sometimes the choices are more important. Invite a couple of car owners to talk about their choice of car and whether they are happy with their decision. Ask a student which A levels they have chosen to take, or which degree course, and a child what they have chosen to do for a birthday treat.

Sometimes we have to choose even more important things than that! Let's look at a very hard choice Jesus had to make, which we heard about in today's Gospel. Jesus knew that he was alive on earth for a very important mission – he was here to save the world, and he really wanted to do that, because he loved the people. But there was a problem. He also knew that saving the world was bound to land him in terrible pain and danger, more pain and agony than anyone has ever faced before or since. It would involve taking on himself all the sin and evil of the world, and going on loving right through it.

So he had the choice – to go ahead with saving the world, taking on the suffering as part of the deal, or to avoid all that appalling suffering by opting

172

out, in which case the world would have no hope of being saved.

And it wasn't an easy thing to choose. Everything human in him screamed out against going through the pain of it all; but everything divine in him pleaded for love and compassion, and selfless giving whatever the cost.

We know what Jesus chose. Love won, and he chose to go through hell, giving up everything, including his life, just so that we could be set free to live.

All-age ideas

- As a form of preparation for the Pentitential Rite, provide everyone with the words of Psalm 50 and play a recording of it (*Miserere* by Allegri) so they can have a time of meditation and sorrow for sin. For children use a larger print and this simplified version:

  > O God, have mercy on me
  > because you are loving.
  > I know about the things I have done wrong
  > and cannot forget them.
  > Please wipe out all my wrong doing.
  > Wash away my guilt
  > and make me clean again.
  > Give me back the joy that comes
  > when you save me.
  > Keep me strong by giving me a willing spirit.

- Use music as a background to the reading from Jeremiah – such as the slow movement from Mozart's *Clarinet Concerto*, or *The Swan* by Saint-Saëns.

Palm (Passion) Sunday

Liturgy of the Palms:
Mark 11:1-10 or
John 12:12-16
Psalm 118:1-2, 19-24

Liturgy of the Passion:
Isaiah 50:4-7
Psalm 21
Philippians 2:6-11
Mark 14:1-15:47 or
 Mark 15:1-39 (40-47)

As the Messiah, Jesus enters Jerusalem, knowing that he rides towards rejection and death in order to save his people.

All-age talk

Beforehand make two large, clear signs, one saying, 'Hosanna! Blessed is he who comes in the name of the Lord!' and the other, 'Crucify him!'

First remind everyone of the way the crowds had welcomed Jesus as he rode into Jerusalem on a donkey. They were all giving him the red carpet welcome, throwing down greenery and their coats for the donkey to walk on, and waving palm branches as flags, cheering and singing. One of the things they shouted was from one of their traditional songs, which we know as Psalms: 'Hosanna! Blessed is he who comes in the name of the Lord!' (Everyone can shout this as loudly as possible.) It meant they were welcoming Jesus as the new King David; they were really excited, expecting Jesus to become their king and throw out all the Romans so they would be free again. They thought they really wanted God's kingdom.

Sometimes we are like the people in this crowd. We get all excited by Jesus, and promise to work with him, and feel ready to do anything to help the kingdom come. 'Let your kingdom come! Let *your* will be done!' we pray, and we really mean it. We work hard at our praying, and do our best to be loving and honest in the way we live. We give God the worship we know he deserves, and we give of ourselves simply because we are filled with love for him.

In today's Gospel we heard what happened to Jesus on Good Friday. It makes us very sad to hear what happened to our friend, and we might find ourselves thinking that we wouldn't have left him alone like his friends did; we would have been there for him; we would at least have prayed with him and not fallen asleep in the garden.

But the crowd remind us of something rather nasty. They weren't singing 'Hosanna!' any more. They were shouting, 'Crucify him!' (All shout this.) And although we wish it wasn't true, we all know there are times when we do that as well. Those times when we know very well what is the right and loving thing to do or say, and we want Jesus out of the way so we can be as unkind and dishonest as we like. It's hard work having Jesus there when we don't want to be loving, or humble, or obedient. At those times we don't much like his kingdom. Every time that happens we are joining the crowd which shouted, 'Crucify him!'

Let's remember that, and pull ourselves together when it next happens so that, instead, we shout with our lives, 'Hosanna! Blessed is he who comes in the name of the Lord!'

All-age ideas

- Involve the whole congregation in the reading of the Passion, giving individuals and small groups their parts to read and having the words the crowds say held up on placards, or shown on a screen using an OHP.

- If you are having an outdoor procession, make it a festal one, with children shaking instruments and waving greenery or streamers, and everyone singing songs they know well and won't need words for. Consider inviting the local schools to take part, and possibly a real donkey.

EASTER DAY

Acts 10:34, 37-43
Psalm 117
Colossians 3:1-4
John 20:1-9

Jesus is alive; God's love has won the victory over sin and death.

All-age talk

Bring along a hot cross bun, a chocolate Easter egg, an ordinary hen's egg, and one of those fluffy Easter chickens.

Ask a volunteer to take the first object (the hot cross bun) around the church so everyone can see what it is. As they go, explain that these buns remind us that because God loves us so much he was prepared to live among us in person, and go on loving us even when he was arrested, tortured and killed on a cross. It's in Jesus' life, and in his experience on the cross, that we can 'taste and see that God is good'.

Now for the next object (another volunteer does the rounds) which is . . . a hen's egg. The egg looks as dead as a smooth oval stone, but we know better. We know that if the egg is fertilised, and kept warm by the mother hen, that hard shell will start to crack, and into the world will climb . . . (a volunteer takes the chick around) a fluffy yellow chick, full of life! So the egg reminds us that what looked dead and hopeless on Good Friday (when Jesus' dead body was taken down from the cross, and it seemed he had failed as a Saviour) was actually full of new life, because on the third day after that, Jesus broke out of death to be alive for ever!

And so our last object (a volunteer walks the chocolate Easter egg around) is what we all enjoy having on Easter Day – chocolate Easter eggs. They're always bright and colourful, fun and delicious, and that's because Easter Day is party time for Christians! Today we celebrate the fantastic truth that Jesus Christ is Lord – Love has won the victory over evil and death for ever!

All-age ideas

- Encourage people to make their own miniature Easter gardens and bring them to church on Easter Day.

- Fill the church with flowers and candles to celebrate – perhaps different groups and clubs could undertake an arrangement each, or work on an Easter banner. Ideas for banners: 'Love is stronger than death'; 'Jesus is alive!'; 'New life'; 'He is not here, he is risen'.

SECOND SUNDAY OF EASTER

Acts 4:32-35
Psalm 117
1 John 5:1-6
John 20:19-31

Our faith in the risen Christ is bound to affect the way we live.

All-age talk

Bring with you some items of clothing which alter the way you move when wearing them, such as a pair of flippers, a pair of very heavy boots, a pair of binoculars and a pair of very high-heeled shoes.

Invite volunteers to demonstrate that when they are wearing (or looking through) these, it changes the way they walk. The changed way of moving is all part of wearing them.

It isn't only clothes and footwear which change our way of going about; it's our thoughts and feelings as well. If we've just won a match, if the person we love has just realised they love us as well, if the mortgage rate has gone down, or if we've just been fed and changed, then the whole day looks rosy and happy, and we'll pass on our feel-good factor in the way we react to those we meet. On the other hand, if the cat's been sick on the new sofa, you've lost your spelling list and know you haven't learnt the words, if the 7:27 is half an hour late, or you're hungry and your bottom feels damp and sore, then those feelings will probably make you less friendly and forgiving, and far more grumpy!

When we look at today's picture of life in the early Church, we're struck by how much love there seems to be in the community. Something is making these people happy to look after one another instead of fighting and arguing, and happy to share everything instead of looking after number one all the time. So what is making them like this? It must be something very good and very powerful!

It's all to do with them knowing something. They *know* that Jesus is alive and among them, so they

178

are living in Jesus' company all the time. Jesus being there changes the way they live.

Now for a big question we all need to ask ourselves. Would anyone guess, just from looking at how we think and speak and behave, that we *knew* Jesus was living here among us?

He is, so it should show!

All-age ideas

- As an introduction, or as an acted reflection, have someone knocking loudly on the outside of the church door. Then in the quietness, someone says:

  If the risen Jesus knocked on the door of our church, would we be happy to let him in?

  (Pause for reflection)

  If he knocked on the door of our home, would we want to let him in?

  (Pause)

  What would he be glad to find?

  (Pause)

  What would he be sad to find?

  (Pause)

  (The door is knocked again)

  Come, Lord Jesus, we welcome you among us!

- Cut out the letters of 'LIFE' from foil and stand lighted candles along them where people will see them.

THIRD SUNDAY OF EASTER

Acts 3:13-15, 17-19
Psalm 4
1 John 2:1-5
Luke 24:35-48

Having redeemed us by his death, Jesus can offer us the forgiveness of our sin, which sets us free to live.

All-age talk

Bring along a dry stick and a growing plant with fresh shoots.

Easter is all about a different, richer sort of life which we can now have, thanks to Jesus going through death for us. It's a bit like the difference between this dry stick (show it) and this one which is full of life and growing (show it).

In today's Gospel we heard that Jesus comes into the locked room where his frightened disciples have met (display a number 1), and puts their minds at rest, so they aren't terrified, even though they are open-mouthed at God's power. Then (display a number 2) Jesus explains things to them so that they begin to understand that Jesus had to die and rise again, and lastly (display a number 3) he commissions them, sending them out to set everyone free to live this way (the shooting plant) instead of that (the dry stick).

We may not have noticed, but there are lots and lots of dry sticks like this walking around. Dry stick people are often disguised. Because they are only interested in money, possessions or following their own wants, they often look attractive, with the latest everything to wear, smear on their face, drive or play. But a look into their eyes will show you that they are hard and dry as people, without any real joy, and may well be full of worries and anxieties, guilt and fear. Many of these dry sticks really know that this way of living is 'second best' but don't know how to get fully alive, or are frightened that God would say they were beyond his help.

Today is great news for all dry sticks! In going

180

through evil and death without love slipping, even for a split second, Jesus has won for us all the victory over the sin and evil which dries us up and stops us living God's full life. All any dry stick needs is God's forgiveness; as they admit to themselves and to God what they are really like, and how they are cut off from him, his forgiveness starts to work on them, turning them into vibrant, warm, joy-filled people, happy to be living God's full life, and no longer bullied and caged by things that don't matter.

All-age ideas

- Use a song such as *Purify my heart* as everyone calls to mind the areas in their lives and attitudes where repentance is needed, or *I'm accepted, I'm forgiven*.

- On a long piece of lining paper, have a dead-looking twig drawn. During the talk the younger children can stick on green leaves (pre-cut) so that this dead branch is given new life.

FOURTH SUNDAY OF EASTER

Acts 4:8-12
Psalm 117
1 John 3:1-2
John 10:11-18

'I am the Good Shepherd and I lay down my life for the sheep.'

All-age talk

Gather all the young children in the aisle and get them doing sheepy things like eating grass, drinking from a stream, sitting and chewing, and bleating. Place a few older children around the edges of the building to be wolves and bears, sheep-watching and hoping for a chance to eat one of the lambs. They can howl sadly as they wait, or growl. One person is a good shepherd, keeping an eye on the flock, and watching out for any signs of wolves and bears.

The wild animals are waiting for the shepherd to go for a break, or doze off, because that's when they might get a chance to grab a lamb or sheep. But this shepherd loves his sheep, and that means he isn't going to give the wild animals any opportunity to attack the flock. He's ready to defend them with his life, if necessary.

Now swap the shepherd for a hired hand. Here's a different flock, with a different shepherd, further up the valley. The wild animals have gathered here now, and they're still waiting. (Howls and growls.) A couple of wolves start to come closer, but this shepherd doesn't frighten them away – he just runs away! The wolves get more confident. They're getting dangerously close, and the sheep are all huddled together, when that good shepherd walks up, with stones in his catapult, and the wolves back off quick!

Thank the sheep and wild animals for their help, and explain that Jesus is like a good shepherd, who cares for us and looks after us, protecting us from evil. He loves us, so he isn't going to let us down, and is even ready to lay down his life for his sheep.

In fact, as we know, Jesus did just that – he was ready to lay down his life to set us free.

All-age ideas

- Have a simple cut-out of a sheep on white paper for everyone and give these out as people come into church. Use them as a focus in a time of prayer, as an alternative form of Prayer of the Faithful. First people write their name on their sheep, and hold it as they pray for people in need of Jesus' shepherding in their own families, in this country and in the world. Then swap the sheep around by collecting them and distributing them again. Now everyone can pray for the person named on the sheep, knowing at the same time that they are being prayed for themselves.

- Incorporate a crook and sheep or lambs in one of the flower arrangements, using meadow flowers and grasses.

FIFTH SUNDAY OF EASTER

Acts 9:26-31
Psalm 21
1 John 3:18-24
John 15:1-8

To produce fruit we need to be joined on to the true vine.

All-age talk

Cut six long strips of green crepe paper, or lengths of green string. Also prepare ten cut-out bunches of grapes from coloured paper.

Begin by suggesting that if you came in and said you were a pair of curtains, everyone would probably tell you to pull yourself together. But in our Gospel today we find Jesus saying, 'I am a grape vine.' Obviously he wasn't really a grape vine, was he? So what on earth did he mean?

To help us understand, we're going to make a kind of grape vine. Ask one volunteer to hold a green string in each hand, and two others to tie the strings round their waists. They can now hold four strings between them, and four others can tie these round their waists. Now for the fruit. Each of the last four people can hold a bunch of grapes in each hand (eight altogether) and the other two bunches can be stuck with a loop of sticky tape to the fronts of the second two volunteers.

In just a short time, and with just a few people, we've grown quite a big vine and ten bunches of fruit! Just imagine how much fruit there would be if everyone here was joined on the vine.

Jesus said he was the true vine and his Father was the gardener, looking after the growing and helping the vine branches to produce as much fruit as possible. Obviously these branches are only able to produce their fruit if they're joined on to the vine, because all the life-giving sap feeds them and if they're cut off they don't get anything to keep them alive.

Jesus was really saying that if we want our lives to produce fruit like love, joy, peace, patience,

184

kindness, goodness, faithfulness, gentleness and self-control (stick these labels on the grapes), then we have to make really sure that we're joined up to Jesus and in touch with him. We need his life in us all the time. We need to keep in touch with him every day!

All-age ideas

- Include some vine leaves, or vine-like plants, and grapes in one of the flower arrangements today.

- Pray particularly for church mission links today, including any updates and specific prayer concerns, photos and maps. Have an airmail open letter for people to add their encouragement and send it off today.

SIXTH SUNDAY OF EASTER

Acts 10:25-26, 34-35,
   44-48
Psalm 97
1 John 4:7-10
John 15:9-17

We are to love one another as Jesus loves us.

All-age talk

Begin with the sketch in All-age Ideas, which looks at the difference between servants and friends.

Invite everyone to spot the differences. Also ask those involved in the sketch what differences they felt. The kind of things which might come up are the sense of involvement and belonging which friend-ship gives, compared with the distance and lack of co-operation in servants; the difference in how they feel valued, and what response is acceptable.

Point out that Jesus said he was no longer think-ing of us as servants but as friends. That means we are people he is happy to talk things over with, co-operate with and involve in the work. There is going to be companionship and perhaps some good-natured teasing. Above all is the sense that we are in this together, and enjoying one another's company.

Another thing Jesus said is that we are to love one another in the way he loves us. So how is that? How does Jesus love us? Collect people's ideas; here are some that occurred to me:

- as friends
- with affection
- treating us seriously
- understanding us
- with honesty
- with forgiveness
- ready to put himself out for us
- with faithfulness
- consistently

186

Is this how we are treating other people? Or is it how we treat the people we like? As Christians we don't have the option to choose certain people to treat with God's love, while behaving how we feel with all the rest. We can't claim to love God and then decide that some people aren't worth treating with respect or understanding.

Of course it isn't easy to love one another like this. Lots of people are difficult to love in God's way – perhaps we are, ourselves! But when we look at how amazingly God treats us, copying his way of loving is the very least we can do. And the often surprising thing is that putting ourselves out and making the effort to live God's way is very rewarding, and makes us feel much happier inside.

All-age ideas

- This sketch can be used to introduce the talk. Write two titles on sheets of paper or slate boards, which are walked around the church before each section, so everyone can see them: 'The Servant' and 'The Friends'.

The Servant

The employer is talking on his mobile phone, pacing up and down, with a file open. He's sorting out some complex problem. The office cleaner comes in with feather duster and starts cleaning.

Mr King   *(Into phone)* Quite . . . Quite . . . But look at these figures on page 24 . . . *(catches sight of Marg the cleaner)* Marg, get me a strong coffee. And a doughnut or something. *(Returns to phone)* Yes, these figures should have warned us . . . Well, the point is what can we do about it now?

(Marg reappears with coffee and doughnut.)

Marg   Coffee, Mr King. It's strong. And a doughnut. *(Puts them on desk)*

187

Mr King   (*Still on phone, listening and making 'mm' noises. Motions with hand for Marg not to interrupt him as he's busy.*) Sorry, Steve, say that again . . . the schedules systematically reduced what? . . . Oh, I see. Yes, of course. So what are you going to do about it?

(*Marg continues dusting.*)

Mr King   (*Still on phone*) Marg, get me the February file – it's there on my desk. (*Talks into phone*) It seems to me we can possibly get ourselves out of this mess, Steve. I've just had an idea.

(*Marg brings the February file to Mr King.*)

Marg   The February file, Mr King.

Mr King   (*Takes it without thanking her and starts looking in it. Into phone he says*) Yes, here it is! I'm looking at these figures for the second week of February . . .

(*Marg goes back to the dusting. The desk phone rings.*)

Mr King   Answer that, Marg.

Marg   (*Picks up phone*) Hello, Mr King's office. Well, he's very busy at the moment, in an important meeting . . . Oh, I've no idea, I'm only the cleaner here. I just do what I'm told.

The Friends

Norman and Pete walk up to a bench and sit down. They put their rucksacks down.

Pete   Phew! That was quite a climb, wasn't it. What a view, though, eh?

Norman   Marvellous, isn't it. (*Pause*) Anyway, you were saying about your interview . . .

Pete   Oh yeah, that's right. So we've got to decide whether to move or not, basically. And that's a big decision to make.

Norman	How does Sheila feel about moving? She's settled here, isn't she?
Pete	Yes, it would be quite a wrench for her, but you know Sheila, she's willing to give it a go if she feels it's what God wants for us.
Norman	Funny, isn't it. This time last year, there you were just made redundant, and no hopes for the future, and now this new door seems to be opening for you. I'm really happy for you, Pete.
Pete	Thanks, Norman. Well, you've been a good friend through all this – it's always good to talk things over with you. Shall we be on our way then? *(They get up and walk off.)*
All four characters	I no longer call you servants, because a servant doesn't know his master's business. Instead I have called you friends.

• As an alternative form of bidding prayers with a smaller group, try the following with a repeated response:

In our homes, at work and at school
help us to love one another.
In what we think and speak and do
help us to love one another.
When there are arguments
and when we disagree
help us to love one another.
When we are tired and not feeling our best
help us to love one another.
Every moment of every day,
whether it's easy or hard,
help us to love one another.

THE ASCENSION OF THE LORD

Acts 1:1-11
Psalm 46
Ephesians 1:17-23
Mark 16:15-20

Having bought back our freedom with the giving of his life, Jesus enters into the full glory to which he is entitled.

All-age talk

Prepare a large cardboard arrow pointer, and have the following things ready to use as signs: a Nativity play manger or a doll wrapped in swaddling clothes; a pair of sandals; a cross; a lit candle.

Explain that today is called Ascension Day (which means 'going up' day). Why is it called that? Because we are remembering the day when Jesus went out to a hill with his disciples this time after Easter, and they watched him returning to heaven. We are told that it looked as if Jesus was going upwards, not so much up into the sky as out of their sight. It was the last time Jesus was seen on the earth.

In a way, today is like being with the disciples on the top of a hill. If we look down one way (point the arrow backwards) we can look back to when Jesus first came to earth, as a newborn baby. (A volunteer takes the baby or crib to stand as far as possible behind the arrow, but where they are still visible.) We're not just looking back to last Christmas (which does seem quite a long time ago!) but right to when Jesus was actually born. From our Ascension hilltop we look back to Jesus' life, and all the travelling around he did. (The sandals are taken behind the arrow, but closer than the crib.) Jesus walked from town to village, healing the sick, teaching and loving the people. We can look back to the cross (the cross is brought behind the arrow, closer than the sandals) which Jesus' love brought him to, and we can remember what a great victory over evil was won there. And we can look back to that first Easter morning (the lit candle is brought close behind the

190

arrow) when death couldn't hold the Lord of life any longer, and Jesus burst into fuller life than ever.

(Turn the arrow to point upwards.) So today marks the end of Jesus' time on earth, tied to a time and a place, and we are celebrating his triumphant return to heaven, having won the victory and defeated the power of evil for us.

(Turn the arrow to face forwards.) From today's Ascension hill we are also looking forward into the future. And what do we find in the future? Among other things, all of us, sitting in this church in this year, with our lives transformed and filled with joy because of our faith in the living Jesus!

All-age ideas

- Have some decorations with clouds cut from white paper and crowns cut from gold wrapping paper.

- After the narrative of the Ascension is read, have a group of people who walk forward as if following Jesus, while music plays. They kneel in worship and then all raise their eyes slowly upwards, till they are staring at the sky. They hold this position for a few moments, and then stand up, amazed and suddenly smiling at one another. As they turn to walk joyfully down the aisle, they shout above the music: 'Let the kingdom come! In every time, in every place, let the kingdom come!' (Suitable music: 'Morning' from Grieg's *Peer Gynt* Suite.)

SEVENTH SUNDAY OF EASTER

Acts 1:15-17, 20-26
Psalm 102
1 John 4:11-16
John 17:11-19

Although now hidden from our sight, Jesus lives for ever, and in him we can live the Resurrection life even while we are on earth.

All-age talk

Prepare two short straws amongst a few full-length ones. Begin by asking for volunteers. Let all those who have offered come out but explain that as you only need two we'll choose by the fairest way – each pulling a straw from your hand. Those who pull the short straws will be the ones chosen.

Label these two Matthias and Joseph, and remind everyone of the problem the disciples had – there had been twelve of them and now there were eleven. Why wasn't Judas with them any more? Because he had helped get Jesus arrested, and afterwards gone and taken his own life.

So Peter organised the believers to choose a replacement for Judas. Who would they choose? If we were going to choose, what kind of person would we look at? What would that person have to have done?

(Collect the ideas, and re-read verses 21 and 22.)

Well, there were two possibilities, Matthias and Joseph, both good people, and both having been with Jesus all through his ministry. So how are they to choose? They did it in two stages:

1. They prayed, asking God to show them the one he wanted.

2. They used the straw method, like we used.

In effect, they had decided not to take on the choosing themselves, but felt it was so important that they should leave it entirely up to God's leading. And the one who drew the short straw was Matthias. That didn't mean that God liked Matthias better; it was just that God had another important job for Joseph, and knew that Matthias was going to be most useful for this one.

Although Jesus has ascended into heaven, and we can't see him here any more, he's very much with us *all* the time. When we have difficult decisions to make and important, scary things to organise, we don't have to do them alone. We can do what the disciples did, and keep in touch with God, wanting only what God wants and asking him to show us what that is. We can practise wanting what God wants at all kinds of times, just by saying in our hearts, 'Let your will be done!'

All-age ideas

- The mime suggested for Ascension Day (All-age Ideas, page 191) could be used today instead.

- Play some quiet, reflective music (either live or recorded) while everyone sits for a few minutes, opening themselves to God's possibilities for them and choosing to commit themselves to their calling as Christians.

PENTECOST

Acts 2:1-11
Psalm 103
1 Corinthians 12:3-7,
   12-13
John 20:19-23

The Holy Spirit of God is poured out in power on the expectant disciples, just as Jesus promised.

All-age talk

Cut flame shapes from red and orange paper (shiny paper is specially good), and have these given out to everyone as they come into church.

Remind everyone of how the Holy Spirit came, with the noise of a gale-force wind (the noise of which they can try making), and looking like fire, which split up into flames resting on each of those in the room. (Everyone holds up the flame they have been given, so there are flames all over the church.) That was how it seemed from the outside.

Inside each person, what was going on?

- (Display an exclamation mark.) The disciples were stunned by this display of the power of God. God meant business, and was clearly way outside their control. God was in charge.

- (Display a red rose or a red heart.) They suddenly knew, at first hand, what God's love really meant. They felt full of it, and it made them very happy and excited. They wanted to tell God all about it!

- (Display an empty speech bubble.) They wanted to tell other people all about it too. They wanted everyone to know God like this, because they knew how wonderful it was. And God's love in them made them want to share the good news, rather than keep it to themselves.

God is still pouring out his Holy Spirit on people, every day. Wherever anyone seriously wants to have the powerful love of God living in them, the Spirit will come and fill them.

Often we don't really want God that close. This may be because we are scared of God being really

194

powerful; but we forget that with power which is full of love and goodness we don't need to be afraid. Mostly we just aren't bothered enough to take God seriously. The disciples were spending all day in God's company, waiting and hoping for the Holy Spirit to come. How much time do we focus our attention on God?

If we want something really badly, it fills our thinking all the time. Suppose we really want a computer, or to be a ballet dancer, or to drive a car. We'll be reading all the advertisements and the magazines, spending out on lessons and working hard at them, making sure we're in touch with the experts and so on.

So if each of us, and all of us as a church, are impressed by today's reading, and serious about wanting a fresh outpouring of the Holy Spirit, what can we do?

We can really want more of God in our lives. We can want that when we wake up, all through the day, and when we lay our heads down on the pillow at night. We can want it so much that we start listening to God and getting our lives ready to receive his gift. We can put God at the centre, instead of somewhere squeezed in at the edge.

And God will come to us, filling us with his Holy Spirit, and transforming our lives.

All-age ideas

- Give the children red, orange and yellow streamers to dance with in one or two of the hymns, or the Gloria.

- Make posters or banners with flame shapes of paper stuck on and words describing the life of the Spirit, such as love, joy and peace, power and gentleness.

- Arrange to have a parish party or picnic, so that the fellowship of the community is enriched. Suggest that everyone wears something flame-coloured.

195

TRINITY SUNDAY

Deuteronomy 4:32-34,
   39-40
Psalm 32
Romans 8:14-17
Matthew 28:16-20

The mysterious and holy nature of the one true God is beyond our understanding, but it is both communal harmony and individual personality, Father, Son and Holy Spirit.

All-age talk

Prepare either an OHP acetate or a very large cut-out triangle, as shown.

Also have three equal strips of card and three paper fasteners, or bring three equal strips of a large-scale construction toy, with the appropriate nuts and bolts – basically any three things which can construct a triangle.

Start by asking a volunteer to help by making a triangle from the separate strips. As they work, do a commentary on the progress, observing the sides move in all directions until that final join, at which point the triangle is a strong shape, with each two sides holding the other firm. It's such a strong shape that it is used in building – bridges, towers, pylons, roof rafters, for example.

Why on earth are we looking at triangles in church today? Explain that today we are exploring the nature of God. Will we be able to end up by bedtime knowing all about God, then? No! Human brains aren't big enough to cope with understanding our great God completely, any more than your hamster can understand completely what it is to be human.

But as your hamster gets to know you and become your friend, little by little he will understand more about you, as much as a hamster can.

So, back to the triangles. Perhaps they can help us understand a little bit more about the great and powerful God of love. (Show your triangle.)

We've seen how strong one three-sided shape can be. Suppose for a minute we look at the threeness and oneness of God as a bit like this triangle. We know that there is only one true God, and here we have one triangle. We know that God is our Father and Creator, Jesus our Saviour and the Holy Spirit. (Turn the triangle round as you refer to each side.) Whichever aspect of God we focus on, we are always looking at God in all his truth and fullness.

And there's another thing. The Son always directs us to see the Father and the Spirit; the Father always directs us to see the Son and the Spirit; and the Spirit always directs us to see the Father and the Son. (Turn the triangle round as you refer to each side.)

Of course, our God is far, far more than a mathematical shape – the God of love and glory is much more than a triangle! But the way a triangle works can help us understand a little more of how, for God, it's no problem to be one God, who is also Father, Son and Spirit. It's as natural for God to be like that as it is for us humans to be able to be in one place and think about being somewhere else, both at the same time.

All-age ideas

- Use the Baptismal promises in place of the Creed.

- The children can wave green streamers in one of the hymns today – not as a performance, or for anyone to see, but simply as part of their own worship offering.

CORPUS CHRISTI

Exodus 24:3-8
Psalm 115
Hebrews 9:11-15
Mark 14:12-16, 22-26

*In bread and wine at the Last Supper,
Jesus offers himself, the Lamb of God
who takes away the sins of the world.*

All-age talk

Show everyone a ten or twenty pound note, and
ask a volunteer to read the promise on it: 'I promise
to pay the bearer on demand the sum of twenty
pounds.' This note may just look like a pretty piece
of paper, but the reason it's a special piece of paper,
worth treating carefully, is that it carries a real
promise. At one time we could have gone to the
Bank of England and demanded the real twenty
pounds worth of gold. It's a bit more complicated
than that now, of course, but in a way our whole
financial system works on the promise, and we pay
one another in promises of twenty pounds.

How do promises work? Collect ideas, and
establish that when people make serious promises
they mean what they say and it is understood that
promises are not for breaking. We should never
make promises we know we won't be able to keep,
and if we do make a promise we should do our
very best to keep it.

A Covenant is a legal promise between two people
or two parties, often sealed by both people signing
their names. Out in the desert, God had made a
Covenant with the people of Israel. God promised
to be their faithful God, and they promised to be his
faithful people, living by God's law of love. As a
kind of signing to seal the Covenant, animals were
sacrificed, and their blood, the sign of their life, was
sprinkled both on the people and on God's altar.

Today we are celebrating the new Covenant, or
promise, which Jesus has made with God's people.
In the bread and the wine Jesus says we can share
his very life, and he seals that promise in blood –

not by just signing his name, but by giving his life on the cross. That's quite a signature.

All-age ideas

- Give everyone a small piece of paper and a pen or pencil when they come in. Following the talk, or as part of the Penitential Rite, have a time of silence for people to look at the cross as Jesus' signature, sealing the promise of his life in us, and when they are ready suggest they recommit themselves to their part in that promise, signing their name on the paper as a sign of their life offered. Collect all these and stick them on to the shape of the cross.

- Have a longer than usual time of thanksgiving after Communion, either with quiet singing, with recorded music or with total stillness and silence, as people savour the gift of the sacrament.

SECOND SUNDAY OF THE YEAR

1 Samuel 3:3-10, 19
Psalm 39
1 Corinthians 6:13-15,
   17-20
John 1:35-42

Christ calls us to follow him and walk his way through our lifetime.

All-age talk

Begin by giving out a few messages as if they are notices, rather like this. 'Is Ali Holden here? I've got a message from Molly, your neighbour's dog. She says when you next take her for a walk could you go past the swimming pool as there are some good smells around there. And then there's another message . . . this is for John Bendkowski. It's a message from the rope you used to climb the tree, asking for another high level outing as it enjoyed the view.' (Use inside information so that the messages match up with real life.)

What do we reckon – are those messages true or not? Does Ali take a dog called Molly out for walks? Did John use a rope to climb a tree? Yes! Then what makes us think the messages aren't quite right? It's because common sense tells us that dogs and ropes can't send messages like that, even if they wanted to. Today we are looking at the way God calls us, and how we can work out whether it's really God calling us, or not.

What first alerted Ali and John to the messages given out? It was their names. When God calls us, he gets our attention and speaks directly to us. Sometimes what happens is that we hear a reading at church, or read a passage of the Bible at home, and suddenly a particular bit hits home, and we know it's meant specially for us. It's as if it has our name on it. God spoke into Jonah's heart so that Jonah knew God had a message for him, whether he chose to obey it or not. The fishermen heard Jesus calling directly to them as they worked in the fishing boats. So one thing we can learn about God's call is that it feels personal to us.

The next thing to look at is this: is this the sort of message that God would give? With our messages from a dog and a rope, we knew they didn't ring true, so we could laugh at the messages and not take them seriously. But what other things might make us suspect that a call is not from God at all? If it's to do with anything unkind, violent, selfish, greedy, lazy, deceitful, or evil, then the call we think we are hearing is not coming from the God of truth and love. But if we feel God is calling us to something loving, selfless, thoughtful, kind, courageous, honest, or good, then it's likely that God is speaking into our hearts, and we should listen carefully.

Then what? Since Samuel realised that God was calling him, he bravely spoke out God's message to Eli, even though it wasn't very good news. As soon as Andrew heard about Jesus he went out of his way to follow him and introduce his brother Simon Peter to Jesus.

So we need to be ready to hear God calling in the quiet of our hearts, check with our experience of God that the call is true, and then be prepared to obey the call, going bravely wherever God is leading us.

All-age ideas

- The reading from 1 Samuel can be mimed as it's narrated.

- During the gospel, have a line of people (mixed ages) holding candles, which are lit one from another until all are alight.

THIRD SUNDAY OF THE YEAR

Jonah 3:1-5, 10
Psalm 24
1 Corinthians 7:29-31
Mark 1:14-20

When we are called we need to respond with obedience so that many may be brought to repentance.

All-age talk

Point out that everyone is sitting with their bodies turned towards the person who's speaking. The same thing happens in a lecture theatre, at a play, and in the cinema. Why is this? Collect ideas, which may well include being able to see and hear better, helping concentration, and being polite. In the aisle provide a few chairs facing in the opposite direction and invite volunteers to sit in them.

Now start rustling a parcel and explaining that you are going to show everyone what's inside it – it's something you are sure they will all be able to enjoy. Slowly unwrap a new toy for the children's corner, and enthuse about it but don't mention what it is. Then address those sitting facing backwards, either pointing out the way they have turned their heads round to be as much facing the right way as possible, or giving them permission to turn round, as you are sure they are feeling they're missing out by facing the wrong way.

In our readings from the Bible today we heard the word *repent*. Jonah was giving God's message to the people of Nineveh to repent, and as Jesus starts his work among the people he goes around telling them to repent. So what does it mean to repent, and why are we told to do it?

To *repent* really means to turn round and start facing the right way. Ask the volunteers to pick up their chairs, turn them around and sit facing the front. It really isn't any fun facing the wrong direction – away from God's love. Sooner or later we shall feel we're missing out, somehow, and we'll be right. When we are facing away from God we *do* miss out. We cut ourselves off from seeing what God is doing and from hearing what he is saying. Sometimes we might swing our heads round to glance in God's direction, but that isn't repenting.

To *repent* we need to choose to turn ourselves round completely and face God. That may well be quite an upheaval for us. It will certainly mean that we'll be facing away from wrong (though perhaps pleasant and exciting) things we're involved with at the moment, and that takes courage. It may mean changing what we think of as most important. It may mean coming clean about some secret fault and apologising to certain people.

The good news is that facing the right way is wonderfully liberating, and takes all that weight and strain of our sin away. It lets us take advantage of all God's help and blessings again.

The disciples were called to help spread this message of Jesus which sets people free: *repent and believe*.

All-age ideas

- Have a flower arrangement focusing on the fishermen, using a flat mirror and some sand, stones and shells, driftwood and netting.

- Give everyone a stone as they come in and suggest they hold it during the Psalm and during the Prayer of the Faithful as a tactile reminder that God is our rock and refuge, whom we can always trust.

FOURTH SUNDAY OF THE YEAR

Deuteronomy
    18:15-20
Psalm 94
1 Corinthians 7:32-35
Mark 1:21-28

Jesus displays all the signs that mark him out to be God's chosen One.

All-age talk

Strike a match and light a candle. Talk about how useful fire is to heat up food and cook it, to keep us warm, melt steel and make steam to generate power. But fire is very powerful, and so it can be very dangerous. Show a picture or a model of a fire engine, and enlist the children's help in talking about what happens when fires get out of control, and how the firemen fight the dangers. We need to have a healthy fear of fire to keep us safe.

God is very powerful. When you think of the power needed to create fire and oceans, ranges of mountains and galaxies of stars, you can't help but be a bit fearful at the thought of getting in touch with such a powerful person.

We are sensible to stand in awe of this great Being, on whom we depend for everything, including life itself. We are right to respect the Lord of life, and think carefully before we speak to him, and give him our full attention whenever we pray. We are right to humble ourselves in his presence and behave well during church services. God sees everything we do and knows everything we think, both the things we are pleased about and the things we are secretly rather ashamed of. Sometimes we behave as if God is more of an easygoing pet than the Lord of the entire universe. We need to take God seriously and recognise that he is very powerful indeed.

(Pick up the candle again.) But that great power of God is only part of the story. Just as a candle is a person-sized fire, which we can hold and which gives us light, but doesn't frighten us like a house on fire, so Jesus is the way we can approach the great creative God in person.

204

All-age ideas

- Have phrases describing God's power written up on the walls and pillars.

- Have the Gospel read by a group of people taking the different parts.

FIFTH SUNDAY OF THE YEAR

Job 7:1-4, 6-7
Psalm 146
1 Corinthians 9:16-19,
  22-23
Mark 1:29-39

The good news about God is far too good to keep to ourselves.

All-age talk

Begin by having the following read out, or having it printed on the weekly sheet. It is an extract from *The Solitaire Mystery* by Jostein Gaarder.

'Tell me about Rainbow Fizz,' I said.

He raised his white eyebrows and whispered, 'It has to be tasted, my boy.'

'Can't you tell me what it tastes like?'

He shook his old head in despair.

'A normal fizzy drink tastes of orange or pear or raspberry – and that's that. That isn't the case with Rainbow Fizz, Albert. You taste all those flavours at the same time with this drink, and you even taste fruits and berries you've never been near with your tongue.'

'Then it must be good,' I said.

'Hah! It's more than just good. You can taste a normal fizzy drink only in your mouth . . . first on your tongue and the roof of your mouth, then a little bit down your throat. You can taste Rainbow Fizz in your nose and head, down through your legs, and out through your arms.'

'I think you're pulling my leg,' I said.

'You think so?'

The old man looked almost dumbfounded, so I decided to ask something which was easier to answer.

'What colour is it?' I asked.

Baker Hans started to laugh. 'You're full of questions, aren't you, boy. And that's good, but it's not always easy to answer. I have to *show* you the drink, you see.'

(© 1996, Phoenix House, a division of the Orion Publishing Group. Reproduced by permission.)

Talk about how hard it is to describe something so wonderful that it is impossible to imagine; the only way Albert is really going to find out how wonderful Rainbow Fizz is, is to experience it for himself.

Today's Psalm is a bit like this. The psalmist is doing his best to describe to us how wonderful God is, but God is simply so incredibly amazing that we find it almost impossible to imagine. There's only one way to find out, and that is to experience God for ourselves. If you ask anyone who has become aware of the great, loving God working in their life, they'll agree that there really aren't any words to describe how wonderful and amazing he is. They just know because they've experienced him in action.

In the Gospel we heard how Jesus had been busy healing lots and lots of people at the house of Peter and Andrew, where he was staying. It started with Peter's mother-in-law, who had a bad fever and was very ill, and Jesus made her better. After she'd made them all supper, full of new energy, no doubt, crowds of visitors came, all wanting Jesus to heal them as well. So he did. Through Jesus, God was working right there in those people's lives, and making them more free and happy than they had ever felt before. It was so exciting to see! We can imagine how happy it made Jesus to see these people suddenly realising at last how wonderful God was! He couldn't wait for everyone else to find out.

Well, people are still finding out that our amazing God can set us free to live happy and joyful lives doing good and standing up for what is right and true. And how are they going to discover God? Only if those of us who have found out already how wonderful he is are prepared to tell them about him, and introduce them to him!

All-age ideas

- Try this wine tasting sketch:

  Presenter   Good morning, everyone, and welcome to today's pick of the bottles with our expert wine

	taster, Jelly Golden! Good morning, Jelly, it's nice to have you with us again for today's tasting.
Jelly Golden	Gosh, yes, we've certainly got some super tastes here. Let's start with this delicious red – just look at that glowing, ruby colour. You can almost smell the sunshine through the glass, can't you?
Presenter	If you say so, Jelly. Shall I pour some out for you?
Jelly Golden	*(Sniffs it)* Mmm! Wonderful aroma . . . warm summer days with a breath of a breeze . . . and just a faintest hint of honey. *(Tastes it)* Oh yes, it's so rich and mellow . . . I can taste loganberry, plum and, yes, strawberry as an exquisite aftertaste, all blended wonderfully in the grape. My word, it's really sun-packed . . . utterly delicious! It must be late summer 1992, and if I'm not mistaken, it's from that little valley a few kilometres northwest of Nuits St Georges. Here, you've simply got to try some for yourself! It's the only way to know how magnificent it really is!
Presenter	OK, if you recommend it so highly, Jelly . . . Cheers!

- As a background to the reading from Job, play some music which speaks of pain and anguish, such as the theme music from *Schindler's List* or a slow movement from a Mahler or Shostakovich symphony.

Sixth Sunday of the Year

Leviticus 13:1-2, 45-46
Psalm 31
1 Corinthians
    10:31-11:1
Mark 1:40-45

Jesus wants to heal us to wholeness, and to him no one is untouchable.

All-age talk

Invite a volunteer to run up the aisle as if they really want to win a race. Then ask them (or another) to run as if they aren't much bothered whether they win or not. Everyone can pick out the differences in the two performances.

Paul tells us that in all we do, we must do it seriously, for the glory of God. What will that mean? We'll be taking our following of Jesus very seriously, and trying very hard at it, practising it every day and building up our stamina. We'll be like 'professionals' instead of wishy-washy drifters. And we'll be getting better and stronger as we practise. If we don't bother, and don't take it seriously, we won't make much progress.

Today in the Gospel we are given another example of what it means to be a follower of Jesus. Let's look at how Jesus behaves with the man who has leprosy. Then we can practise living like that, as we try to follow Jesus.

But first, what does it mean to be a leper? (Lepers and leopards both have spots, but there the similarity ends, so make this clear!) Leprosy is a skin disease. When people get leprosy, they first find they lose the feeling in a finger, or a bit of the foot, and gradually the skin turns very white in patches. It is a bad illness, and people die of it if they don't get the medicines which can cure it. In Jesus' time, lepers were sent off to live on their own because they were thought of as 'unclean'. No one else was allowed to touch them. If they did, the law said they would become unclean as well.

So what did Jesus do? There was the leper, knowing Jesus had the power to heal him, but not

209

sure that Jesus would want to have anything to do with someone as unclean as he was. And there was Jesus, so much wanting the man to be healed that he did something very shocking. He reached out . . . and *touched* the leper! Jesus wasn't afraid of the law saying he would be unclean; he just knew that this man, who had been untouchable for years, more than anything needed to feel touchable again. We know what happened – the man's skin was made better straightaway, so he could go and show the priest and have it all made official; he was no longer unclean.

As Christians, we are followers of Jesus, so now we know a bit more about how we must try to live. We must try wanting the best for people, and we must try not to shut people off or have nothing to do with them just because they are poorer than us, or richer than us, ill, smelly or just different. Even if other people avoid them, as Christians we must never think of anyone as unclean or untouchable, because God made and loves every one of us.

All-age ideas

• Have some information displayed on leprosy aid, and have a collection for this important work. For more details contact: St Francis Leprosy Guild, 26 Inglis Road, London W5 3RL.

• Act out the Gospel, with the healed leper going down the aisle, telling individuals and groups in the congregation all about it at the end.

• Following the Gospel, try this mime. An 'untouchable' moves around in a group of people, who shrink away from him whenever he comes near, and turn their backs on him when he asks for their help. Then Jesus moves behind one of the group and gradually their actions fall in step with Jesus'. This time, when the untouchable comes near, Jesus stretches out his hands towards him, and so the person he is shadowing also reaches out. Through this touch, the untouchable realises he is accepted, and the others gradually come closer, losing their fear.

SEVENTH SUNDAY OF THE YEAR

Isaiah 43:18-19, 21-22,
  24-25
Psalm 40
2 Corinthians 1:18-22
Mark 2:1-12

The Son of Man has authority on earth to forgive sins.

All-age talk

Start by explaining that you have a list of hard things to do, and you are going to ask everyone which they think is easiest of two options. They can have a moment to think or confer, and then a show of hands should indicate their communal decision. Here are the options:

1. Learning to ride a bike, or learning to talk.

2. Earning money, or saving your money up without spending any.

3. Doing something brave, or doing something thoughtful.

4. Talking non-stop for an hour, or being completely quiet for an hour.

In today's Gospel we heard Jesus ask a similar question. Remind them of the circumstances – the crowds, the paralysed man let down through the roof, Jesus telling him his sins are forgiven, and the scribes, knowing that only God can forgive sins, horrified that Jesus has done what only God can do. This was his question – which is it easier to say to the paralysed man: 'Your sins are forgiven you' or 'Stand up, take your bed and walk'?

Let's try and work out an answer. First we need to make a few things clear. Who is the only one who can forgive sins? It's God. And what about a paralysed man suddenly being able to get up and walk home – who's the only one able to do that? Once again, it's God. So in a way, Jesus is saying to the scribes, 'Is it easier for me to act like God, or to act like God?' And what would be the answer to that? There'd be no difference; both are a natural way for God to behave.

211

The man's body was paralysed – that meant he couldn't make it move freely. When Jesus healed him he was free to move about again. It's like that when our lives are jammed by sin and guilt about bad things we've done in the past. When God forgives us completely, he unjams us, so we are free to live happily again.

All-age ideas

- Have the Isaiah passage read chorally, with a mixed group of voice tones – low, medium and high. Experiment with what helps unlock the mood of the words, using sometimes the whole group and sometimes one section, or one voice.

- Have the Gospel printed out, with movement directions, so everyone can join in. Jesus and the scribes know who they are beforehand. The scribes stand in a group a little apart from the congregation, and Jesus stands in the centre of the crowd. At verse 2 everyone moves out from their seats into the aisle. In verse 4 everyone looks up, and their eyes follow an imaginary bed as it comes down at Jesus' feet. Jesus says the words to the imaginary paralysed man, and the scribes pull their beards and look offended. Jesus looks over to them and says his words (verses 8-11). As the narrator reads about the man getting up, all the crowd gasp in amazement and say together their words in verse 12.

EIGHTH SUNDAY OF THE YEAR

Hosea 2:16-17, 21-22
Psalm 102
2 Corinthians 3:1-6
Mark 2:18-22

The long-expected bridegroom is Christ, and the Church is his bride. We cannot half-attend the wedding feast, but must wholeheartedly join in the celebrations.

All-age talk

Bring along an old supermarket carrier bag, with the handles weak and split. Also some freshly bought glass bottles of wine or fruit juice – the posher the better. Beforehand, prepare a child or young person to interrupt you at the appropriate point. We'll call the person Phoebe. Give someone else in the congregation a strong new bag to have ready.

Show off your purchases and explain that you now need a bag to put them in to carry them home. Wave the old carrier bag around, mentioning how old it is and how the handles don't look too strong, but decide that it'll probably do, and start loading the bottles in, resting the bag on the ground as you load.

Now Phoebe comes and gets your attention, suggesting that it's stupid to put those new things in such a useless bag. Why? Well, it'll break, and then the bottles could break as well, and you'd have wasted all the wine and fruit juice!

Ask the rest of the congregation whether they think Phoebe is right. What would be more sensible? To put the new bottles in a strong new bag. Does anyone happen to have a strong new carrier bag? Well, that's a relief!

As you pack the bottles safely in this bag, explain that Jesus said it's no good – and can be dangerous – to think we can pack the new life of God into ourselves if we're still wanting to stay the same old bags we've always been! That won't work. We should never let Jesus into our hearts unless we are prepared for change.

Otherwise, after a quick froth of excitement as

213

new Christians, we'll find it too much of a strain to be living a new life in an old lifestyle, and the danger is that we crack up, and end up feeling loads of guilt, loads of failure and think Jesus has let us down badly. In fact, all we need to do is go to Jesus and ask him to turn us into completely new containers to house the new life safely.

He's an expert at doing just that, and, however long or short time we've been Christians, we all regularly need God's transforming of our whole selves if we are to join fully in the celebration.

All-age ideas

- Have a flower arrangement on a wedding theme, focusing on the bridegroom aspect, with a button hole, top hat and gloves among the flowers, ribbon and wine.

- Invite everyone to share the celebration with a poster on the church notice board, made to look like a wedding invitation. The children will be providing some wedding garlands they have made.

NINTH SUNDAY OF THE YEAR

Deuteronomy 5:12-15
Psalm 80
2 Corinthians 4:6-11
Mark 2:23-3:6

Jesus has the words of eternal life – he sheds light on a right attitude to the Law.

All-age talk

Bring along a piggy bank and some money to put in it. Some people keep their treasure safe in one of these, adding to it each week. (Drop some more money in.) Sometimes people will get an ordinary jar and fill it up with coins, so that soon it's full of treasure. The pot or jar is often very ordinary – it's the treasure inside which makes it special. People in Roman times used to use clay pots to keep their silver jewellery safe – archaeologists have found them, still guarding their treasure!

In one of the letters Saint Paul wrote, he said he thought we were all a bit like clay pots holding special treasure. As people we're just ordinary, but we've got something as Christians which is extraordinary – real treasure. It's being friends with God through Jesus which changes our lives from being ordinary to extra-special, because we're actually holding in us the love of the living God.

What does that look like?

We saw a bit of what it looks like in today's Gospel. Jesus notices a man whose arm is withered and shrunk so he can't use it, and immediately his heart goes out to that man, and more than anything he wants to set the man's arm free to wave and lift things, touch and hold things. His love for the man makes Jesus sad for him having to struggle, and he sets about mending him.

What Jesus doesn't do is look at the man and think, 'Ah yes, a man with an arm which doesn't work. But it's the Sabbath, so that's too bad; he'll have to stay like that – I'm not going to break the rules and heal him today.'

Well, of course he wouldn't think like that,

because you can't be full of God's love and yet shut off your compassion. What Jesus did was the Godly, loving thing – he used his power of healing and set that man free, there and then, rules or no rules. And that offended the teachers of the Law. They had become so keen to keep the Law that they'd actually blocked God's light out, and couldn't see that Jesus was keeping the real spirit of the Law completely – love God and love one another.

So here we are as ordinary human pots, holding in us the light of God, and that's going to affect the way we live. We'll have to reach out in love and mercy to those around us, and that might mean we end up offending some people. But who cares? If we're living God's way, then we won't be offending God, and if living that way makes us unpopular sometimes, we'll be in very good company.

All-age ideas

- Collect the offering today in earthenware pots, such as unglazed flower pots.

- Have a flower arrangement expressing God's love and mercy, using warm colours and gentle, delicate foliage. Label it 'Jesus displays God's love and mercy'.

TENTH SUNDAY OF THE YEAR

Genesis 3:9-15
Psalm 129
2 Corinthians
4:13-5:1
Mark 3:20-35

Anyone who does God's will is considered a close family member of Jesus.

All-age talk

Whether we live on our own or with others, most of us have family; we may not see them that often, or we may see them every day. Some of them may no longer be alive, but they are still our family. Mothers and fathers, stepmothers and stepfathers, parents-in-law and children-in-law, sons and daughters, grandchildren and grandparents, aunts and uncles, brothers, sisters and cousins, are all family. We share the same genes (and sometimes the same jeans).

In every family there is something called a family resemblance – a family likeness. (Some family members may be willing to demonstrate this likeness.) The DNA within our families shows up right across the generations; in my family there's the Morris nose, the Rackett musicality, and the Orme stubborn determination, for instance!

In our Gospel reading today, Jesus says something rather amazing. He's sitting teaching, surrounded by a closely packed circle of faces, people from all kinds of different families and backgrounds, with all kinds of different looks and personalities. They are there because they sense that in Jesus they can get closer to the true, living God than they've ever been before. They are so keen that they are hanging on every word Jesus speaks, listening to him intently.

And as he looks around at them sitting there, and sees in their eyes their love of God, Jesus happily counts all of them – and everyone else who does the will of God – as members of his close family. He is saying that any of us, however ordinary or damaged, whatever natural family we belong to, or are separated from, are close members of Jesus'

217

family! So you can think of yourself as closely related to Jesus. And that makes all of us in the Church part of the same family, distinguished by the family likeness of doing God's will – living the loving way.

All-age ideas

- As a Penitential Rite:

  Father, there have been times
  when we have seen your will but failed to do it.
  Lord, have mercy.
  Lord, have mercy.

  Jesus, there have been times
  when we have behaved more as your enemies
  than members of your close family.
  Christ, have mercy.
  Christ, have mercy.

  Spirit, there have been times
  when we have ignored your prompting
  and preferred to live selfishly.
  Lord, have mercy.
  Lord, have mercy.

- Have the reading from Genesis read by a group of people, so that the different voices are clearly brought out.

Eleventh Sunday of the Year

Ezekiel 17:22-24
Psalm 91
2 Corinthians 5:6-10
Mark 4:26-34

From small beginnings, and by God's power, the kingdom of heaven grows.

All-age talk

Ask everyone to look at the mustard seeds they were given when they came into church (see All-age Ideas), and have a couple of tall people (or children on chairs) to stand back to back, spreading their arms out. In Israel, where Jesus was living, mustard seeds often grow as big as this, and local people will even use the mustard branches for firewood, so that tiny seed really does grow into a spreading tree, and all the birds love to sit in the shelter of its branches. The mustard plant provides spicy flavour, fuel and shelter.

Why did Jesus talk to the people about mustard? He often used things that were all around to help describe spiritual things which can't be seen. Perhaps there was a shady mustard plant right there where they were sitting, and some of its seeds scattered on the ground.

Anyway, Jesus said that the way God's kingdom grows is a bit like the way a mustard seed grows. It starts off very little, and gradually grows very big. The little seed may be an act of kindness you do which makes someone think to themselves, 'I wonder! She's become a Christian, and it seems to be changing her for the better. Perhaps there's something in this Jesus person after all!' Or perhaps you're the one in the office who insists on honesty, even if you'd gain from being less than honest, and someone notices and starts thinking. Or perhaps someone notices that you aren't that impressed by the labels people are wearing, even though you're cool.

The little seed of God's kingdom is someone opening themselves up a tiny bit to the possibility of God being real and active in their lives. Gradually

219

it grows in them. Perhaps they begin to ask more questions about God, perhaps they read some Bible stories or start coming with you to church sometimes. Then they start to pray! Now that little seed can really begin to grow, because God can lead the person step by step as they get in touch with him more and more. Sometimes the kingdom of God grows gradually as they pick up teaching week by week, or look at God's world with new eyes. At other times there's a sudden growth spurt. Perhaps a verse of scripture hits home and they realise how their life needs to change, or they suddenly sense God real and close to them in a time of sadness or joy.

Perhaps over a few years, or a lifetime, that little seed has grown in the person until they are so full of God in their life that they are standing tall and strong in faith, and many come to them, now, for spiritual help and comfort, like the birds coming to the mustard plant's spreading branches.

How is the kingdom of God's growing coming on in us? Is it still a tiny seed, full of hope but not yet developed very much? Has it just started to sprout, putting out roots and shoots? Is it not growing very much at all at the moment, or has it recently had a big surge of growth and is excitedly stretching upwards and outwards in the knowledge of God's love and forgiveness? Or is it already tall and strong, providing spiritual shelter for others, scattering other seeds all around, and happy to be full of God's life?

What a world it would be, with churchfuls of people in it, in whom the kingdom of God was growing strong as mustard trees! It could happen. The people could be us.

All-age ideas

- Have bowls of mustard seeds and invite people to take one as they come in. They can plant their mustard seed when they get home.

- If practical, include some mustard plant in one of the flower arrangements.

TWELFTH SUNDAY OF THE YEAR

Job 38:1, 8-11
Psalm 106
2 Corinthians 5:14-17
Mark 4:35-41

What kind of person is this? Even the wind and waves obey him.

All-age talk

If practical, arrange for a couple of people to bring their (well-controlled) pet into church this morning. If this isn't possible, interview a couple of pet owners.

Look at the animals and talk to the owners about what they like to eat, and how they like to play. Then ask them about how their pets behave when they are frightened or feel threatened, and how they calm them down.

It isn't just pets who get worried, angry and upset – it's humans as well. Today we heard about a time when Jesus' friends were so frightened they were panicking, and we saw how Jesus calmed them down. Remind them that Jesus was actually asleep, and the disciples woke him up to tell him to start worrying! With the stormy waves pitching the boat up and down, and the water coming in over the side it was beginning to look like a *Titanic* situation, and there was Jesus fast asleep in the bottom of the boat!

Sometimes we do that, too, if life seems very scary, and everything seems to be going wildly out of control. We scream out to Jesus, demanding that he notices and *does* something, instead of being so calm about it all. It's almost as if we want him to panic as well.

Jesus, once he's been thoroughly shaken awake, doesn't seem to be caught up in the excitement. But he can see that it isn't only the disciples who are churned up – it's the weather as well. And perhaps he sees here a good way to help the disciples understand more about who he is. The disciples are so scared at the moment that they can't take anything in. So instead of calming them down, Jesus calms

221

the wind and the waves. As the howling wind eases and settles quietly again, and the pounding waves flatten back to a gentle lapping around the battered boat, the disciples calm down as well. In this lull they recover themselves and stop panicking.

What does Jesus do next – wait for their applause? Go back to sleep? In fact we find he now starts teaching them, because they are now calm enough to listen. He talks to them about trusting God, even in the middle of raging storms.

Often in life we will find that when we have invited Jesus into our boat – into our life – we don't get so thrown by all the stormy problems (things like quarrels in friendships, loved ones moving away, financial problems, pressure and stress at work). And if we're panicking about them so much that we can't hear Jesus helping us to weather the storm, then often we'll find we're given a breather – a bit of space – where things are calmed down long enough for us to realise that, with God in charge, we don't actually need to be terrified.

All-age ideas

- As an introduction to the talk, try this eye-opener to the wonder of God:

    Voice 1   The highest waterfall on earth is Angel in Venezuela, where the water plunges down 979 metres. The River Nile in Africa is 6,695 kilometres long. At its greatest depth the Pacific Ocean is 11,034 metres deep.

    What a universe.
    What a God!

    Voice 2   Adult salmon in the open sea find their way by rivers and streams and up waterfalls, to the actual pool they hatched in, years before.

    What a universe.
    What a God!

    Voice 3   Our Milky Way galaxy is one of

thousands of millions of galaxies, all apparently rushing away from one another at tremendous speeds. The nearest neighbour star to our solar system is 24 million million miles away.

What a universe.
What a God!

- During the reading of the Gospel, some of the children can interpret the mood of the sea by moving a length of blue fabric, first gently, then increasingly stormily until Jesus' calming of the waves, to which they quickly react, restoring the gentle calm once more.

THIRTEENTH SUNDAY OF THE YEAR

Wisdom of Solomon
  1:13-15; 2:23-24
Psalm 29
2 Corinthians 8:7, 9,
  13-15
Mark 5:21-43

God's power can reach even into death and draw out life.

All-age talk

Make a circle of chairs near where you are talking, or a circle of rope – something which is clearly visible.

Explain that this circle is like our life here on earth. How do we get into it? By being born. (Invite a couple of people to make their way in.) While we're here what do we do? We eat, play, work, talk, make friends (and perhaps some enemies), watch TV, learn things and so on. (Everyone can add to the list.) Invite the people in the circle of life to mime some of those things as they are suggested.

How do we get out of the circle of life? By being born backwards? We get out of this life by dying. (The volunteers make their way out of the circle.) Point out that they're not in the circle any more, but they're in a huge space, much bigger than they might have imagined, if they'd only ever known life in the circle. And outside this space is the whole outdoors, stretching outwards and upwards, and full of light and colour, better than anything we could imagine if we'd only ever known the circle as 'life'. Just as the circle isn't the only place, so this earthly life isn't all there is to complete life – Jesus told us that life after our death can be full, rich and wonderful; and it's Jesus who has made that possible for us.

Remind everyone of the story in today's Gospel, about a twelve-year-old girl dying. Everyone is specially sad when a young person dies, because they haven't had a chance to live very long here and enjoy our world. But Jesus brings that young girl back to life again. It's as if from inside the circle of life he calls to her on the outside and she comes back in again, completely better, and hungry. He could do that because Jesus *is* life. When she next died, perhaps after a long and happy time on earth, she closed her eyes on earthly life and heard Jesus calling her name again into life – but this time from heaven, into the life with Jesus that lasts for ever.

When we get to the point of our death, Jesus will be there, calling us out into that life, and welcoming us. And because we know his voice, from a lifetime of prayer, we'll be very happy to move towards it and find him, waiting for us there.

All-age ideas

- Act out the Gospel for today, either miming it as it is narrated, or preparing it with spoken parts.

- As a reflective preparation for a penitential rite try this dialogue:

    Left side   If we were praying for rain, would we bring our umbrellas?

    All   Forgive us, Lord; we place limitations on what is possible with you.

    Right side   If we pray for others, are we ready to be part of the answer?

    All   Forgive us, Lord; we mark off boundaries where your kingdom is not welcome, because it makes demands on our time.

    Play some reflective music during which the following is said:

    Voice 1   Come, Holy Spirit and draw us into full life.

    Voice 2   Come, Holy Spirit and melt our hearts of stone.

FOURTEENTH SUNDAY OF THE YEAR

Ezekiel 2:2-5
Psalm 122
2 Corinthians 12:7-10
Mark 6:1-6

If we are not ready to listen to the truth, we will not hear it.

All-age talk

You will need a sieve – either a culinary or a gardening one. Also some appropriate thing to sieve – such as flour or earth.

First talk about the way we tend to hear if someone offers us a second chocolate biscuit, a raise in our pay, or a special discount, but not if we're being told to clean out the rabbit, work late, empty the washing machine or make a dental appointment. As the saying goes, 'There's none so deaf as those who won't hear'.

Explain that what our minds do is to sieve information which comes in through the ears and the eyes. Produce the sieve and start sieving so that everyone can see this process in action. The holes are a particular size so that everything is sorted automatically. Big lumps are not wanted, so they won't fit through the holes. Fine flour or earth can get through quite easily. The rest only gets through if we process it a bit first (breaking it down to a suitable size) and if it can't be broken down (like stones in the earth or a free sticker in the flour) then it doesn't get through the sieve at all.

In just the same way we are selective about what we hear, and mostly that is very useful to us. It stops us turning into nervous wrecks by the daily news items, for instance.

But sometimes we try to keep out what God is trying to make us hear. Just because it may mean us changing something in our lives, we treat it as a threat, and shut it out, when really it is helping us to get rid of a way of thinking or behaving which is not healthy to us or others, physically, mentally or spiritually. What we need is to have 'God's Word'-shaped holes in our sieves, so that God's Word can always get through.

All-age ideas

- As a response to the All-age Talk, suggest that we trace the cross on our ears and eyes (or do this to one another) as a sign that we really want to see and hear what God is telling us, whether it is comforting or challenging.

- Cover the base of a flat sieve with paper which has a cross cut out of it. Place this where people will see it as they come to receive Communion, or as they leave the church, and label it: 'Lord, may we hear and receive your Word'.

- In the Ezekiel reading, mime the prophet walking about trying to tell people good news. Each in turn starts to listen, but some shrug and shake their heads, getting on with what they were doing before, and others look affronted or angry, and deliberately turn their backs on the prophet, folding their arms and sticking their chins in the air.

FIFTEENTH SUNDAY OF THE YEAR

Amos 7:12-15
Psalm 84
Ephesians 1:3-14
Mark 6:7-13

Those who speak out God's will are bound to be vulnerable to rejection and abuse.

All-age talk

As everyone comes into church give them a length of thin wool or string and a paper clip.

Begin by inviting everyone to fix one end of the wool or string into the paper-clip so that they have made a plumb-line. Explain that this can be used to check whether things which are supposed to be upright are as straight as they should be. (They can try out their plumb-lines on the pews and chairs around them, and some volunteers can check other uprights in the building.)

Suppose we were to find that one of our upright walls was actually leaning over – would it be useful to know that? Yes, because then we could get in the workmen and pay them to put it right.

Suppose we just got angry and offended at being told our wall wasn't as upright as it should be? We could tell the person with the plumb-line to go away and not talk about it to us any more. That way we could go on pretending our wall was upright, and we wouldn't have to pay to put it right. But if we did that, the upright wall might go on leaning more and more until in the end the whole building crashed down in rubble.

Plumb-lines for checking how straight and upright things are can be very useful indeed. Being told where things aren't as upright as they should be can also be very useful indeed.

One of the things prophets do is draw our attention to places in our lives or our society or our church community which are leaning dangerously and are nowhere near as upright as they should be. How do people react to being told? We heard today how the people shouted at the prophet Amos to go and leave them alone. They didn't want to hear, because they didn't want the bother of putting things right. We also hear how Jesus prepares the disciples for rejection and not to be surprised when people don't want to listen to them. People don't want to hear because they don't want to put things right.

How good are we at hearing God whispering lovingly into our hearts about the places in our lives that should be standing tall and upright but are instead leaning a little, or leaning dangerously? Do we thank him for showing it to us so we can quickly put things right again, or do we get sulky or angry and pretend we haven't heard?

All-age ideas

- On upright pillars or walls stick strips of coloured paper with Bible verses on them which emphasise the importance and joy of living upright lives in God's love and strength. Here are some possible verses: Psalm 84:11 – Love and faithfulness meet together; Psalm 23:1 – The earth is the Lord's and everything in it; Psalm 31:11 – Sing, all you who are upright in heart; Psalm 111:2 – The generation of the upright will be blessed; Proverbs 3:32 – The Lord takes the upright into his confidence; Ephesians 1:4 – He chose us in him before the creation of the world to be holy and blameless in his sight; Matthew 22:37-39 – Love God and love one another.

- Have a display with a pair of sandals, a staff and, separately, a tunic, or jacket, a bag, bread and some copper coins, with the note, 'Leave behind'.

SIXTEENTH SUNDAY OF THE YEAR

Jeremiah 23:1-6
Psalm 22
Ephesians 2:13-18
Mark 6:30-34

Like a good shepherd, Jesus sees the needs of his people and always responds with love.

All-age talk

Bring along a crowded diary or calendar, and other gadgets for coping with busy lifestyles, such as a computerised notebook, a laptop, mobile phone, alarm clock or fax message.

Ask a few children to walk up and down pretending to be talking on their mobiles or driving their cars, while you talk about the way we can now continue our office work walking along the High Street or on the train. We can send messages by e-mail or fax so that they get there almost immediately. All this enables us to spend more and more of our time being fully at work if we happen to have a job, with increasing pressure and decreasing space in our lives. People have either far too much work than is healthy or none at all, and leisure activities often have to slot in some frantic physical activity to compensate for all the physically inactive work of brain and adrenaline. Advertisements shout at us to buy this, choose that, look like them; the newspapers and magazines advise us what to think and how to behave, and often we believe their lies. We are like a scattered flock of sheep racing in different directions, without knowing where we are or where we are going.

(Stop the children and have them sit down very still wherever they are.)

Today we heard in the Gospel about Jesus' busy ministry of teaching and healing, listening and encouraging. When he and his disciples had been hard at work for days, and were really tired and drained, they'd get into a boat to sail across the lake for a bit of peace and quiet – only to find all the crowds had run round the edge of the lake and were already there waiting for them! Jesus didn't send them away and tell them what the office hours were, or put them on hold. He didn't ask Peter to change course and sail off somewhere else instead.

Instead, Jesus saw the lost and struggling lives, the need for reassurance and practical, wise teaching, the longing for healing and wholeness, and the hearts attracted to God but needing help to find him. And seeing all that, he loved them, with the deep affection of God's love; he climbed wearily out of the boat and fed them with the teaching and comforting they so badly needed. From stories like this of Jesus' ministry we know with certainty that God never ever turns any of us away. None of our needs or wounds or sorrows are hidden from him. Whenever we run around the lake to be there waiting for him, he will step on to our beach and minister to us, because he loves us. Like a good shepherd he is concerned for our well-being and leads us carefully and safely through time into the eternity of heaven.

All-age ideas

- Have a time of peace and reflection after the talk, where people can simply be still and settle themselves in God's loving company. Music is helpful at such times – possibly the music group singing *Be still, for the presence of the Lord*, or a recording of Beethoven's *Pastoral Symphony* (No. 6) – the song of thanksgiving after the storm, for instance.

- Consider a parish away-day for some relaxation and spiritual refreshment together.

SEVENTEENTH SUNDAY OF THE YEAR

2 Kings 4:42-44
Psalm 144
Ephesians 4:1-6
John 6:1-15

Out of God's riches, a great crowd is fed and satisfied from a small offering of food.

All-age talk

If you have an ancient building you can direct people to look at how steps or pews are worn away by generations of people simply walking on the step or holding the end of the pew. Or you could show a well-used copy of a Bible, worn out and falling apart just by being handled and read every day. (It is said that Bibles which are falling apart are read by people who are not.) You could show an old and well-loved teddy, threadbare through daily loving.

Each step, each picking up of a book, each cuddling of a bear is in itself only a slight action which we can't imagine would do much. But day by day, over the years, the effect of all those little actions starts to show quite dramatically. Little actions turn out to be very important. Even a smile can spread wider than we might think. There's an old children's poem about that:

> Smile awhile, and when you smile
> another smiles, and soon
> there's miles and miles of smiles
> and life's worthwhile
> because you smile!

Today we heard about one boy and his packed lunch. What was the point of him offering that when there were so many thousands of people to feed? Perhaps we think he might as well have just eaten it himself! But look at what happened when, instead of that, the boy wanted to offer what he had to share. Jesus used it. He blessed the gift that was offered and then all the people were fed, with some left over.

Those who have been God's friends for a long time will have noticed that God is very good at giving us more than we asked for, and giving in ways we hadn't thought of! But he does need us to offer what we have, whether that's time, money or talents and skills. Basically what we have to offer is ourselves. And when we do that, God can use the rest of our life here in ways we haven't even thought of, blessing people who perhaps we haven't even met yet, and may not meet till heaven. If we offer ourselves at the start of every day, then every day can be used for some wonderful good that wouldn't otherwise happen.

All-age ideas

- Have written on the day's handout, or displayed on a board or OHP, the words from John 6:14 – 'This must be the Prophet who's to come into the world!' Ask everyone to turn to those round them when you get to that section of the Gospel and whisper these words to one another a few times, getting louder each time.

- Have a flower arrangement incorporating a child's lunch box.

EIGHTEENTH SUNDAY OF THE YEAR

Exodus 16:2-4, 12-15
Psalm 77
Ephesians 4:17, 20-24
John 6:24-35

Jesus is the Bread of Life who satisfies our hunger and sustains us on our journey to heaven.

All-age talk

Ask who had a meal yesterday, and express surprise that they are thinking of having another meal today – some have already eaten today and are still planning to eat lunch! They can explain to you that our bodies need food every day for them to stay strong and healthy, and for the children to grow. We run on food like a car runs on petrol.

Remind everyone of how Jesus had fed all those people with enough bread and fish, and they had all enjoyed their meal. Now they are all running after Jesus the next day as well. Some of them want to hear what Jesus says, some want to come and be healed, some want to come because it's exciting going where everyone else is going and they don't want to miss out on anything. And lots are going because they remember those nice tuna sandwiches – the meal they ate with Jesus.

Why does Jesus want them to have come? Collect various ideas, and draw out that Jesus wants them to be there because they know they will meet with God if they're here with Jesus.

But Jesus knows all too well why some of them have really come, and he tells them so – 'You're looking for me because you ate the bread and were satisfied.'

And then he helps them to understand how God feeds us not just with bread for our bodies, while we live on this earth for seventy years or so, but in another way as well. He gives us spiritual food which keeps us alive through this life and right on into life beyond physical death. With that feeding we won't be finishing as soon as we die, but going on living for ever.

The people thought that sounded pretty good bread to have, and asked Jesus if he would give them some, so they could be fed spiritually as well as physically. And Jesus told them, 'I am the Bread of Life!' So it's Jesus himself who we feed on.

What does that mean? Obviously we're not like cannibals, eating Jesus up – he didn't mean that. But if we think how satisfied we feel when we have been very hungry and then eat a good meal, that's how our spirits feel when we spend time with Jesus and receive him in the Eucharist – contented and satisfied, happy and full of energy and health. And just as we need to keep eating ordinary food every day, so we need to keep spending time with Jesus every day, so that, spiritually as well as physically, we will be growing strong and healthy, and we'll stay that way even when our physical bodies get old and weak, and when they stop working so that we die. Even then we'll be spiritually bounding with life and energy, ready to spend eternity alive in God's company.

All-age ideas

- Have wheat and bread as the focus of one of the flower arrangements today.

- Have the words of the Gospel written out in full, with the people's words in bold, and the priest or deacon reading the words of Jesus, so that the Gospel becomes a lively teaching conversation.

NINETEENTH SUNDAY OF THE YEAR

1 Kings 19:4-8
Psalm 33
Ephesians 4:30-5:2
John 6:41-51

Just as bread is the visible form of life-giving nourishment, so Jesus is the visible form of God's life-giving love.

All-age talk

Tell everyone that you are about to show them some vitamin B and some energy, some life-giving essence and some potential penicillin. Have a drum roll or dramatic chords on the organ as you whip out of a supermarket bag a loaf of bread.

But this is just an ordinary loaf of bread – how can something so natural and ordinary be all that clever, invisible, scientific stuff? Well, it is! If we were really hungry we could try it and find out how much better it made our bodies feel. (A hungry person can do this.) We eat our way through loaves and loaves of bread every day because we have found that it does us so much good and comes in a form we can easily take naturally – by eating!

So bread is the visible form of all kinds of good-ness and life-giving nourishment. And when Jesus talked of himself being the Bread of Life, he was describing how he is the invisible God in visible form – in the familiar shape of a human being, who we can talk to, watch, touch and listen to.

So why couldn't the religious leaders understand? Why did they find it offensive that Jesus said this?

- Jesus seemed too normal and familiar – they knew him as their carpenter.
- They thought the Son of God should look greater than Moses.
- Their expectations blinded them to seeing the very person they had been waiting generations to meet, when he was standing there right in front of their eyes.

We too need to make sure we don't miss God in the

ordinary. In fact, God made everything, so nothing is just ordinary, and God can speak to us through his creation, as long as we are ready to notice and listen. Here are some examples.

We often see heavy rain, but usually just moan about it spoiling our hair or stopping a match. Suppose we start actually looking at it and seeing there a picture of how generous and fulsome God is; so many individual droplets of rain – or petals in a tree full of blossom!

Or think of the wide night sky describing God's overarching love; the regular days, nights and seasons showing his faithfulness.

In a dog's dogginess and a young child's openness we can see God showing us the importance of being honestly ourselves; when we see weeds and wild flowers growing over a rubbish dump we see God telling us about redemption, and how everything can be made new and beautiful.

All we need to do is train our spiritual eyes to look, so that we don't miss out on anything God is wanting to say to us, even through the ordinary things.

All-age ideas

- Try this dance/mime of having our eyes and ears opened to notice God. Have a group (of mixed ages and genders) being very bustly and busy – perhaps miming the jobs they themselves do during the week. Walking around between them is someone who keeps tapping people on the arm to show them something, but they are just brushed aside, in a rather irritated way. Finally one person is alerted and shown a flower, so that they really look at it and then in wonder upwards, giving God thanks and praise. They too now wander around trying to alert others, until one by one they are all able to enjoy the world and recognise God's love in it. The mime ends with all raising their hands in worship and moving off back to their places, looking expectantly around them as they go.

- The Penitential Rite could be based on the reading from Ephesians:

Therefore each of you must put off falsehood and speak truthfully to his neighbour.

Lord, have mercy.
Lord, have mercy.

Do not let the sun go down
while you are still angry,
and do not give the devil a foothold.

Christ, have mercy.
Christ, have mercy.

Do not let any unwholesome talk
come out of your mouths,
but only what is helpful for building others up.

Lord, have mercy.
Lord, have mercy.

TWENTIETH SUNDAY OF THE YEAR

Proverbs 9:1-6
Psalm 33
Ephesians 5:15-20
John 6:51-58

God's wisdom may appear foolishness without the God-given grace to understand.

All-age talk

Begin with the short quiz given in the All-age Ideas.

Are the people who knew the answers to our quiz necessarily the wisest people here? No. (Though of course they may be!) Real wisdom is different from knowing lots of facts. Remind everyone of the Brownie story about the wise owl. The children are sent to her because they want to find out who will be the little people who do secret good turns all around their house, and wise owl tells them to go to a pond in the woods and recite a poem. (Any Brownies, present and past, can join in the poem!)

Twist me and turn me and show me the elf;
I looked in the water and there saw ... MYSELF!

The owl had been very wise because she had been able to help the children understand a deep kind of magic – whenever they did their good turns, they would be not just Imogen and Rebecca, but real Brownies! And they'd go on being Brownies whenever they did their good turns, long after they'd become Guides and grown up and had their own children who were learning the wisdom of the wise owl!

Wise people are good to go to when you want to talk things over, but you don't want to be told exactly what to do. Wise people are those who really listen to you – to how you are feeling inside as well as what you are saying. Wise people think carefully before they speak, and like learning from their mistakes.

We could say that WISDOM is all about
Walking In Simplicity Dreaming Of More

239

or we could say that to become WISE we need to
Wonder and ask questions
Imagine
Seek God
Expect to learn from him.

All-age ideas

- Have lady Wisdom and lady Folly both calling out to invite people their way, as a group walks up and down deciding, one by one. Each lady has a big sign on a stick. On the front these say 'Wisdom' and 'Folly', and on the back there are pictures of a rising sun with rays of light, and a skull. As each person decides to go down one way or the other, the lady in the chosen place turns her notice around so that the person can't see it but the rest of the congregation can.

- The quiz:
  1. What is H_2O?
  2. How many legs does a spider have?
  3. What animal pretended to be Red Riding Hood's grandma?
  4. What is the current exchange rate for dollars?
  5. What do you call a cake made with eggs, flour and sugar but no fat?
  6. Who scored for Manchester United in their last match?
  7. What are nine sevens?
  8. What comes straight after a red light?
  9. What is another name for Rose of Sharon?
  10. How many balls in one over?

(Answers: 1. water; 2. 8; 3. wolf; 4. check in newspaper; 5. sponge; 6. check in newspaper; 7. 63; 8. red and amber; 9. St John's Wort/hypericum; 10. 6)

TWENTY-FIRST SUNDAY OF THE YEAR

Joshua 24:1-2a, 15-18
Psalm 33
Ephesians 5:21-32
John 6:60-69

'To whom else could we go? You alone have the words of eternal life.'

All-age talk

Have a show of hands for a few choices – Who's for football, who's for rugby? Who's a lark and loves the early mornings, who's an owl and loves to stay up late? Who's a 'dog' person, who's a 'cat' person?

All these are a matter of choice, and happily we are all different so we all like to choose different toppings on our pizzas, different music to listen to and different colours to wear. It's wonderful and important that we are all different.

But there are some things we can't choose, because it's been decided that there is a collective good way of going on. So we all drive on the same side of the road whatever part of the country we're in; we all go to school and learn how to read and write and do maths and science; we all pay taxes on what we earn so everyone, both poor and rich, can use schools and hospitals and so on.

In our first reading, from the Old Testament, Joshua wants the people to decide, before they go in to the promised land, whether they really do want to serve the Lord their God or not. He makes it quite clear that they will only be choosing wisely if they do choose to worship God, as he is real and powerful, and the other gods are not. It's a little bit like asking a football team if they are going to choose to play with a football or a matchbox in an international match. There really isn't much point in playing with anything other than the real thing!

In the Gospel we heard of some of the crowds choosing not to walk with Jesus any more because he seemed to be making out that he was the Holy One of God. Jesus asked his disciples if they were

241

going to turn away as well, and Peter spoke for them all, and for us as well. 'Lord, who else could we go to,' he asked, 'seeing that you are the one with the words of eternal life?' When we know that God is real, and that Jesus really is the Holy One of God, what else can we do but make the sensible, wise choice and commit ourselves to following him? That's the wisest, most important choice we make in the whole of our life.

All-age ideas

• As a follow-up to the All-age Talk, it may be helpful to provide the opportunity for making a renewed commitment to serve God and become a follower of Jesus Christ. Depending on the style and tradition of your church this could involve a time of worship before the Blessed Sacrament; or you could have a time of silent reflection followed by the baptismal declaration of faith.

• With the focus in the reading from Ephesians being on marriage, have a display of photographs of the couples in the parish preparing for marriage, or of those celebrating particular anniversaries.

Twenty-second Sunday of the Year

Deuteronomy 4:1-2,
  6-8
Psalm 14
James 1:17-18, 21-22,
  27
Mark 7:1-8, 14-15,
  21-23

We need to be careful never to replace the timeless commands of God with man-made traditions.

All-age talk

Probably quite a lot of us washed before we came out today. Why do we keep ourselves clean by regular washing? (Collect ideas and reasons.) Conclude that there are good reasons for washing. It's all to do with keeping healthy as well as being pleasant to sit next to! Our Gospel reading today was talking about what makes us unclean. If we are talking about our bodies, what sort of things make us unclean, or dirty? (Collect a few ideas.)

Now it was traditional for Jewish religious people to do lots and lots of washing. Some of this was to keep everything clean and healthy, and, having lived as wandering nomads in hot desert country, all that was very important. But there was another kind of 'being unclean' which wasn't to do with bodies but souls. Sin is your soul, or spiritual nature, being unclean and in need of a good clean-up. They believed that eating certain foods or not following special rituals would make you unclean.

But whereas it's *outside* things that make our bodies unclean and in need of washing, Jesus explained that with our souls it's thoughts and wants from deep *inside* us that often lead us into sin, making us unclean. Like what, for instance?

- Like when we have mean, unkind thoughts;
- when we feel like hating or despising people because they've got what we want;
- whenever we want what we know is wrong and against God's way of living;

243

- when it seems like a clever idea to lie our way out of trouble;
- when doing something unselfish seems too much hard work and we can't be bothered with it.

When we are baptised, we're dunked in water, partly as a sign that we're being washed clean from sin. (The priest washes his hands just after the bread and wine are brought to the altar, as an outward sign that he wants God to wash him clean of sin, ready for this special part of the service.)

So if those wrong and bad thoughts and drives make us sin, so that our souls are unclean, how on earth can we get clean again? Can we scrub our souls with soap and water, or soak all our nastiness away in a hot bath? No, we can't. But there is a way of getting our souls clean without leaving any stain of sin at all. It's a two-stage washing process, rather like putting stuff out for the laundry because we know it's dirty, and then having it washed clean. And it's called *repentance* and *forgiveness*.

Once we realise that our souls are messy and dirty with sin, and that makes us sad, we bring all of it to Jesus, tell him how sorry we are and how we would love our souls to be completely clean again. That's *repentance*.

What Jesus does is to take our souls and soak away all the sin in a wonderful bath of *forgiveness*, that leaves us feeling free and happy and spiritually clean.

All-age ideas

- Have an arrangement of washing products, such as a laundry bag with some clothes in it, washing powder/liquid, a laundry basket and some pegs.

- Give everyone a peg to hold. While a song or hymn is sung, focusing on repentance and forgiveness, suggest we all look over our souls to see what needs a good wash, and bring it to Jesus for his cleansing forgiveness.

TWENTY-THIRD SUNDAY OF THE YEAR

Isaiah 35:4-7a
Psalm 145
James 2:1-5
Mark 7:31-37

Jesus comes fulfilling the hope of healing to wholeness; he shows that mercy has triumphed over judgement.

All-age talk

Introduce the talk with the short sketch given in the All-age Ideas. Bring along a couple of different masks and ask volunteers to come and put them on. Point out how Farouk has now turned into a fierce tiger, and we might be scared of him; Mazin is now a clown and looks even funnier than usual! Thank the volunteers and restore them to their normal identities.

One of the things that all grown-ups do is to put on different masks for different people. We need to learn from the children, especially the very young children, how not to. What sort of masks do grown-ups wear? Not usually animal or clown masks, but masks all the same!

Like the woman answering the phone in the sketch, we put on a special voice for people we want to impress, we wear special clothes and try to give the other person the impression that we are efficient, cool, witty, deep or dependable. Why do we do that? Because we know that most people are influenced by outward appearances, and most people are fairly judgemental. If we can persuade them that we are worth respecting, then we reckon they will be more likely to listen to us and take notice of us.

Is that how we want it to be? Think instead of young children, who simply act as themselves, and haven't yet learnt the game of pretending who they are. You can see in the direct look in a young child's eyes that there is something there which grown-ups call innocence, because they are real;

245

and we all regret losing that in all the clever pretending and wearing of masks.

As Christians, we are called to break that destructive cycle. We are *not* to judge from outward appearances, or just be friendly and respectful to wealthy, important-looking people. For us it's different because we know that every person we set eyes on is made and loved by God. And if we treat every person with the respect and love which they deserve as God-made human beings, they won't feel that they need to put on masks when they are with us. We will be joining Jesus in allowing people to be who they are, so that they are helped to wholeness and integrity.

All-age ideas

• Here is the sketch to introduce the All-age Talk.

Pauline Carter is sitting at her office desk working and answering the telephone. She can have the script in front of her, so she won't have to learn it.

(Phone rings. Pauline answers it in bored, automatic voice.)

Good morning, Pauline Carter speaking, how can I help you? . . . *(Suddenly sits up straight and adjusts hair, changes voice to be very efficient and respectful.)* Oh Mr Townsend, good morning. How can I be of assistance? . . . Yes, certainly, I'm sure that would be convenient . . . I'll just check the date . . . Yes, Monday at eleven forty would be fine . . . Certainly, I'll arrange that . . . And you, too, Mr Townsend . . . Thank you so much . . . Goodbye.

(Carries on working. Phone rings again. Pauline answers it in efficient, friendly mode.)

Good morning! It's Pauline Carter here. How can I help you? . . . *(Suddenly raises eyebrows and slumps back in seat, getting on with work while the other person talks. She's obviously not really listening.)* Ah . . . oh, hi . . . mmm . . . ah . . . ah . . . no . . . look, I'm really busy here . . . yeah. OK . . . Bye.

(Carries on working. Phone rings again. Pauline answers it in bored auto voice.)

Good morning. Pauline Carter here. How can I help you?

- Beneath the words of the Alleluia verse have a display. To one side have a radio, some newspapers and a TV listings guide. On the other side have an open Bible. In the middle of the display have a question mark.

TWENTY-FOURTH SUNDAY OF THE YEAR

Isaiah 50:5-9
Psalm 114
James 2:14-18
Mark 8:27-35

Loving obedience to God is shown by Jesus to be a quality rich in courage and wisdom, a quality to be highly respected.

All-age talk

Ask for some volunteers and spread them around. Explain that all you want is for them to do as they're told. Then give a series of instructions, such as right hand in the air, stand still, run on the spot, stretch arms out to the sides, touch your toes, touch your nose, and so on. Hardly give them time to think. Finish by telling them to go back to their seats and everyone can give them a round of applause for giving us such a stunning example of perfect obedience.

Point out that it's quite easy to be obedient when someone's shouting out instructions, and the things aren't too hard. But if you had told them to push everyone off their chairs, or give all their money to the priest, would they have rushed to be obedient and carry out the instructions? Hopefully not! God forbid that we should be so keen to obey anyone that we fall in with any dangerous or wrong instruction. Teachers often come across children who have done something really stupid, and give the excuse that their friend told them to. Is that a good excuse? No, of course it isn't, because we have to think when we are asked to do anything, and refuse to do it if it seems selfish, dangerous or wrong. (It isn't just children, either – grown-ups will give as an excuse that everybody else does it, which is just as foolish an excuse, since everybody else could well be doing something dangerous or wrong.)

So where have we got to with obedience? That we are not meant to leave our brains and consciences behind. That means we are measuring every instruction up against the one we really trust to know what is right and good – underneath all the other obedient things we do there is a deep solid rock of obedience to God. That is what keeps us obedient wherever the instructions we are given are sensible and good, because measured up against the solid rock of our God we can see clearly that it's right to do what we're told here. In being obedient we are also being obedient to God.

And it's also what stops us obeying foolish, dangerous or wrong instructions which we might get from other people. Because when measured up against the solid rock of our God we can see clearly that to obey in those cases would make us disobedient to God.

Obedience to God is what matters more than anything, and Jesus showed us that.

All-age ideas

- Have different voices reading today's Gospel.

- Use part of the letter of James as the basis for a Penitential Rite.

  For the times when we have failed to respond to the needs of our neighbour,

  Lord, have mercy.
  Lord, have mercy.

  For the times when we have failed to clothe the naked,

  Christ, have mercy.
  Christ, have mercy.

  For the times when we have failed to feed the hungry.

  Lord, have mercy.
  Lord, have mercy.

TWENTY-FIFTH SUNDAY OF THE YEAR

Wisdom of Solomon
   2:12, 17-20
Psalm 53
James 3:16-4:3
Mark 9:30-37

The truly great in God's eyes are those who are prepared to be last of all and servant of all.

All-age talk

You will need to bring along a Christening gift of some kind (Peter Rabbit bowl, silver spoon or locket), a 5 or 10 metre swimming badge, an item of school uniform, several cups or trophies, a graduation certificate or gown, and a driving licence, a few brown envelopes and a clock.

Ask for a volunteer to help take everyone on a whistlestop tour of a lifetime. Work through a person's life (you can call them the name of the volunteer), presenting them with the trophies which mark each stage of the climb to power and greatness. As a baby they are presented with special presents. As they grow up they start doing clever things like swimming and riding bikes. They wear special clothes to show they're old enough and clever enough to be going to school and learning loads more things every morning. Perhaps they have a hobby – in sport or music – and they do so well that they keep winning cups and trophies for it. As they get older still, they're off to university, and a few years later, here they are at their graduation. It's congratulations time again. And then there are the driving lessons and the practice and the extra insurance, and suddenly it's the test, and a smart new driving licence. All they need now is the car to drive. But the work's going well and the money's coming in, so they can buy all the things they've always wanted, and here are the bills to prove it. And then, after a good many years of work, this highly respected person is old enough to retire.

They have become a powerful and important pillar of society.

The volunteer is now loaded. Help unload them and thank them for their assistance.

We all have ambitions; we all hope our lives will turn out like our dreams. We want to be successful, liked, appreciated, fit and good-looking. And often we secretly want to be best. Jesus sees all of our dreams, even the secret ones. He knew what the disciples had been muttering about on their way as they walked along. They probably hoped he couldn't hear, because, like all of us, they had a strong suspicion that discussing who had most status was not really Jesus talk. Jesus really didn't care if the important people disapproved of him. He wasn't out to impress anybody, or work his way up, or gain status – he was just there to get on with the work of loving people to wholeness.

And that's what he wants for his followers as well. He wants us to have that freedom, so we can get on with what's really important, instead of wasting our time and energy empire-building in our particular area, impressing people, or collecting status symbols to wear or drive in. What do they matter when we compare them with God's values? Let's learn to be happy and content with nothing but being last, being unnoticed and the servant of all.

All-age ideas

- Act out the Gospel while it is narrated, using a young child. Have the child's parent taking Jesus' part.

- *Secrets.* Give everyone a small piece of paper and invite them to think of some act of loving service they could do without anyone knowing. When they have thought, they fold the pieces of paper up and bring them out to a collection point near the cross. They can enjoy carrying this out during the coming week – a secret between them and God.

TWENTY-SIXTH SUNDAY OF THE YEAR

Numbers 11:25-29
Psalm 18
James 5:1-6
Mark 9:38-43, 45,
    47-48

Don't let your body lead you into sin and risk exchanging eternal life for eternal punishment.

All-age talk

Bring along some scissors and some thick garden wire, and something which has been ruined by being used in the wrong way – such as a spoon, buckled after being used as a trowel, or a tray which has gone rusty from being used under the Christmas tree.

Ask people what they think would happen if you were to use this good pair of scissors to cut the wire. Although you'd probably be able to cut through it eventually, you'd probably spoil the scissors for ever – they aren't made to cut wire, so the wire would ruin them. Show your example of something you have already ruined through using it in a way it wasn't designed for.

It's just the same with human beings. We were all made in the image and likeness of our loving God. We were designed to love God and love one another, and we work at our best like this.

But our readings today are full of the sad truth that we often live in a selfish and wrong way. If we insist on living this wrong way again and again, we're setting out on a self-destruction course. Jesus wants all his followers (including us) to know that it isn't worth choosing wrong ways of living all the time because that way we'll end up being destroyed instead of having the wonderful everlasting life we were made for, and Jesus wants the very best for us all.

And there's another thing. God is very concerned about all the other people who don't realise how dangerous and destructive it is to live wrongly, and he needs those who know God's love to help them all. God badly needs some volunteers living in this world, and this parish, going to the local school, shopping in the local supermarket, working wherever you work, and belonging to the clubs you belong to.

To be of any use, we'll need God to sort out our own sin, and we mustn't let our minds or bodies lead us into wrong thinking and doing. We need to get that done, however much it hurts and however difficult it seems – even if it feels as painful as chopping off a hand or a foot. Turning from sin hurts, but it won't kill your eternal life, like the sin will. Let's live instead as we were designed to live – growing in love day by day, looking out for one another's needs, and working together for the coming of God's kingdom.

All-age ideas

- Have a display with, on one side, a moth-eaten or very grubby garment, with the sign 'Original price £xxx – value now £???'. On the other side have a glass of water with the caption 'Your gift to a thirsty person' and the sign 'Value £???'.

- As a poster or banner, have a selection of many and various pictures of people, with the words: 'Humans – designed for loving'.

- For the Penitential Rite give everyone a piece of paper with a '1' written on it. Invite them to reflect on what they have made number 1 in their time, loving and spending, instead of putting God first.

TWENTY-SEVENTH SUNDAY OF THE YEAR

Genesis 2:18-24
Psalm 127
Hebrews 2:9-11
Mark 10:2-16

Human beings are made responsible for the care of creation but are subject to God in all aspects of their lives.

All-age talk

Invite people to share what jobs they are responsible for, including household chores, professional responsibilities and so on. Have people of all ages contributing so that it is clear that we all have responsibilities of some sort, whatever our age. You could also draw attention to those responsible for particular jobs in church, making it an opportunity for everyone to thank the flower arrangers, servers and choir, cleaners and pastoral team.

Point out that right from the beginning, when Adam was naming the animals, God has made us human beings responsible for looking after this world and each other. That is the important job that God has given us to do. If we all did our bit and everyone acted responsibly to the planet and to one another, under God's guiding hand, we would find that our life together here would be greatly blessed. People would have enough to eat, and many disasters and much suffering would be avoided.

So why doesn't that happen, when it seems such good sense for us to live according to the Maker's instructions?

The trouble is that we all let our own wants and selfishness get in the way. If we, as rich nations, started acting more responsibly, then things we've become used to getting cheaply would be more expensive, and we might have to make do with less. Our greed stops us acting responsibly. So does our short-sightedness, when we want 'lots, now!' instead of considering those who haven't yet been born.

It's even the same in our friendships and marriages. If we are responsible in these, we will be caring for the other person and looking after their needs, sensitive to their feelings and wanting to help them. If one or other or both stop doing that, the relationship becomes hurtful and wearing instead of rewarding. The answer may not be to get out of the friendship or marriage, but change our way of behaving with each other, talking things over with each other and with God, learning to be responsible again. It is grown-up and sensible to know that life can't always be happy, and the person we love can't always agree with us. Giving one another space, understanding that we all have bad days, forgiving one another and working at our friendships – all this is part of being the responsible people God created us to be.

He doesn't expect us to do it without help. God is there with us in all the bad patches as well as the easy rides, and as a community we are to look after one another properly, making sure we're all OK and coming to the rescue whenever someone isn't.

All-age ideas

- If the church hasn't already got a system for community caring, today is a good time to start one. This might involve grouping people to keep an eye on one another's needs, looking out for them and being there for them in any rough patches. Spreading the responsibility like this makes for a realistic expectation of care without overload.

- Married couples may like to affirm their marriage vows today, with the whole community affirming their commitment to the support and nurture of families.

TWENTY-EIGHTH SUNDAY OF THE YEAR

Wisdom 7:7-11
Psalm 89
Hebrews 4:12-13
Mark 10:17-30

The most valuable possession is not the wealth that owns us, but is Christ, the Wisdom of God, who gives us untold riches.

All-age talk

Beforehand set up a kind of treasure hunt, like this. Prepare the following envelopes, numbered clearly, and place them all around the church.

1. Contains the reference Wisdom 7:7 and a Bible with a bookmark in the right place.

2. Contains a charity envelope with a description of the need for fresh water in many villages, or an immediate crisis concern.

3. Contains a flag of our nation.

Ask for a couple of volunteers, old enough to read, and send them off to search for envelope number 1. When they bring it back, ask them to open it and look up the reference in the Bible. This was part of our first reading today, and in order to understand what seeking God involves, we're doing it. The author knew that seeking God actually changes us, helping us to find God. Already our search has led us to pick up a Bible and read it. All of us need to do that – it's no good having a Bible at home if we never open it up and read it! As we heard in our second reading today, the word of God is living and active. If we are really seeking God, we'll have to find out what the word of God says, every day.

Ask for another couple of volunteers to search for envelope number 2. They open it and show the contents. Either describe the needs in the present crisis, or explain how (CAFOD) is trying to provide the basic need of fresh water for villages in Africa and India, where the children die because the water is so bad. We have fresh water there in our taps all the time! What can we do to help these people? God is leading us to see with his eyes of compassion and love. Explain how the parish may already be responding through its concern for the developing world.

Another couple of volunteers search for envelope number 3. Inside is the national flag. Invite people to think about their country – the things that make them happy about it and the things which sadden them. As we seek God's goodness, truth and justice, we'll find that we notice things that need to be changed. Our country needs us to stand up for what is right and fight what is evil. Are we doing that, or leaving it to other people?

The young man in the Gospel was seeking God, and Jesus helped him. The next stage of that young man's journey into God would be to change things in his life. If we set out to seek God, we must expect the same.

All-age ideas

- Outside the church have a large sign with an arrow, saying, 'God-seekers this way!'

- Have the Gospel acted out, with people taking parts.

TWENTY-NINTH SUNDAY OF THE YEAR

Isaiah 53:10-11
Psalm 32
Hebrews 4:14-16
Mark 10:35-45

Even the Son of Man himself came not to be served but to serve, and to give his life as a ransom for many.

All-age talk

Have three chairs placed in front of the altar, in the obvious place of honour. Prepare three 'Reserved' signs.

In the Gospel today we watched two of Jesus' disciples – James and John – coming up to him with a question they wanted to ask. They wanted to make sure Jesus would give them what they wanted, so instead of starting with the real question, they first said, 'We want you to do for us whatever we ask.' Perhaps we try that one with parents or spouses, or the boss sometimes. Like this.

Invite a child and adult to come and read the following script:

Child Dad, you love me, don't you?

Dad Yes, son.

Child You'd give me anything I wanted, wouldn't you?

Dad Mmm . . . maybe I would.

Child Well, can I have this really good educational computer game?

Dad No.

Child Oh, but Dad, you said . . .

Dad I only said maybe!

Child Oh well, it was worth a try.

Jesus didn't say yes either. He asked James and John what they wanted, and was pretty gobsmacked by

258

what it was. Invite two children to read out James and John's question – have it printed out in large, clear letters for them: 'Let one of us sit at your right and the other at your left in your glory.'

What on earth was Jesus to say to that? Point out the three chairs, and have someone place a reserved sign on the main, middle one. Who was this place in glory reserved for? Jesus. Had he pushed for it or even asked for it? No! He was given it by Almighty God, his Father. It was being a servant and being willing to give up his life for us all that brought Jesus to reign in glory. If James and John were to be granted their wish (invite them to go and sit either side of the main seat), what would it show about them, and about Jesus? (Collect ideas. It might show that they were the most important of the disciples, that Jesus liked them better than the others, that pushy people get their way in God's kingdom, for instance.)

Jesus pointed out to them that those places are not his to give anyway as they have reserved signs on them. (Invite someone to move James and John off the thrones and place reserved signs on them.) No one, not even Jesus, knew who they are reserved for. It could be for someone here! What we can be sure of is that the people they're reserved for would be the very last people to ask to sit there, or count themselves more worthy than anyone else!

Jesus tells us that we are all here to bother about serving others, not to bother about being served. Even Jesus himself, the Son of the living God, came as a servant, and gave up his life for the good of others. That's the example we're to follow, not resigning ourselves to it, grudgingly, but happy to have the honour of giving up our lives to serve others in love.

All-age ideas

- The Gospel works well read with different voices, especially if the readers have prepared by studying the text and thinking through the subscript, rather as actors would, so that they can act it in the expressions and body language, pauses and so on, as well as the words themselves.

• While the first reading is read, have a cross brought from the back to the front of the church, or project an image of the cross from a painting on an OHP screen.

Thirtieth Sunday of the Year

Jeremiah 31:7-9
Psalm 125
Hebrews 5:1-6
Mark 10:46-52

In Jesus, God gathers his scattered people and opens their eyes to see.

All-age talk

Begin by asking people to imagine a child who has gone outside to play. She has been learning to ride her bike, and is quite good at it now, with a few wobbles. She's happy out there, riding up and down, until she takes a corner a bit steeply, brakes sharply, and she and the bike crash down. The child has a nasty graze on her leg, and is upset and a bit frightened by the fall. All she can think of is getting back home, to the person she knows will make it all better, and there she is, limping up the road, with her leg bleeding, crying out for her mum as she goes.

Most of us have been there. Whenever we're badly hurt, even when we've grown up, there's a young child inside us limping back home, crying, to the place we feel safe, and to the person we know will look after us and make it all better.

It's a good picture of our loving parent God, who is always there, waiting for his hurt and limping children to walk back home to the one who can and does make it all better, however old or young we are, and however we got our wounds. What that walk back home shows is that the child trusts. What our walk back to God shows is that we know and love and trust God to help us.

In today's Gospel we met a blind man called Bartimaeus. He knew he was blind. He knew he missed out in life because he couldn't see. When he heard that Jesus was passing by, he shouted and kept on shouting, so he wouldn't miss his chance. Never mind if the disciples told him to be quiet, he knew this was too important an opportunity to miss, and he shouted hard until Jesus himself heard him. That gave him the chance to do his 'limping home' – he made his way to the person he knew could help him. And, sure enough, Jesus did just that.

All-age ideas

- The reading from Jeremiah can be read chorally, with a group of voices such as men, women and children, or a mixed group of high, medium and low voice tones. Work through the passage experimenting with who reads what, bearing in mind that the object is to help bring out the meaning in the best way.

- The Gospel can be acted out, with a narrator and mime, or with the different voices. In a small group, everyone could be involved by creating the Jericho street scene, with the people all standing there, crowding round the action as it happens.

THIRTY-FIRST SUNDAY OF THE YEAR

Deuteronomy 6:2-6
Psalm 17
Hebrews 7:23-28
Mark 12:28-34

To love the living God with heart, soul and strength, and to love our neighbour as ourselves means far more than any sacrificial offerings.

All-age talk

Beforehand ask three people to practise saying the same sentence, each emphasising a different word so that the meaning is slightly changed.

- WE go to church on Sunday – (as opposed to other people)
- We go to CHURCH on Sunday – (that's our destination)
- We go to church on SUNDAY – (rather than another day)

Also they need to practise saying the same sentence meaning something different.

- Yes, I believe so – (but you're not at all sure about it)
- Yes, I believe so – (automatically because it's written for you to say, but absent-mindedly)
- Yes, I believe so – (after much thought and with deep conviction)

Begin by pointing out how jokes can be really funny if you tell them right, but fall completely flat if you don't. How we say things is as important as what we say. Somebody can be saying nice things but you know they really don't like you and are trying to be nasty. Your friend could say the same things and you'd be happy and pleased instead of upset.

Invite the sentence-speakers to the front and invite everyone to spot the difference in what they are saying. (We go to church on Sunday.) Through

263

stressing different words, they changed the meaning, even though the words stayed the same.

In the Gospel today we met a well-educated person, who had been quoting the scriptures every day of his life for a good number of years. He was thought of as fairly expert in his field of understanding God's law. He's been sitting listening to Jesus discussing the matters of law and faith with other experts, and he's impressed. He thinks it sounds as if Jesus really knows what he's talking about. He's so impressed that he asks Jesus a question, addressing him very respectfully as Rabbi, or Teacher. And the question he asks is this (have a volunteer, or everyone, read it out clearly and loudly): 'Which is the most important of the Commandments?'

The trouble was there were so many commandments now (as you speak, gradually unroll a very long roll of paper labelled 'Commandments') that it was all rather complicated and confusing. The scribe needed some help to sort it all out.

And what Jesus does is this. He recites the special statement of faith which every Jewish person knew by heart from childhood. It was this (everyone reads it out clearly): 'Hear, O Israel! The Lord our God is the one Lord.'

Just imagine how God's Son, a Jewish young man, would say that! The scribe could hear, in the way he said it, all Jesus' complete trust in God. He could tell it meant everything to Jesus, and he wasn't just rattling it off by heart. He meant it, completely and joyfully. And that got the scribe excited about his own faith – Jesus' love of God was catching!

When we talk about Jesus, does our love for him show?

All-age ideas

- A credal statement today could be this:
  The Lord our God is the one Lord,
  and Jesus is Lord!
  Glory be to the Father and to the Son

and to the Holy Spirit,
as God was in the beginning,
is now and shall be for ever. Amen.

- The summary of the law can be sung to the tune
  of *London's burning*, in a round:

  You shall love the Lord your God with
  all your heart and all your mind and
  all your strength! All your strength!
  And love your neighbour,
  and love your neighbour.

THIRTY-SECOND SUNDAY OF THE YEAR

1 Kings 17:10-16
Psalm 145
Hebrews 9:24-28
Mark 12:38-44

Loving generosity is the hallmark of Godly giving.

All-age talk

Ask for two or three volunteers and give each of them a thick wad of monopoly money, a posh hat to wear, and a car key for a posh car (an ordinary key with a flashy cardboard key ring marked Rolls or BMW, for instance). Explain to everyone that they have their hats and flashy car keys because they all have lots and lots of money. Now invite another person and give them a supermarket bag and two pennies. This is all she has left for the week.

Have another volunteer holding the collection plate, and go over the Gospel with the rich people miming their giving (several notes from their wad). Encourage everyone to be impressed by how much each one has given. When the poor person comes to the collection plate, she gives two pennies (everyone listens to hear them clatter in). That isn't nearly as much as the others gave, is it? But Jesus reckoned the woman who gave two coins had given most. Why?

Collect their ideas and draw out Jesus' reasoning. God is not interested in the actual amount we give but in how lovingly generous we are, and that turns our way of thinking upside down. Sacrificial, or costly giving, out of love, will vary enormously in the actual amount. And there's another thing, too. Sometimes we are tempted to spend much more than we can afford, not really because we're so generous, but through a kind of pride. We feel pressurised to give the same quantity and quality of presents at Christmas, for instance, or all the trimmings at weddings, which richer people can

266

easily afford. Many end up working themselves ill to keep up such giving, or running up huge credit card bills with massive interest to pay.

That is not what Jesus means by generosity.

If our giving is sliding in that direction we need to check our motives in giving. Are we giving so that our children will like us better, or stop nagging us? Are we hoping for other people's respect and admiration? If so, we need to ask God in to change things. Loving generosity is a way of thinking, of giving time and attention to others, as well as looking after needs. It is even learning the humility to receive as well as give, and to love without being possessive.

The readings today teach us how to give in a Godly way – freely and willingly, not through pressure but through love.

All-age ideas

- Have the children singing *Love is something if you give it away* at the offering of the gifts.

- Have the first reading read by three people – Elijah, the widow and the narrator.

THIRTY-THIRD SUNDAY OF THE YEAR

Daniel 12:1-3
Psalm 15
Hebrews 10:11-14, 18
Mark 13:24-32

We are to be on our guard; great anguish will accompany the last days, but all that is good and loving, wise and true will be saved and celebrated for ever.

All-age talk

Bring along a well-loved and very well-worn companion – teddy or pyjama case. Introduce him to everyone and point out how we can all see just how well loved he is! He bears the signs of being well loved. Probably most of us older ones feel a bit like this – loving has worn us to the shape we are, a bit threadbare and squashed maybe, but perhaps a little wiser and softer and less selfish as a result. Although we know from experience that loving hasn't always been easy, we can say with certainty that it's well worth living lovingly.

Our readings today are helping us to look forward to the end of time, when the sky is wrapped up and the moon folded away. It can sound very frightening, to think of everything we know coming to an end. Whenever there are terrible disasters and famines and wars it can feel as if things are spinning out of control – even out of God's control. Is the end going to be some huge ghastly mistake, brought about by our greed and selfishness?

The Bible reassures us that, however it may look as evil grows and temporarily gains the upper hand, God is always ultimately in charge. As we know, God's way is not to crash into our blundering and force us to change so that disasters are prevented. He has given us that great gift of free will, so that we can choose good or evil in the small and large decisions of life. He longs for us to choose the good that will bring us blessing and peace, but is always there weeping with us in the chaos and suffering that evil leads to, ready to redeem it for good.

And it is that buffeted and battered loving which will last and last for ever. The prophet Daniel gives us a lovely picture of that. All those who have guided others in the right path, he says, will shine like the stars of heaven for ever. All the wise leaders will show up brightly for all to see. If we have set ourselves to live lives of faith and love, there is no way we need be frightened by the last days. After the feeding of the five thousand Jesus told his disciples to gather up the fragments so that nothing is lost. That's how it will be at the end; every scrap of goodness and love will be gathered safely in, so that nothing of it is lost.

All-age ideas

- Have a display with the well-loved friend, together with a sign which reads 'Love remains for ever'.

- Have the passage from Daniel read by a group of adults and children, reading alternately, like this:

Children: Verse 1 up to 'your people . . .'

Adults: 'There will be a time . . . came into existence.'

Children: 'When that time comes . . . written in the Book.'

Adults: 'Of those who are sleeping . . . shame and everlasting disgrace.'

Children: Verse 3.

CHRIST THE KING

Daniel 7:13-14
Psalm 92
Apocalypse 1:5-8
John 18:33-37

Jesus Christ is the everlasting King whose kingdom is not of this world, but grows in the hearts of his people and lasts for ever.

All-age talk

Beforehand prepare a long length of lining paper on which the alphabet is written clearly. Fix it up where everyone can see it, or ask people to hold it. (Please don't make them hold it high or their arms will drop off!)

Claim that on this sheet you have the whole of the Bible, the complete works of Shakespeare, every love letter ever written, every postcard and Christmas letter ever sent. You also have the names of every person and every place.

At this point a pre-arranged person walks out to protest. Preachers are supposed to tell the truth and here you are telling porky pies. You can't possibly have all that on this sheet of paper. You've only got a few letters!

Meet the challenge by inviting them to find their own name from the sheet, which they spell out letter by letter, and have to admit that they are on the sheet after all. Get someone else to find 'To be or not to be' and 'Come, Lord Jesus'. These are also found to be there.

Our God is like A to Z – the beginning and the end of everything, all thoughts and ideas, all creation, all love, all hope, all existence. That's why we worship God – God has always been. God is, at this very moment now. (Pause for everyone to become aware of that amazing fact.) And God will always be, for ever. God's kingdom is wherever Jesus reigns as our King. And that means wherever people say, 'Yes!' to Jesus, 'I really want to be in your kingdom!'

And we know what being in Jesus' kingdom is

like, don't we? It's full of love and joy and peace, full of forgiveness and patience, full of hope and healing. Today it's as if we've brought out our flags to wave as we celebrate Jesus as our wonderful, everlasting King, who sets our lives dancing!

All-age ideas

- If you have bunting stored away for summer fairs, bring it out today and festoon the entrance to the church.

- Make the flower arrangements reflect the royal dignity and power of Jesus, with gold and scarlet colours, and perhaps including a gold crown.

- Use two voices in the Gospel for the conversation between Jesus and Pilate.

YEAR C

First Sunday of Advent

Jeremiah 33:14-16
Psalm 24
1 Thessalonians
   3:12-4:2
Luke 21:25-28, 34-36

The gathered hopes of generations remind us to get ourselves ready, so that Christ's return will be a day of excitement and great joy.

All-age talk

Have ready a good supply of inflated balloons on strings. These will be needed later.

Bring out three sweets or apples and explain that three people are going to get them. Give them out completely randomly and then ask if that was fair. Agree with them that it wasn't fair, and often life seems unfair to us. (This is something that all ages know about.) Explain how our world is full of injustice and sometimes cruel and terrible things happen which don't make sense.

Now ask anyone who would like a balloon to raise a hand. Invite these people to come and collect a balloon and return to their seats. You will need them to gather with their balloons later on, when you beckon them.

As Christians we don't have to pretend the bad things aren't there, or try to work out easy answers that don't make sense. God knows there are sad and bad things happening in our world as well. They happened just the same when Jesus was walking around in Galilee. A tower fell on some people and killed them. The people asked Jesus to explain it, but he didn't. He felt very, very sorry for anyone who was ill or whose child had died, and, instead of explaining why, he set about comforting them and doing everything he could to make things better. So that's what we need to do as well while we are alive.

But Jesus did tell us that life wouldn't always be unjust. One day, he said, everything as we know it will finish, and on that day everything you, and everyone else, have ever done which is good or kind, or helpful, friendly or honest will be gathered in, like harvest, and kept. (As you say this, gather all those with balloons together in the centre.) It will be an exciting and very beautiful harvest!

Let's make sure that we grow plenty of love and thoughtfulness and honesty and integrity in our lives, however old or young we are, so that whenever that last day comes, we'll be helping to make it a bumper harvest.

All-age ideas

- If you have a set of advent candles, have the candles lit each week by representatives of different age groups, so that by the fourth Sunday in Advent there is a child, a teenager, a working-age adult and a senior citizen.

- Ask a few people to write these words on large posters for the walls or pillars: 'Heaven and earth will pass away but my words will never pass away.'

SECOND SUNDAY OF ADVENT

Baruch 5:1-9
Psalm 125
Philippians 1:3-6, 8-11
Luke 3:1-6

It had been prophesied that there would be a messenger to prepare the way for the coming of the Messiah. Now John the Baptist appears with his urgent message of repentance.

All-age talk

Beforehand arrange for a local builder/decorator to be interviewed, preferably in working clothes and carrying his tools.

Introduce the guest, and ask his advice about a structural problem (either real or imagined). When the builder talks about the importance of all the 'making good', suggest that surely he could just smear some more plaster over the top, and wouldn't that be as good? Or put on thick wallpaper to hide the cracks? Let the builder explain what will eventually happen if the real problem isn't sorted out.

Thank the guest builder and have a couple of the children bring him a mug of tea as it's time for his tea break.

While the builder drinks his tea, explain how what is true for walls and windows is true for us as well. If we have been mean or a pain, or lazy, or if we've been telling lies or living lies, or if there is anything at all in the way we behave which is not right, loving and honest, then we are like a building with bad cracks and damp. As the builder told us, the only way to put it right is to have the wrong things cleared away, and then be built up soundly again.

God can do that in us if we want. He will help us put our lives right, however bad a state they are in. Tell him you are sorry you tell lies, and want to be more honest. He will help you become an honest person who others can trust. Tell God your sister/father-in-law/colleague winds you up and you hate

276

all the rows and want to be more able to cope. God will help you improve those relationships. Tell God you find it hard to share your toys or your money, and want to be more generous. He will help you do it.

But we can't put anything right until we see that there is a problem. It was only when the damp and cracks were noticed that the builder was called in.

John the Baptist spoke about 'repentance'. That means he is saying to us: 'Look at your lives; see those cracks and damp patches; and get them sorted out.'

All-age ideas

- Instead of a flower arrangement or as a separate display, have an arrangement of an open DIY manual, and various tools and materials, with a title: 'Get your life sorted out!' This can be done by someone doing their own property up at the moment, or a student on a building course.

- Give everyone a small paper house shape. Ask everyone to look at their house as their life, and listen to what God is saying needs putting in order or sorting out. Then the houses are collected up and placed in front of the cross (or people can bring them up to the cross). At the end they can be given out for people to take home and remind them of what they and God are going to tackle together.

THIRD SUNDAY OF ADVENT

Zephaniah 3:14-18
Canticle: Isaiah
    12:2-6
Philippians 4:4-7
Luke 3:10-18

Our period of preparation shifts from repentance and forgiveness to the freed exhilaration of hope, as the momentous truth of God's immanence begins to dawn on us.

All-age talk

Bring with you a sealed envelope containing an invitation to a very special party or wedding. The date for the celebration needs to say 'to be arranged'.

Tell everyone how you have received this letter, and it looked so exciting that you thought you'd bring it to church and open it there. Invite someone to come and help you open the envelope, and someone a bit older to read it out. Show your excitement and start planning what to give as a present, and what to wear, getting suggestions from people and scribbling it all down on a list. Such a lot to think about!

Then stop as you ask to check the date of the celebration. Realise that it only says 'Date to be arranged'. *Date to be arranged!* That means you have no idea when to get ready. It might be ages to wait. It might be next week! Suppose it's next week!

Come to the conclusion that the only way you can be sure to be ready is to get ready straightaway.

Put the invitation down and pick up a Bible. As you flick through the pages talk about how you are sure there is an invitation to a party somewhere in here as well. Find the Zephaniah reading and discover that it's the one we heard this morning, with all the dancing and singing in it.

It's going to be quite a day, and we'll need to make sure we're ready for it. But what was the date again? Look and find it's another case of 'Date to be arranged'. Only God knows the actual date. That means it could be a long time ahead or it could be very close, so the best thing to do is to get ready straightaway.

What kind of presents would be in order for this party?

Collect ideas like loving kindness, peacemaking, compassion, forgiveness, goodness and self-control. If we start now, we can grow those in our lives.

What kind of clothes would be suitable?

Clean clothes and good habits like honesty, faithfulness, humility, just or fair behaviour, and thoughtfulness. If we haven't got any yet, we can go to God's wardrobe and he'll make them to fit us perfectly. And if we have got them, but haven't worn them lately, now is the time to get them out and put them on again. These clothes get more and more beautiful as you wear them.

The second coming will be a wonderful celebration, and whether we are alive here or the other side of death, we will all be able to see it and take part.

All-age ideas

- Continue lighting the Advent candles with representatives from different age groups.

- Have the Luke passage read by a group of voices as appropriate.

FOURTH SUNDAY OF ADVENT

Micah 5:1-4
Psalm 79
Hebrews 10:5-10
Luke 1:39-44

When we co-operate with God amazing things happen.

All-age talk

Try a kind of Mexican wave, first with one side of the church and then the other. The side not involved can enjoy the effect. Row by row, starting with the front row, everyone stands together and then sits together. The row behind gets up as soon as the row in front of them has sat down. Point out that for this to work they all needed to co-operate with one another and also with you, in agreeing to try it in the first place. Today we are watching what can happen when people are willing to co-operate with God.

Last week we found John the Baptist challenging people to sort out their lives and giving them some practical advice. Those who went away and did as John suggested found that once they had started to co-operate with God their lives took on a new sparkle and freshness many had lost. Those of us who took last week's teaching to heart and started looking seriously at what needed changing in our lives will also be here this morning with a new lightness in our step and a more positive sparkle in our lives because co-operating with God is very exhilarating and liberating. Working together with God sets us free. (And if we haven't yet got round to that there is still time for us to shake ourselves awake and use Advent profitably.)

Mary was one of those people who had decided to work together with God. And that meant that God could use her. So he did. It was through Mary co-operating with God that Jesus could come into the world.

Mary and Elizabeth are both pregnant. Mary is expecting Jesus, and her cousin Elizabeth is expecting John the Baptist. It's the same John the Baptist we met

280

last week when he was grown up, teaching people by the River Jordan. Today we have a flashback to before he was born. Any mothers here will know that exciting feeling when the baby you are carrying first moves. Luke tells us that the unborn baby John was so excited at sensing the unborn Jesus, brought along in Mary, that he leapt about in his mother's womb!

Never before had God come among his people so closely. And now his birth into the world was less than a year away. No wonder Elizabeth and Mary were so excited. Having agreed to co-operate with God they found themselves being used for such an extraordinary and important job that they could hardly believe it. And they weren't even rich or powerful! They probably weren't even that well educated!

When anyone (and that includes you and me) says to God, 'I want to spend my life working together with you', God takes us up on our offer. If we don't opt out as soon as he asks of us things we may not want to give, he will be able to work with us in our lives to do amazing things. Imagine if everyone here in church decided to work with God. He could get us making waves in our community which would completely transform people's lives.

All-age ideas

- Continue the lighting of the Advent candles using representatives from different age groups. Or you could have a child dressed as Mary lighting today's candle.

- The meeting of Mary and Elizabeth in Luke's Gospel can be mimed while it is being read, using nativity costumes if you have them. It always seems a pity to have these packed away for most of the year when they are such a useful resource.

- If you have a member of the congregation who is pregnant, it would be valuable to have her lead the intercessions, or take part in a short interview about the way the baby moves, as she will be able to add insights which will help our understanding.

CHRISTMAS DAY

Isaiah 9:2-7
Psalm 97
Titus 2:11-14
Luke 2:1-14 (15-20)

Emmanuel – 'God with us' – is born at Bethlehem into the human family. Now we will be able to understand, in human terms, what God is really like.

All-age talk

You will need to borrow a mobile phone (unless you have received one as a Christmas present!) and a helper who is expert at sorting out OHPs.

Begin by telling everyone you want to show them something on the OHP, and then find that you can't work the equipment properly. Before anyone rushes to your aid, produce the mobile phone, delighted that this is an opportunity to use it to get in touch with an expert. Pretend to use the phone to get through to the expert, and have a mock conversation with them about how to work the apparatus, during which the expert suggests coming to help in person.

Welcome the help and pretend to talk through their (speedy) journey, which can be from anywhere in the world. As you get to guiding the expert down the road and into the church your helper arrives in person, mobile phone to his/her ear. (They have been standing hidden somewhere at the back of the building.)

The expert is able to get the apparatus going, and you enthuse about how much more helpful it is to have them there in person. You can now show the OHP acetate, which says: 'EMMANUEL = God with us in person.' The helper can point out that you've just been saying that it's much more helpful having them there in person. Is that what Emmanuel means?

You can then draw out the similarities – that with Jesus being born into the world as one of us, we have God with us in person to help us live good lives, make good decisions and guide us in all the tricky places. It's not that things won't ever go wrong any more, but it does mean we can always be in touch with the one who can help us sort things out. And that is a truth well worth celebrating in style! Suggest that over the Christmas festivities we live out this truth to one another. It will mean being generous-hearted, thankful, available and willing to meet people where they are, whether that is a group of friends at a party, or relatives we find it less easy to relate to. Welcome God in person to your home this Christmas and enjoy yourselves in his company.

All-age ideas

- The Advent candles will all be lit today, together with a white one in the centre. Continue to use representatives from different age groups for this. Perhaps the centre candle can be lit during the singing of the Christmas Day verse of *O come, all ye faithful*.

- Have people dressed in costume to mime the Gospel. Have a narrator who is sensitive to the actors and is able to give them the cues they need if necessary.

- Have a nativity tableau during a carol and children standing round the altar with candles during the consecration.

FIRST SUNDAY OF CHRISTMAS: THE HOLY FAMILY

Ecclesiasticus 3:2-6,
   12-14
Psalm 127
Colossians 3:12-21
Luke 2:41-52

Jesus' perception and understanding of his purpose and work begins to take shape throughout his childhood in the Holy Family.

All-age talk

Beforehand cut out two simple white cloth tunics like this, one to fit a three- or four-year-old and a larger one for a twelve-year-old.

Invite a couple of toddlers and their parents to the front and interview them about the coats or jackets the children are wearing. Admire them and ask where they were bought, and what size was needed compared with their last coat.

When God came to earth at Christmas as a baby, it was like him putting on the clothing of being human, and it was God's way of showing how much he loves us and is with us. It also helps us to see what God is like, because we cannot see God, but in Jesus we can see how God behaves. We can see that he enjoys people's company, wants to help them and shares their sadness and joy.

And Jesus didn't suddenly arrive on earth as a grown-up. He was born as a baby (draw attention to the size of someone very small in the congregation) and grew to be a toddler and a child (use other people of appropriate ages to demonstrate), so by the time he was a grown-up twelve-year-old he had experienced all the sort of human things that we experience.

Use the larger tunic with the word 'Humanity' written on it to clothe a twelve(ish)-year-old. All twelve-year-olds start asking questions about God and themselves, and so did Jesus. Part of wearing humanity meant that he developed as a human person and now he was grown-up he was fascinated to know who he was and why he was alive, just as we are. Those questions are important, and need to be asked. They are a sign of growing up. The answers for Jesus (and the answers for us) didn't come all at once. But that visit to the temple seems to have been a very important one for him. He began to understand that he was on earth to carry out God's purposes. That was why he was wearing the clothing of humanity. Perhaps for some of us this Christmas is an important one for finding out God's purpose for us in our lives. We need to come into God's presence wearing the clothes of honesty and openness, and ask our questions.

All-age ideas

- The Gospel can be acted out with a narrator leading the miming.

- The tunic with the word 'Humanity' written on it can be laid down near the altar for people to see and remember as they come to receive communion.

SECOND SUNDAY OF CHRISTMAS

Sirach 24:1-4, 12-16
Psalm 147
Ephesians 1:3-6, 15-18
John 1:1-18

Christ is the way God tells people about himself.

All-age talk

You will need a hairdrier or a fan, or a lit candle to blow out.

Start with a riddle. You're thinking of something which is all around us, pressing against our faces and bodies at 15 pounds per square inch. It goes in and out of us all the time we're alive, and there's lots of it right in front of our eyes. What is it? (Air.) But we can't see it, so how do we know it's there?

Put on the hairdrier or fan, or ask someone to blow the candle out. When air moves, we can see what it does. When we try to hold our breath we realise how much our bodies need air to live.

God is here as well, and we can't see him. No one has ever seen God while they are alive on earth. So how can God tell us what he is like, when we can't see him?

There are ways we can see what God is like by what he does and by what he creates. If we look at the world we can see that God must be generous, imaginative, careful, clever, organised, hopeful and happy to let us work with him.

But God had an even better idea. If he could walk among humans as a human, then all the humans who lived at the time or at any time afterwards would be able to see exactly how God behaves. We could see it in our own human language. The language of doing, thinking, feeling and speaking.

In the Gospel today Jesus is talked about as being the Word, or the Message of God. When we look at how Jesus lived and died, we are looking straight at God, even though we can't see God with our eyes.

And what do we see? John describes Jesus as being 'full of grace and truth'. Have this written up on a sheet. Around it you can add other people's ideas. Head the page 'Jesus is' and display it for the rest of the service.

All-age ideas

- Have on a banner or poster the words from John 1:18: 'No one has ever seen God . . . But the Son has shown us what God is like.'

- If you have an OHP, try making up some Christmas cards into acetates as a parish resource. These can be placed behind the words of hymns and carols to reflect their meaning.

THE EPIPHANY OF THE LORD

Isaiah 60:1-6
Psalm 71
Ephesians 3:2-3a, 5-6
Matthew 2:1-12

Jesus, the hope of the nations, is shown to the world.

All-age talk

Beforehand arrange for a knitter to bring a completed garment to church, together with a ball of wool and needles. Also prepare a large paper cut-out of a similar garment, which is folded up so that the first bit that would be made is the only piece showing. Alternatively use the actual garment, folded up at that point.

Begin by showing everyone the wonderful garment that the knitter has made and asking how long it took to make and who it is for. What did it look like at first, when they started making it? The knitter can show the ball of wool and needles, and do a couple of stitches. Hold up the needles with these stitches and point out that it doesn't look much like a jumper/scarf yet! But the knitter went on working at it, knowing that one day it would be ready.

God knew that one day everything would be ready for Jesus to come into the world, but he, too, took a long time making things ready. He started by calling one person, Abraham. (Show the folded garment, but don't refer to it – it is there to be visual reinforcement of what you are saying.) Over the years God went on to prepare all Abraham's family. (More of the garment is revealed.) Until over more years that family became one nation. (Reveal some more of the garment.) But God's plan still wasn't finished. He went on to include not one nation but all the nations and everyone in them. (Shake the whole garment out and display it.) Today is called the Epiphany because the word 'epiphany' means 'showing' or 'revealing' or 'manifesting', and when those wise men arrived at Bethlehem with their presents, God was showing or revealing himself not just to Abraham or his family, not just to the whole nation of Israel, but to all the rest of us in the world as well.

Whatever country you come from, whatever you look like and whatever language you speak, God is saying to us today that he is there for you and no one is left out. You don't have to have the right ancestors to know God. You don't have to pass any exams to know God.

We sometimes get so interested in the presents the wise men were bringing to Jesus that we forget what brought them there in the first place. It was God who called these wise men from other nations to be there when Jesus was still a baby, so he could welcome them as well. They were there representing all the nations, so when God welcomed them he was welcoming each of us.

All-age ideas

- Today's Gospel can be acted out, preferably with costumes, as these may well be available from a nativity play. I am not suggesting a full-blown production with hours of rehearsal. All that is needed is a sensitive narrator, and the characters to mime what the narrator says.

- The wise men can take the collection and offer the gifts today. This emphasises their role as representatives of all the nations coming to be welcomed and offer their gifts. A globe can be offered at the same time.

- Have a bowl of burning incense, gold and myrrh arranged among flowers as a display either as people come in or near where they will come to receive communion.

THE BAPTISM OF THE LORD

Isaiah 42:1-4, 6-7
Psalm 28
Acts 10:34-38
Luke 3:15-16, 21-22

Jesus is baptised, and God confirms his identity and his calling.

All-age talk

Using a flipchart, OHP or large sheet of paper and thick pens, collect everyone's suggestions about what water can do. Some of the suggestions can be drawn rather than written, so that the non-readers can also join in.

Read through all the suggestions to celebrate them, and talk about how Baptism picks up on these qualities of water and uses them to teach us spiritual things. When we are baptised we are 'drowned' to the old ways, given new life, washed clean, and refreshed. If it is practical, have water in the font and pour it as you explain each quality and its spiritual meaning.

Remind everyone that today we have heard about Jesus being baptised, and as he was praying the Holy Spirit came upon him, looking rather like a dove flying down to rest on him. And God told Jesus that he was God's Son, and God was well pleased with him.

Point out any dove symbols there are in the church – in carvings, pictures or windows – and have a cut-out dove shape (you can use the picture below) to show everyone. The dove has become a sign or symbol for the Holy Spirit because of what happened at the Baptism of Jesus.

When we are baptised God calls us actually by name to follow him, and sets us apart to love and serve him through the whole of our life. We can only do that with the gift of the Holy Spirit, so that is what we are given. The more we use it, the more it will grow. The sign of the dove will remind us. Whenever we see a dove or a pigeon, or a wild goose, it will remind us that we belong to God, and have chosen to follow him.

All-age ideas

- Give everyone a simple cut-out paper dove as they come in. Ask people to hold their doves in the palm of their hands during the intercessions.

- Decorate the font with flowers to give the sense of a cascade of water.

- Use the Renewal of Baptismal Vows in place of the Creed.

FIRST SUNDAY OF LENT

Deuteronomy 26:4-10
Psalm 90
Romans 10:8b-13
Luke 4:1-13

Following his baptism, Jesus is severely tempted out in the desert, and shows us how to overcome temptation.

All-age talk

On matching sets of three graded sizes of card, from A5 to huge, write these two messages, with the print and thickness increasing with the card size.

I want it and I want it now.
Love God and love one another.

Begin by explaining that Jesus went into the desert after he had been baptised, and had a very hard time out there being tempted. We all know what it feels like to be tempted. It's when we want something or want to do something which we know is wrong. (Show the middle-sized 'I want it and I want it now' card.) Ask someone to hold this card, but don't make them stand with their arms in the air for ages.

Jesus was being tempted to turn the stones into bread so he could eat them, but he knew that this would be using his power in a selfish way. He remembered that he loved God and he loved other people (display the largest 'Love God and love one another' sign). Ask someone else to hold this up.

As you can see, the love for God and other people stayed bigger than the temptation, and so Jesus was able to stand firm and not let the temptation get the better of him.

Whenever Jesus was tempted he always remembered that his love for God and other people was much stronger than the 'I want'. Put these signs down.

Now let's see what happens with us. First we get a little temptation inside us. (Give one helper the smallest 'I want' sign.) It isn't very big and we remember the right way to live (give the other helper the middle-sized 'Love God' sign) so we don't give way to the temptation.

But as we think about it more, this happens. (Exchange the small 'I want' for the middle-sized one.) And now there's a battle going on inside us, because the 'I want' is the same size as the 'Love God'. If we're not careful the 'I want' will get even bigger! (Swap it for the largest 'I want' sign.) And when we let the 'I want' get bigger than the 'Love God', even for a minute, we're in danger of falling into temptation, and doing or saying what we really know is wrong.

Jesus shows us how not to do this. As soon as you feel a little 'I want' coming on (show it), remember that you love God and you love other people more than you want what is wrong. (Display the middle-sized 'Love God' sign.) And if the 'I want' gets bigger in you (show the middle-sized 'I want') think hard about how you and God love each other (show the largest 'Love God' sign) so that the 'I want' is less strong and you can fight it; and instead of giving in and doing or saying what you know is wrong, God will be helping you to stand up to temptation and win.

All-age ideas

- On the walls have poster-sized versions of the advertisements below so that people can see how temptations use truth but distort it.

  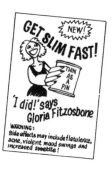

With the posters have a heading: 'Always read the small print!'

- During the first reading have a family bringing baskets of fruit and vegetables to lay in front of the altar.

SECOND SUNDAY OF LENT

Genesis 15:5-12, 17-18
Psalm 26
Philippians 3:17-4:1
Luke 9:28-36

God's glory transfigures Jesus as he prays on the mountain. Our lives, too, can become increasingly radiant as the Spirit transforms us.

All-age talk

You will need a hand mirror.

Begin by asking everyone if they have noticed how people often look like their pets, particularly dogs! Perhaps they choose a pet which reflects their own character. Today we are looking at how spending our lives with God makes us more and more like him.

Use the mirror to catch the light and throw it on to people's faces. Mirrors are excellent at spreading light around, because they are able to reflect light. In the Gospel today we hear of Moses, who was a close friend of God. He was the person who led the people of Israel out of Egypt, where they had been slaves, and through the desert to the promised land. When Moses had been on a mountain in God's company and was given the Ten Commandments, he came down from the mountain with his face glowing and radiant. Like a mirror, he was reflecting some of the glory of God. Sometimes if people are really happy – a bride and bridegroom getting married to the one they love, students hearing they have passed all their exams really well, or children on their birthday – we talk about them looking radiant, or glowing with happiness. How we are feeling and thinking inside changes the way we look.

When Jesus was on earth, three of his close friends were on a mountain with him when he was praying, and they saw him not just with a radiant face, but completely shining, or transfigured. What they were seeing was the glory of God in Jesus, who was and is completely at one with God, his Father. They heard

God's voice explaining who Jesus was and telling them to listen to him. Not like listening to music in the background, but really attentive listening, like you would listen to instructions for flying an aeroplane if you were the only person on board able to bring it safely to land.

When we live our lives close to Jesus like this, listening to his quiet voice guiding us, talking over our problems and happiness with him, and working at living a good life, then gradually our faces will start to show some of God's glory, and our lives will start to shine, reflecting God's loving nature like mirrors (flash the light again) reflecting the light.

All-age ideas

- Have a mirror on the floor with a flower arrangement and lots of small candles on it, so that the picture of reflecting light and beauty is expressed.

- During the reading of the Gospel, have music playing, starting at verse 29. This can be provided by the organ or music group, or you could use taped music.

- For the penitential rite, give out small pieces of shiny paper (cut from wrapping paper). Explain that the cleaner, smoother and shinier the mirror, the better it works. Ask people to bring to mind anything in their life which needs cleaning, smoothing down or polishing. Give them time to tell God about it, and receive his forgiveness, so that they are all able to reflect God's love better.

THIRD SUNDAY OF LENT

Exodus 3:1-8, 13-15
Psalm 102
1 Corinthians 10:1-6,
   10-12
Luke 13:1-9

The great 'I AM' calls people in every generation to repent so that God's kingdom can be established and grow.

All-age talk

Bring along a pot plant which is drooping and unhealthy, some plant food and water, a larger pot, trowel and some potting compost. Also a label – 'A Christian' – on a string, and some fruit shapes on strings.

Show everyone the plant and point out how pathetic it looks. Arrange for someone practical and organised to come and pick up the plant, assuring you they'll just get rid of it for you as it's messing up the nice clean church. Protest and stop them taking the plant away, explaining that you still have great hopes for this plant, and you intend doing all you can to help it thrive.

Invite a keen gardener and helper to come and sort the plant out, pruning it, watering and feeding it, and giving its roots more space in a bigger pot. As they do so (protecting the floor as they work), explain how Jesus told a story about a hopeful gardener who did this rather than throw a fig tree out. Jesus wasn't really talking about unproductive fig trees – he was talking about people.

Invite someone to help explain Jesus' story. Stand them in a pot or bowl and hang a label round their neck which says 'A Christian'. If we were plants, producing fruit, our fruit as Christians would be things like loving kindness, truth, patience, joy, hope, self-control and so on. (Drape labelled cut-out fruits on the person's arms as you speak.) We can all see that this Christian is thriving and producing lots of spiritual fruit. But suppose they never produced any good fruit at all? (Take away the 'fruits'.) Does

God just give up on them and have them thrown into hell for ever? What does Jesus' story tell us about this?

Gather ideas, and draw everyone to see that in the story we are shown a picture of what God is like – longing and longing for us to flourish and live, and willing to do everything he possibly can to help us start fruiting.

All-age ideas

- For the Penitential Rite:

  Persistently you call us, and we shut our ears to your voice.
  Lord, have mercy.
  Lord, have mercy.

  Always you are with us, yet we fail to recognise your presence.
  Christ, have mercy.
  Christ, have mercy.

  Patiently you coax us on, as we hold back and make our excuses.
  Lord, have mercy.
  Lord, have mercy.

- Have the words 'I AM WHO I AM' written large on the walls and pillars.

- At the offering of the gifts, invite everyone to offer who they are at the moment, so that the whole church makes an act of commitment to being *available* to God in a new way. As music plays or a hymn or chorus is sung, everyone who wants to writes their signature on a piece of paper and brings it to a basket placed near the altar. Everyone can then join in the prayer of offering – 'Blessed are you, Lord God of all creation, of your goodness we have ourselves to offer . . .'

Fourth Sunday of Lent

Joshua 5:9-12
Psalm 33
2 Corinthians 5:17-21
Luke 15:1-3, 11-32

Be reconciled with God. He is waiting to welcome us.

All-age talk

Bring along some balloons and party streamers, hiding them out of sight until the right moment!

Talk about how we all have times when we fall out with someone in our family, or with one of our friends, or with someone we work with. It feels rather as if a big crack has opened up between us and this other person. Sometimes it just lasts a few minutes, and sometimes, sadly, there can be unhealed rifts between people for years. Invite everyone to think of times we've fallen out with someone, and remember how we get to make up again, or seal up the gap that has opened up between us.

Collect suggestions of things we've found help heal those gaps. (These might include such things as saying sorry, or the other person apologising, making a joke of it, some kind of gift or kind letter, playing a different game, talking it through.) As humans we can get quite good at ways of making up because we get lots of practice! We often think it's worth the hard work of making up with people because we don't actually like the feeling of living with a great chasm between us and someone else.

In our Gospel today we heard Jesus' story about the young man who decided to come back to his father, even though he knew he'd really made a mess of things in his life. As that young man set off to walk back to his father's house, he wasn't pretending he hadn't done anything wrong. He hadn't come to ask for a loan or a new set of clothes so he could go back and carry on spending again. What actually happened was that the young man had suddenly realised what a mess he was in, and who he really was – the son of a wealthy and generous farmer. So then it made sense to go back home and ask to be treated not like a son, but like one of his father's servants.

And what happened? Bring out all the balloons and streamers as you remind everyone of the way the father welcomed his son back home again, because he loved him so much and was so very happy the gap between them could be healed. God our Father is waiting to welcome every person who has got to the point of realising there's a gap between them and God, and who badly wants things to be put right.

All-age ideas

- An alternative Penitential Rite:

  Let us go to our Father and say, 'Father, we have sinned against heaven and against you'.
  Lord, have mercy.
  Lord, have mercy.

  Let us go to the One who welcomes sinners and eats with them.
  Christ, have mercy.
  Christ, have mercy.

  Let us come, trusting in our Father's mercy and forgiveness.
  Lord, have mercy.
  Lord, have mercy.

- Have the Gospel acted out as it is read.

FIFTH SUNDAY OF LENT

Isaiah 43:16-21
Psalm 125
Philippians 3:8-14
John 8:1-11

It is not God's wish to condemn anyone, but he longs for us to turn to him and live.

All-age talk

You will need some lengths of rope, chain or thick string, a blindfold and a bicycle security chain with padlock.

Talk about how we often tie our lives up in knots. We may remember having done something wrong and then having told a few lies to cover up. Or there may be someone we've once had a row with and now we dread bumping into that person ever again. Those kinds of experiences are rather like pieces of rope tying us up and preventing us from moving freely. (Ask a volunteer to help explain this by allowing you to tie them up here and there.)

There are other things which chain us as well. Pick out a really strong rope or chain and explain how selfishness ties us up and restricts our movement dreadfully – we're so busy thinking about ourselves, our own needs and wants, our own rights and so on, that we can't reach out to other people at all. (Tie up the arms firmly.)

Arrogance and vanity make us think we're so wonderful that they stop us seeing the truth about ourselves (put on blindfold), and fear and guilt can make us too terrified to move forward (tie up the legs). So we end up spiritually trussed up, living a compromise and never living life as fully as we could.

God loves us and hates seeing us like this; he yearns to set us free. We heard that message loud and clear in all our readings today – God is not out to condemn us, but to set us free to live. As soon as we hesitantly let him into our lives he will start untying our ropes of selfishness, taking off our blindfolds of arrogance and vanity and prejudice,

300

unchaining our fear and guilt (do this as you talk), until he has set us free to live happily and love others. (The volunteer can leap and run around a bit to demonstrate.)

All-age ideas

- Write out the following message with the words on separate pieces of card: LET IN JESUS AND HIS LOVE WILL SET YOU FREE. Mix the words up, lay down the first word in place, and then, during one of the hymns, invite some of the children to put the words in order to make an important message. If they arrange this on the floor near the altar, everyone will see it as they come to receive Communion.

- Cradle one hand in the other. Love that hand and its owner as Jesus does, with understanding and affection. Then use those same hands to reach out to others in the sharing of the Peace.

Palm (Passion) Sunday

Liturgy of the Palms:
Luke 19:28-40

Liturgy of the
  Passion:
Isaiah 50:4-7
Psalm 21
Philippians 2:6-11
Luke 22:14-23:56 or
  Luke 23:1-49

As Jesus rides into Jerusalem on a donkey, and the crowds welcome him, we sense both the joy at the Messiah being acclaimed, and the heaviness of his suffering which follows. Jesus' mission is drawing to its fulfilment.

All-age talk

Ask about football matches people have watched which have been really memorable and exciting. If you happen to have any players in the congregation, ask them to talk about a particularly memorable moment of triumph, and how it felt to have the spectators sharing the exhilaration.

When Jesus rode into Jerusalem all the crowds were on his side, cheering, waving and singing, pushing for the best view, and excited not just with Jesus as a hero but at what was a turning point for their side – their country. There would have been some there on that first Palm Sunday who saw it as a political statement, others as religious revival, others as a festive carnival of some kind.

So why did Jesus ride into Jerusalem on a donkey?

He was doing something the scriptures had said would happen to the promised Messiah. This meant he was giving a very strong hint to the people about who he was. He was saying that the Messiah had now come and was entering the holy city of Jerusalem as a king. But instead of all the rich clothes and grandeur of an earthly king, Jesus was riding on a very humble animal that was often piled high with people's luggage and shopping. It was a bit like using a shopper bike rather than a Rolls Royce, stretched limo or BMW.

All the crowds that day cheered Jesus, but a few days later, once he didn't look like a winner any more, many of the same people had turned against him and were yelling for his blood.

What kind of supporters are we? Do we support our team only when it's doing really well, or do we hang in there even after a run of lost games? Do we stick with our friends even when they go through a bad patch? Do we keep trying even when a marriage gets shaky? And, perhaps most important of all, are we happy to sing God's praise in church on Sunday but ignore him or deny him by our behaviour and language and choices during the week?

These are Palm Sunday questions which we need to ask ourselves today.

All-age ideas

- Give the children coloured crêpe-paper streamers to wave in the procession, and choose songs which are joyful and don't need books for at least part of the route. Encourage the children to shout and dance and sing – children were very noticeable on the first Palm Sunday.

- Look at some imaginative ways of presenting the Gospel using different voices, singing it, using slides as a visual focus, changing the lighting during the narrative, or using expressive mime during the narration.

EASTER DAY

Acts 10:34, 37-43
Psalm 117
Colossians 3:1-4
John 20:1-9

It is true. Jesus is alive for all time. The Lord of life cannot be held by death. God's victory over sin and death means that new life for us is a reality.

All-age talk

Take along a few Easter cards you have received, and show them around, describing the pictures on them. There are probably some fluffy new chicks, young lambs skipping about in the spring fields, lots of flowers, and some decorated eggs. And we probably all gave and received a chocolate Easter egg today. So all this says that Easter is a happy, festive occasion, in tune with the new life of springtime, with all the new birds, animals and flowers.

What else? Some cards have a garden with an empty tomb, and three crosses on a hill in the distance. Others have made all the flowers into the shape of a cross. So what do these cards tell us about Easter? They tell us about another kind of new life, which doesn't happen naturally every time winter is over, but only ever happened once. It wasn't an ordinary thing at all. It was so completely amazing and impossible that people are still talking about it two thousand years after it happened! Do you know what it was? (Let them tell you.)

Well, that's impossible, surely. People can't come back to life again. It just doesn't happen. The fact that it actually did happen – that Jesus really did die on the Friday, and he really was alive again on the Sunday – shows us that Jesus must be more than a human being. He must be God as well as human. And he must be still just as much alive now as he was then. No wonder we want to celebrate and give one another flowers and cards and Easter eggs! Spring is nice to celebrate, but this is the most wonderful event ever. It means that nothing, not even death itself, is out of God's reach for saving and transforming.

When you eat your chocolate eggs, and open your Easter cards, remember what we're really celebrating today: Jesus is risen. Alleluia! (Everyone can shout back: 'He is risen indeed. Alleluia!')

All-age ideas

- Have one flower arrangement consisting of three levels. The lowest arrangement has rich dark purples with only a few hints of gold. Gradually the colours blend into the gold, yellow and white of Easter at the top arrangement. This will be a visual reminder of the journey to Easter through the suffering of Good Friday.

- Part of the children's day during Holy Week could be given over to creating a banner proclaiming the message of Easter. This can be made of fabric, with the design stuck (with double-sided sticky tape) or appliquéd on to the background, or of heavyweight wallpaper using either paint or collage work.

- The Easter garden presents a wonderful opportunity for different age groups to work together. Consider having a garden outside the church as well as inside.

- Encourage everyone to bring bells to ring in a burst of praise with the organ or music group just before singing the Gloria.

SECOND SUNDAY OF EASTER

Acts 2:42-47
Psalm 117
1 Peter 1:3-9
John 20:19-31

Having seen Jesus in person, the disciples are convinced of the Resurrection. We too can meet him personally.

All-age talk

Beforehand place a tape or CD in your pocket. Begin by telling everyone that you have got an orchestra in your pocket and asking them if they believe you. Then show them the tape or CD. Now they have seen with their eyes they know exactly what was in your pocket. And now that they understand what it is, they can see that you were right – you did have an orchestra in your pocket, but not in the way they expected!

Jesus had told his friends that he would have to suffer and die before rising to new life, and they hadn't understood what he meant. Even when Jesus was dying, nailed to the cross, they didn't realise that this had to happen if we were to be saved from sin and death. Instead they felt miserable and let down and lost and confused. They didn't believe because they hadn't seen for themselves. (Put the tape back in your pocket.)

Then, on the first Easter evening, Jesus was suddenly there with them. He was alive, talking with them and they were so excited and overjoyed to have him there again. Now that they had seen him they knew it was true that he was alive. (As you say this bring out the tape from your pocket again, but don't refer to it. It will simply help them make connections.)

But it was also different from what they might have thought. Jesus wasn't exactly the same as before. With this new life he was able to be there without having unlocked the doors. He could appear and disappear. But he was a real person, not a ghost.

306

He didn't make the disciples feel scared; he filled them with peace and happiness.

At last they began to understand what he had meant when he had talked to them about dying and rising again. They began to understand that God's love had to go right through death, loving and forgiving the whole way, so as to win the battle against evil. When Jesus came through death and out into the light of new life, he was like a butterfly coming out of its chrysalis – the same but completely different, free and beautiful.

Thomas and the others needed to see Jesus with their eyes for quite a few times after the Resurrection. They now had to learn that he was always there with them, even if they couldn't see him.

All-age ideas

- While singing the *Caterpillar* song, have a few children with painted net butterfly wings and wrapped in green towels to look like caterpillars. They are squirming around, pretending to eat plants and then curling up during the chrysalis part. Then they throw off their towels and fly about all over the church, ending with arms raised in front of the altar.

- Today's reading works well with different voices and a narrator.

THIRD SUNDAY OF EASTER

Acts 5:27-32, 40-41
Psalm 29
Apocalypse 5:11-14
John 21:1-19

Those who know Jesus and recognise that he is the anointed Saviour are commissioned to go out as his witnesses to proclaim the good news.

All-age talk

Beforehand prepare some masks from thin card, and mount them on sticks so that they can be held up in front of people's faces. Here is the pattern.

Begin by asking for two volunteers (of different age groups) and giving them a brief interview: What is your name? What is your favourite colour? What do you enjoy doing? How did you get to church today?

Explain that it's nice for us all to know who these people are, and suggest that we all get to know the name of someone in church today. We may see them there regularly but have never actually discovered their name!

Notice how Jesus made a point of calling Simon Peter by his name in today's Gospel. 'Simon, son of John, do you love me?' And on the first Easter Day when Jesus met Mary in the garden he called her by her name, and that's when she recognised him as Jesus.

Produce the 'happy' mask and ask for a volunteer to 'wear' it. Talk about the way we sometimes pretend we're different from the person we really are, because we think God and other people will like us better. This person is pretending to be happy. But if we are pretending, and God knows that inside we are really feeling very grumpy or sad, then the mask we are wearing makes him sad. This person is pretending to be very holy and good. But if we are pretending, and God knows that inside we are feeling angry and resentful, then the mask we are wearing makes him sad.

Jesus wants us to trust him with our real selves, even the bits where we make mistakes and get our lives in a mess. He speaks to us by our real name and will spend our lifetime teaching us who we really are. (Take the mask away.)

All-age ideas

- Have this written on the handout, or displayed on the OHP so that each person is able to join in with the responses.

  Leader My child, where are you?

  All Here I am, Lord, right beside you.

  Leader That is not the person I know and love. Where is the real you, my child?

  All Here I am, Lord. Surely you recognise me now?

  Leader I recognise the face you wear, but where is the real you that I love?

  All Suppose I showed you and it was unacceptable?

  Leader It is the real you that I love.

  All Then just as I am, O Lamb of God, I come!

- Alternatively, this can be done by a hidden voice and someone wearing a mask, which is put aside at the end.

- The Gospel can be mimed as it is narrated.

FOURTH SUNDAY OF EASTER

Acts 13:14, 43-52
Psalm 99
Apocalypse 7:9, 14-17
John 10:27-30

Jesus, the Good Shepherd, leads his flock into eternal life.

All-age talk

First ask for an intrepid explorer and blindfold the valiant person who volunteers. Now set out an obstacle course which ends with building a tower of three cartons at the far end, which are to be brought through the obstacles one by one.

Ask for three other volunteers and explain to the explorer that s/he can choose any one of these guides to help them build the tower by going through the obstacle course. The first guide is blindfolded and has his legs tied together. The second guide can see but can only see the place where the tower will be built. The third guide can see and is able to move around wherever s/he likes. The big question is . . . which guide will the explorer choose? Before the explorer chooses, invite everyone to tell someone near them which guide they would choose and why. Then ask the explorer to decide and set them off, timing their task to create urgency.

Afterwards explain how Jesus the Good Shepherd is like the guide who can see and move anywhere he likes. He is both in time and eternity, and this makes him by far the wisest choice in our lives, because he can see the whole situation. He knows where we are and what our limitations and weaknesses are. He can come alongside us and help us through even the most frightening or difficult times in our lives, and, at the time of our death, he can lead us safely into heaven. To be part of his flock we have only to listen to his voice and to follow him wherever he leads us.

All-age ideas

- Have two or three 'stations' of prayer focus on situations where Christians are being harassed or persecuted for living and preaching the Gospel. While music is playing, invite people to walk round and look at the displays, adding their names to encouraging letters provided, or writing letters or cards to those in authority.

- Include a sheep and/or a shepherd's crook in one of the flower arrangements today, and have some wheat and spring meadow flowers, with a written heading: 'Jesus the Good Shepherd leads his sheep through life into eternity.'

FIFTH SUNDAY OF EASTER

Acts 14:21-27
Psalm 144
Apocalypse 21:1-5
John 13:31-35

Christ, breaking through the barrier of sin and death, allows us to break into an entirely new way of living which continues into eternity.

All-age talk

Beforehand ask a family to help you by providing a couple of clothing items which are now too small for their child to wear. Or you could borrow a cub/brownie sweater which once you would have been able to get into. Also find a sprouting acorn, or a similar example of life bursting out of confines.

Begin by talking about the way we grow out of our clothes. Sometimes we like a sweater or jacket so much that we want to go on wearing it even when it's a bit short or tight, but eventually we realise that we just can't get into it any more, and we'll have to hand it down to someone younger or smaller. As you talk about this, use the children and their skimpy clothes to illustrate how silly it looks and how uncomfortable it feels to wear something which is much too small for us, and then try the same garment on someone it fits to see the difference.

Remind everyone that we are spiritual as well as physical, and we can grow out of things spiritually as well. Some of the early Christians thought that it wasn't right for non-Jewish people to be allowed to join the Church. Today we heard how Paul and Barnabas set off to continue preaching the Gospel to the Gentiles, those who weren't Jews. God wanted everyone to be part of his love, with no one left out. So the early church very sensibly took off that outgrown idea.

When we are very young, we are taught to pray prayers we can understand. That's wonderful. But if we are still praying like a three-year-old when we are thirteen or twenty-three, or fifty-three, we

312

are wearing skimpy spiritual clothes that we have really outgrown. Unless we realise that, and take them off, and find ways of praying that fit, we won't be able to move forward where God wants us to go.

Take a look at the acorn. Acorns are lovely to hold and play with, just as they are. But the oak tree can't become its huge, leafy self unless it breaks out of the acorn, and leaves that behind.

Jesus gives us all a rule, or command. We are to love one another. As soon as we start this kind of responsible, caring love for one another, we are bound to start growing. Sometimes the growing hurts. Sometimes the growing feels exciting. Sometimes the growing is hard work. And always the growing will be breaking out of where we were before. This means that, like children growing taller year by year, we will not be able to keep wearing the same old spiritual clothes. God won't let us get set in our ways because he goes on having exciting plans for us right through our lives, no matter how old we get.

All-age ideas

- Have a display of Paul's missionary journeys.

- Have everyone holding hands, either as they sing *A new commandment* or during the Lord's Prayer.

SIXTH SUNDAY OF EASTER

Acts 15:1-2, 22-29
Psalm 66
Apocalypse 21:10-14,
  22-23
John 14:23-29

The continuing presence of God, as Holy Spirit, leads us, as Jesus promised, into a personally guided outreach to all nations.

All-age talk

First fill the space of the centre aisle with chairs and obstacles. If yours is a fixed pews building, have people to sit down as obstacles in the aisle. Remind everyone of how, in today's Gospel, Jesus was talking to his friends at the last supper they had together before he was crucified. Jesus knew his friends were dreading the future without him being there with them. Perhaps they thought it would be a bit like this.

Ask for a volunteer and blindfold them, twizzle them round and send them off down the aisle. As they walk hesitantly, bumping into the obstacles, you talk about Jesus' friends thinking that living without Jesus around would be like trying to get round the difficulties of life blindfolded, and with no one to help or guide them.

Rescue the volunteer and remove their blindfold. As this person knows, you don't feel very safe all on your own and unable to see where the obstacles are. It is frightening and could be dangerous. Sometimes our life can feel like that, and it isn't a comfortable place to be.

What Jesus wants his friends to know is that God doesn't have that in mind for them at all. Although Jesus knew he wouldn't be there physically with his friends for ever, he promised them that they (and we) would have a personal guide right there with us. Let's see how that changes things for us.

Blindfold the volunteer again, but this time appoint a sensible, caring guide who steers them round the obstacles, talking to them and helping them along. (You may want to have primed this person beforehand.)

Watch them together, and then talk alongside the rest of their journey about God's Holy Spirit being with us to teach and explain things to us, to guide us and help us through the dangerous parts of life, so that we are not left alone, but working in partnership with our loving God.

All-age ideas

• Have labelled paper flags from many different nations displayed around the church. Or focus on a few countries and have displays of the needs and problems facing the people there, examples of their bread, and pictures of their people, together with the national flag. During the intercessions people can be encouraged to walk around the church, praying for the needs as music from the countries is played or sung.

• The meaning of the reading from Apocalypse is brought out well if it is read chorally by a group of people who have prepared it prayerfully, splitting the phrases among different voice tones – high, medium and low. If you have an OHP consider making some acetates from coloured pictures of light and water to show during the reading.

THE ASCENSION OF THE LORD

Acts 1:1-11
Psalm 46
Ephesians 1:17-23
Luke 24:46-53

Having bought back our freedom with the giving of his life, Jesus enters into the full glory to which he is entitled.

All-age talk

Begin by staging a Mexican wave, which runs through the whole church or assembly. Point out how it only worked so well because all of us as individuals were working together as a unit of energy.

Remind everyone of the events leading up to today, giving them a whistle-stop tour of Jesus' life, death, Resurrection and post-Resurrection appearances. Explain how the disciples needed that time to get used to Jesus being alive and around, though not always visible or physically present.

Now they were ready for the next stage in the plan. Jesus leads them out of the city and he gives them his blessing, telling them to hang around Jerusalem without rushing off to do their own bit of mission work. (Enthusiasm is wonderful but it can sometimes make us race off to start before we've got everything we need.) The disciples have got to wait because God is going to send the Holy Spirit to empower them and equip them for the work they will be doing. It will make it possible for the news of God's love to spread out through the world like our Mexican wave.

When Jesus had finished giving the disciples their instructions and his encouragement, we are told that the disciples watched him being taken into heaven, until a cloud hid him from their sight. Those are the only practical details we have, so we don't know exactly how it happened. But we do know that the disciples were in no doubt about where Jesus had gone, and they were full of joy and excitement as they made their way back to the city to wait for the Holy Spirit, as Jesus had told them to.

A lot of years have gone by since Jesus ascended into heaven – about two thousand years. But that isn't much if you aren't stuck in time as we are, and God isn't stuck in time. He's prepared to wait to give us humans the chance to turn to him in our lives, and we don't know the date when Jesus will return. We do know that in God's good time he will come back, and everyone will see his glory together, both the living and those who have finished the earthly part of their life.

In the meantime, we have been given the Holy Spirit, so that God can be with us in person every moment of our life, helping us and guiding our choices, steering us safely through temptations, and teaching us more and more about our amazing God. All he waits for is to be invited.

All-age ideas

- Any artwork or writing that the children have done on what the Ascension is about can be displayed around the building.

- Have a beautiful helium balloon at the ready. Write on it an Ascension message that the children would like to send. After the service two representative children can let the balloon float away.

- Children can wave white and yellow streamers during some of the hymns.

SEVENTH SUNDAY OF EASTER

Acts 7:55-60
Psalm 96
Apocalypse 22:12-14,
   16-17, 20
John 17:20-26

Jesus lives for all time in glory; we can live the fullness of Resurrection life straightaway.

All-age talk

Beforehand ask a few people to bring awards they have been given. These should include things that probably lots of others have as well, such as a five-metre swimming badge and a driving licence. There may also be a darts cup or a music certificate.

Begin by showing the awards and talking briefly to the award-holders about how these have been well earned, and give us an idea of the standard that has been achieved, so they are something to celebrate. Probably lots of us have similar awards that we have been honoured with, which is well worth celebrating. (A round of applause may be in order.)

When Jesus entered heaven, about forty days after he had come back to life on the first Easter Day, the whole of heaven gave him a hero's welcome. They said he was worthy to receive power and wealth and wisdom and strength, honour and glory and praise – everything good they could think of.

They wanted to honour him like this because Jesus had managed to do such an incredible thing. He had lived a human life and gone on loving all the way through it without once giving in to temptation, turning against God's will or putting his own wants first. Through loving people enough to die for them, he had been able to break the hold death has over all of us, so we can live freely and happily in God's company. (Another huge round of applause for Jesus.)

Now go back to the swimming badge. This badge proves that Susie is able to swim. What God is saying to us today is that Jesus has won the victory for us,

318

so we are all able to live this incredible new, free and happy life in his company.

It is as if there's a wonderful pool just waiting for us to enjoy, but perhaps we're only holding our badges at the edge of the pool, instead of getting into the water and using them. Let's plunge into the life Jesus has won for us and enjoy it to the full!

All-age ideas

- Banners celebrating the fullness of God's glory in heaven and earth can fill the church with colour today, and the flowers, too, can express the colour and variety of full life in Christ.

- If you have some banners in church, don't leave them leaning against walls. Have them carried round the church during the entrance hymn, interspersed with others proclaiming the words: 'The Lord reigns!'

- The Acts reading needs to be really imaginatively read so that everyone is caught up in the excitement and drama of it. Have it acted out, or read with different people taking the parts.

PENTECOST

Acts 2:1-11
Psalm 103
1 Corinthians 12:3-7,
    12-13
John 20:19-23

As Jesus promised, the Holy Spirit is poured out on the apostles and the Church is born.

All-age talk

Beforehand make five red, yellow and orange flame shapes (about 30 centimetres high) and hide them around the church.

Begin by asking for examples of flames, such as on a gas hob, bonfire, forest fire, log fire, candle, acetylene torch, fire-eater, house on fire, match, oil lamp, steel works, steam engine, lighter, Bunsen burner. Draw people's attention to the tremendous power of some of these and the quiet, gentle nature and soft light of others. Fire is something we all have to respect, as it can burn and destroy as well as giving us light and heat.

Send the children off to search for the five flames that are hidden in the church, and tell the adults about our need to seek out the Spirit expecting to find, just as the children are doing now. They trust that what they have been told to search for will be there, and it will. We need to believe that if we seek God we will find him – and we will.

When the children return with the five flames, you can remind everyone of the way the Holy Spirit is described as being like tongues of fire, with the sound of a rushing wind. (You can get everyone to make this sound as the flame-carriers move round the church.)

Like fire, the Spirit can be strong and powerful in our lives. (The first flame is held up.) Sometimes the Spirit is gentle and quiet, whispering deep into our needs and telling us what is right. (The second flame is held up.) Like fire, the Spirit is warming, spreading love and a real desire to put things right, and stand up for goodness and truth. (The third flame is held up.) Like fire the Spirit is purifying, burning away all that is evil and selfish in us, so that we can become like pure refined gold, glowing with the light of God's love. (The fourth flame is held up.) And, like fire, the Spirit is enlightening, shedding light for us on the Bible, our conversations and relationships and the events of our lives, so that we can see God more clearly through them. (The fifth flame is held up.)

All-age ideas

- Make three flags using yellow, orange and red lining material and bean sticks. During one of the hymns have three people standing in a triangle waving the flags gradually upwards and downwards. Or they can be used individually at different parts of the church to express worship as people sing.

- Have each side of the congregation facing each other and praying for each other to receive the Holy Spirit in their lives afresh. They can pray silently or aloud, or in unison with this prayer, said once loudly and then whispered softly.

  Holy Spirit of God,
  come upon these people
  whom you know and love so well,
  and fill them to overflowing!
  Amen; let it be so.

- Have a time of shared expectant quietness after the prayer, with some quiet music being played and sung by the music group or choir.

- Have the church decorated with flame-coloured flowers, ribbons, streamers and balloons.

TRINITY SUNDAY

Proverbs 8:22-31
Psalm 8
Romans 5:1-5
John 16:12-15

The unique nature of God is celebrated today, as we reflect on the truth that God is Creator, Redeemer and Life-giver.

All-age talk

Beforehand prepare a cake. Also get together two eggs, a bag of sugar, a bag of flour and some margarine, and a mixing bowl, cake tin and wooden spoon.

Set the cake tin down and tell everyone that today we are going to have a cake again, because it was so nice last week having the children's cakes, and today is another important day, Trinity Sunday. So we are going to have a Trinity cake. Ask various helpers to bring the eggs, sugar and flour and margarine and place them in the cake tin.

Proudly present the cake, inviting everyone to take a slice, and let the children point out to you that you haven't got a cake at all. You've just got the ingredients. But isn't a cake just ingredients, then? Let them help you understand that you'd have to mix them together and cook them before you had a cake.

Now let it suddenly dawn on you that it's a bit like that with the nature of God. God is the Father who created the world, Jesus Christ who saved us, and the Holy Spirit who gives life to the people of God. But they aren't separate from each other, any more than these separate ingredients are a cake. To be a cake all the ingredients need to be co-operating and working together. Then they become something which is not just eggs, flour, sugar and margarine. Produce the real cake and point out that you wouldn't say, 'Have a slice of eggs, flour, margarine and sugar with your cup of tea.' You'd call it by its name: a cake.

In the same kind of way, when we talk about

God we are talking about our Maker, and we're talking about the risen Jesus who has rescued us from sin and death, and we're talking about the Holy Spirit who brings us into new life. We know that the word 'God' means all three persons in a wonderful harmony, a community which is still One.

Give the Trinity cake to whoever is in charge of refreshments after the service, so it can be shared out then.

All-age ideas

- Use three different voices for the Proverbs reading. Work through the text prayerfully and listen to the places where single voices or a group of voices seem to be indicated. Split the single voice sections between the three people, according to the sense of the phrases and linking meaning with voice type.

- Put clover and shamrock among the flower arrangements today to express the 'three in one' nature of God.

- Use the baptismal statements of belief for the Creed.

CORPUS CHRISTI

Genesis 14:18-20
Psalm 109
1 Corinthians 11:23-26
Luke 9:11-17

Jesus is the Living Bread, who brings us eternal life through Communion with him.

All-age talk

Give everyone a stalk of grass or wheat, and ask them to look at the seeds on it. For thousands and thousands of years the earth has been producing this stuff, all over the world. Our great-great-grandparents would have been able to pick stalks like this, and so would their great-great-grandparents. And there will still be plenty there for the great-great-grandchildren of the youngest child here! That's quite a lot of grass, and it's all done by the grass seeds falling into the earth and growing more seeds which fall into the earth and grow more seeds . . . Bread is made out of flour, and flour is squashed posh grass seed. (Produce some bread.) It's good food – very tasty and full of energy to keep you alive. It was bread and fish which Jesus took to feed all those people in the Gospel reading today. First he accepted the bread which was offered (and it wasn't very much at all), then he looked up to heaven and thanked God for what they had, and started to break it up to share it out among everyone. And the love that wanted all those people to be fed was so strong in Jesus that he went on breaking and sharing out, breaking and sharing out, until every person there had eaten as much as they needed – and *still* there was more!

Today we've gathered to meet with Jesus in our particular country, in our particular town, on this particular date, at this particular time of day, just like all those people beside the lake. We've come because we know that God is worth knowing, and we love him.

So, in a very special way, we are all part of that big picnic by the lake. When we bring bread and

324

wine to the altar we will be offering to God what we have – all that we are and all we've done and said, and all the time ahead of us. When the priest takes the bread and thanks God for it, consecrates it, breaks it and shares it with us, we are reliving Jesus doing what he did at the lake, and then in a special way at the last meal he ate before he was crucified. That breaking and sharing of the bread has been going on and on right down through the centuries, and there's still plenty of Jesus' life for every one of us to share it!

All-age ideas

- If you have anyone who bakes their own bread, they could make a loaf to be part of a flower arrangement on the theme of the day, which can be shared afterwards.

- Precede or follow the Mass with a time of shared silent prayer in front of the Blessed Sacrament.

SECOND SUNDAY OF THE YEAR

Isaiah 62:1-5
Psalm 95
1 Corinthians 12:4-11
John 2:1-12

As a marriage celebrates the beginning of a changed, new life for the bride and groom, so our loving, faithful God has chosen us and is ready to transform our lives for the good of the world.

All-age talk

Beforehand ask someone in the congregation who still has their wedding dress or bridesmaid's dress to bring it along. Several people could do this – they won't have to wear them unless they want to! Ask a happily married couple to be prepared to talk about their wedding day.

Introduce the people and their wedding dresses, bringing out how special they are because of it being such a special day in their lives. Talk to the married couple so that they show how their love for one another brought them to marriage and how the wedding day emphasised the important step they were taking. If there are couples soon to be married, this would be a good time to pray for them as they start their new life together.

Through the prophet Isaiah, God tells his people that his love and faithfulness is a bit like that of a devoted bride and groom. We have been loved and called, and chosen to live a new life together with our God. He will take us just as we are and gradually change us into being more richly ourselves than we could ever be on our own.

Today's Gospel was all about something changing. Water was changed into wine. That happens naturally every year as the rain falls and gets drawn into the vine to make grape juice, and then the grape juice is fermented carefully to make that new drink – wine. But that wedding day in the town of Cana was different because the change happened straight

326

away. Ask the married couple if they had ordered enough wine for their wedding, and then go over the wedding story and the way Jesus transformed the whole situation. John, who wrote this account, tells us that it showed the disciples they could put their trust in Jesus.

That is true for us as well. Whatever has gone wrong in your life, whatever makes you really sad or angry or disappointed, God will take and change so it can be used for good. Nothing you have to suffer will ever be wasted if you stick with Jesus, and do as he tells you.

All-age ideas

- Have the main flower arrangement with a wedding theme, with ribbon and a framed wedding photograph, a bottle of wine and two glasses among the flowers.

- Have the Isaiah passage read chorally with a group of men, women, boys and girls. Work through the passage together, listening for ways to bring out both the meaning and the poetry through the different combinations of voices. The easiest way to record this is with different coloured highlighter pens on copied sheets. Arrange for one of the group to take the lead and that will keep everyone together.

THIRD SUNDAY OF THE YEAR

Nehemiah 8:2-6, 8-10
Psalm 18
1 Corinthians 12:12-30
Luke 1:1-4; 4:14-21

The meaning of the scriptures is revealed to the people.

All-age talk

Begin by telling everyone you are going to drop a pin. Ask people to raise their hand if they hear it. (If the building is large, choose something slightly noisier to drop.) Point out how they all listened to be able to hear it. Today we are thinking about careful listening. Tell everyone you are going to drop the pin again, and this time ask them to notice what their bodies are doing to hear such a little sound. When you have dropped the pin, collect some of the things people have noticed. (These might include things like concentrating, waiting, being very still, cutting out our own noises, putting our best ear forward, turning our hearing aid up a bit.)

Today we are told that God is often revealed or shown to us through the scriptures – through the words in the Bible. (Hold a Bible and open it as you talk about it.) In our first reading we heard how all the people gathered in the square in front of the temple and had God's law read out clearly to them so they could really understand it. And when they heard it like this, they couldn't wait to start living the way they knew God wanted them to live. The reason they heard God's voice that day was because they were really trying to listen, like us trying to hear the pin drop.

When Jesus went to preach at his local synagogue he taught the people that the prophecy from Isaiah was coming true that very day. The ones who were listening as carefully as you listened for the pin dropping would have been very excited. Jesus was giving them a very strong clue about who he really was. And it isn't every day you have the promised

328

Messiah turning out to be someone you grew up with!

The trouble is that lots of them weren't listening at all. And in our lives we are often so busy and preoccupied with things that don't really matter that we make too much noise to hear the still, small voice of God telling us really important things about what is right and what is wrong, and how we can live good lives, full of honest, loving behaviour.

God will always whisper what is good and true and loving to help us. We won't hear an actual voice because God can speak straight into our hearts and minds, so we will just know, suddenly, that what we are doing is very good or very bad, very thoughtful or rather selfish and unkind. Once we know, we can stop the wrong behaviour and change it. But we do need to get used to listening so we can hear God clearly.

All-age ideas

- Make a large card jigsaw of a body outline and a church. During the reading from Corinthians, have two groups of children working on these in the aisle so that the shapes are being built up visually in line with our understanding. The puzzles can be left on the floor so that people walk past (or over) them on their way to communion as one body.

- Act out the Gospel by having it fixed on a scroll. The Gospel reader reads the first section from the Bible as he walks to the lectern. A scroll is handed over and verses 17b to 20a are read from this. When it is handed back the reader takes up the Bible again and walks over to sit down for the rest of the passage.

FOURTH SUNDAY OF THE YEAR

Jeremiah 1:4-5, 17-19
Psalm 70
1 Corinthians 12:31-
    13:13
Luke 4:21-30

As a prophet, Jesus' work is to proclaim the reign of God's love, not only to the Jewish people but to the whole world.

All-age talk

Bring along some sentimental love music, red heart balloons and so on, and show them, explaining that in today's readings there is a lot about love.

The only trouble is, the love we've been hearing about doesn't sound much like all these audio-visual aids. The love we've heard about sounds more like this . . . Bring out a pair of rubber gloves, a bucket and mop and an apron. This love sounds much more like hard work, the kind of thing we need to roll up our sleeves to start on; the kind of thing that always needs doing, even though we did it yesterday and last week and twenty years ago.

We heard Jeremiah the prophet being reminded of the way God had always known and loved him, right from before he was born, and part of that love is going to be Jeremiah taking a message which is bound to make him very unpopular indeed. That's hard work love.

We heard Paul's letter describing love as always patient and always kind, never jealous, never taking offence. That sounds like hard work love, too.

And in the Gospel we find Jesus refusing to go along with what the people in his town wanted him to do because he knew it would lead them away from God, and not be helpful for them. He also knew that this would make the people angry and possibly violent towards him. So that was hard work love.

That means we have to ask: is hard work love actually worth all the effort? Why don't we just go for the sloppy, comfortable sort instead, and do what

330

feels nice instead of putting ourselves out for people and risking our popularity or image?

The truth is that although the sloppy, indulgent sort of love feels nice for a while, it doesn't satisfy us deep down to our human roots, because we are made in the image of God, and God's nature is full of the expensive, costly loving. When we love this way it may be much more hard work, and it will almost certainly hurt, but it will satisfy us as the humans we were made to be, in every corner of our being.

All-age ideas

- Arrange the props for both sorts of love for people to see. With them put labels: 'LOVE?' and 'LOVE!'.

- Have a globe surrounded with flowers or votive candles, with the words between the candles: 'Let the whole world be filled with your love.'

FIFTH SUNDAY OF THE YEAR

Isaiah 6:1-8
Psalm 137
1 Corinthians 15:1-11
Luke 5:1-11

God calls his people and commissions them.

All-age talk

You will need a mirror. First do a spot of face-painting on a volunteer, writing their own name in mirror-writing across their face. Then show them their face in the mirror. They will be surprised at what they look like because it isn't their familiar face looking back at them. Yet it is their own named self they are looking at.

Whenever Jesus met up with people he seems to have been able to show them who they were; what they were really like. By the things he said, the stories he told, and by the signs and miracles he did, people were able to look at him and suddenly see something about themselves they hadn't realised before. Some suddenly realised that they were lovable and important, when they had always thought they were rubbish. Others suddenly saw that they were living very mean, selfish lives, and knew they wanted to change.

In the event we hear about today, Simon Peter has been fishing all night long without any success at all. It's possible that Jesus had watched them, and noticed how they carried on even when they were tired and disappointed. Perhaps Jesus brought that into his teaching, and the fishermen would have sat up on the beach and thought, 'This man really knows what it's like to be a fisherman like me, working all night with nothing to show for it!' So when Jesus suggested they try again, Simon was doubtful, but willing to give it a go. The huge catch of fish, coming suddenly after all that time they had worked in vain, must have given Simon a shock. It was a bit like looking in a mirror and seeing who he really was for the first time.

He saw that this man Jesus, who had been sitting in Simon's own fishing boat talking to the crowds, was different from anyone he had ever met before. His goodness, his wise teaching and his knowledge of where the fish were, all made Simon suddenly ashamed. We don't know what it was in Simon's life that went through his mind. It might have been some particular sin he still felt guilty about, or it might have been remembering all the general meanness and selfishness, or the bad temper he knew he had.

The important thing for us to look at is how Jesus helped him see himself, and then said, 'Don't be afraid, follow me.' That is what Jesus does with us today as well. So be ready for it. If something makes you suddenly see yourself and you don't like everything you see, Jesus will not be standing at your elbow, saying, 'There's no hope for you, then, is there? You might as well give up.' He will be there, speaking into your heart words of love and comfort and hope: 'Don't be afraid of what you really are. Come and follow me.'

All-age ideas

- For the Gospel have different voices for Simon and Jesus.

- Have a fishing net, sand and shells incorporated into the main flower arrangement, or make a boaty display with oars, life jackets, oilskins and waders at the entrance, with a prayer for those who work on the sea.

- Have music played as background to the reading from Isaiah which reflects the sense of over-whelming holiness and wonder of God. Begin with the music on its own, then lower the volume as the reading starts. The reader leaves longer spaces between sentences than usual and the music gives people time to reflect on the vision. Fade the music out during verse 7.

SIXTH SUNDAY OF THE YEAR

Jeremiah 17:5-8
Psalm 1
1 Corinthians 15:12,
    16-20
Luke 6:17, 20-26

The challenges and rewards of living by faith.

All-age talk

Beforehand gather a selection of brand-name items relevant to each age group in the congregation.

Begin by displaying each item and drawing attention to the brand name to impress people. Talk about how we are sometimes made to feel we have to have a particular thing in order to be thought normal or worth anything. Sometimes we are teased if we haven't got them. Sometimes we go out shopping to cheer ourselves up, thinking that having more will make us happy. Sometimes we spend money we can't afford to keep up with our friends or neighbours.

Put all the items into a carton labelled 'Very Important' and close the lid. Explain that Jesus turns our ideas of what is important upside down. As you say this, turn the carton upside down. Today we have heard Jesus telling the people that trust in what you can buy and possess is not the good thing the advertisements say it is, and these things don't give us long-term happiness at all.

So what does he offer instead?

Jesus says that we will be much happier if we trust in God rather than in things people say about us, and things people make and sell. Getting stuck in the 'wanting something else' mode or the 'everybody else does it' mode just ends up making us dissatisfied and greedy and selfish, which doesn't bring happiness to us or those we live with. But if we put our trust in God, all the riches of the kingdom of God will be ours. We'll enjoy the lovely and surprising ways God provides for our needs. We'll be able to see what is good and right, and want to work enthusiastically again instead of just going through the motions. We won't be frantically running to keep up with the latest fashion. We won't be so anxious about material things.

Jesus doesn't say we'll have lots of comforts or fame or money if we live like this. In fact he says we will run into insults and people will think we're crazy, and they will laugh at us and make life difficult for us. We can't say we haven't been warned!

But the rewards far outweigh the disadvantages. Putting our trust in God will enable us to live as free, contented and generous-hearted people – the kind of people we would, deep down, probably prefer to be.

All-age ideas

- Have a twin flower arrangement of a dry, dead branch set in sand, and a bonsai tree or a cluster of flowering pot plants, standing in a wide, shallow tray filled with water and a few pebbles. Have a quotation from Jeremiah or Psalm 1 beside the arrangement.

- Have a collection of actual items needed, rather than money, for a local project to help the homeless, for example.

SEVENTH SUNDAY OF THE YEAR

1 Samuel 26:2, 7-9,
    12-13, 22-23
Psalm 102
1 Corinthians 15:45-49
Luke 6:27-38

Jesus teaches us to love our enemies and forgive those who sin against us.

All-age talk

Beforehand ask the children to make lots of paper chains.

Remind everyone of what Jesus teaches us in today's Gospel: to love our enemies and forgive those who sin against us. How on earth are we supposed to do it? Surely enemies are people you hate? Why does Jesus tell us to love them, then?

Ask a volunteer to run and skip around a bit and talk about how life can feel when we are happy with ourselves, and everything is going well for us. But sooner or later we get into a mood with some-one, someone upsets us and annoys us, someone else winds us up, someone makes our life a real misery, someone lets us down and spoils our plans, someone hurts a person we love, or someone steals from us a close friend or a marriage partner, or our dignity in old age. (At each suggestion, drape a chain around the volunteer until s/he is smothered in chains.) And if we haven't forgiven these people who have sinned against us and hurt us, we end up still carrying invisible chains which weigh us down. The volunteer can walk around bowed down with the heavy chains.

So when Jesus says to us, 'Love your enemies and forgive those who wrong you', he knows it is hard, but he also knows it will set us free to live fully again. Every time we say (and really mean it) 'I forgive you for what you did', a chain drops off. (Pull a chain off the volunteer.) Every time we wrestle with our feelings of hate for someone and ask God to help us sort things out, a chain drops off. (Pull off another chain.) Pull off the remaining

336

chains, with everyone saying 'I forgive you!' for each one.

Jesus doesn't like to see us weighed down with heavy invisible chains of hate and resentment and bitterness against people. He wants us to be free to enjoy life, and he will always help us to do the forgiving. Forgiving is not easy; it's very hard work. If you know there is someone you are finding it very hard to forgive, ask God for the grace to forgive and then work at the forgiving. Don't live with the chains any more.

All-age ideas

- The very dramatic first reading can be acted out while being narrated. Saul lies asleep at the front of the church. David and Abishai creep up the aisle and take the spear, running off to the back, side or balcony, from where David shouts his words to the awakened Saul.

- A chant. Have the following words written on the weekly handout or on an OHP: 'Love your enemies. Do good to those who hate you. Pray for those who hurt you.' Very quietly the congregation recites these words, repeating them six times. Above this hushed chanting of Jesus' teaching, have three people, standing in different parts of the church, to call out their protests. They should leave enough space between each protest for the teaching to be heard through, and the chant should be the last thing left in people's minds. Here are the protests:

  1. 'But you can't expect me to forgive them! Not after what they've done!'

  2. 'It was terrible.
     It was unforgivable.
     How can I possibly love them now?'

  3. 'But they've ruined my whole life.
     Why should I forgive them?'

EIGHTH SUNDAY OF THE YEAR

Ecclesiasticus 27:4-7
Psalm 91
1 Corinthians 15:54-58
Luke 6:39-45

What we think important flows out in the way we speak.

All-age talk

Beforehand arrange for two volunteers to say they are sorry – one sounding not at all interested or bothered, and the other angry and resentful, rather than sorry. Start by telling everyone that you are going to test their powers of detection in a short experiment. Introduce your team, and ask everyone to listen to what is *really* being said by each of them. Now point out to the first person something they've done which is very thoughtless or unkind, such as not feeding the rabbit for two days, or wiping their filthy hands on a clean towel without washing first. The person says they're sorry. But can people detect what they are *really* saying? (Such as 'Do you really think I care about that?' or 'So what?')

Now say the same thing to the other helper, and they also say their 'sorry'. But what are they *really* saying? (Such as 'You're always getting at me and I've had enough of it' or 'Good – I'm glad I did it and upset you because I don't like you'.)

In the Gospel today Jesus is teaching us that God can see what we really mean, whatever we actually say, and it saddens him to see us pretending to be good when we're really being quite selfish, cruel, deceitful, unfaithful or bullying. We can't get away with pretending to God, and often we can't get away with pretending to other people either.

Jesus says we're a bit like fruit trees. If we're rotten trees, then that will show in our rotten fruit. If our hearts are lying and selfish, then what we say and do will show that up, whether we are Christians or not, and whether we go to Mass each week or not. As far as God is concerned, we are to be honest about what we are really like, and when we don't like what we see in ourselves, God will help us to change.

All-age ideas

- As a penitential rite, try using *Come, Spirit, come, prise open my heart*, the words and music for which can be found on page 415. This can be sung by a single voice, or a small group of singers, or even said if there are no singers, giving everyone the space to reflect on areas in their own hearts where openness and healing are needed.

- Try this sketch. Have a sign up with the doctor's name on it and the doctor wearing a stethoscope. A patient walks in with wads of cotton wool plastered over his eyes so that he can barely see. He gropes around, bumping into the wall, and finds his way to the chair, with the doctor guiding him, something like this:

Doc   Ah, good morning, Mr Henning! Do take a seat . . . no, that's the table . . . the seat's over to the right a bit.

Patient   All right, all right, I know where I'm going. What do you think I am . . . blind or something?

Doc   Now, how can I help you?

Patient   Help me? How on earth would you be able to help me? Anyone would think there was something wrong with me!

Doc   Er . . . Perhaps I could examine your eyes?

Patient   (*jumping up*) Oh no, you don't! I've heard about people like you. As if I'd trust my eyes to your interfering fingers. They're my own eyes, aren't they?

Doc   Well, yes, of course, but . . .

Patient   There you are, then, my eyes are my own private business, thanks very much.

Now, why don't you get a move on and stamp these library books. *(He puts some books on the table.)*

Doc   But, Mr Henning . . .

Patient   *(getting up and groping round walls to the door)* I don't know . . . the library system isn't what it used to be . . .

Doc   *(shrugs his shoulders and shakes his head. Outside there is the sound of a horn blaring, a screech of brakes and a loud cry.)* There's no helping some people!

NINTH SUNDAY OF THE YEAR

1 Kings 8:41-43
Psalm 116
Galatians 1:1-2, 6-10
Luke 7:1-10

The good news we have been given is not just for us, but to pass on to the rest of the world.

All-age talk

Bring with you a newspaper, a TV remote control, a mobile phone, an airmail letter and, if possible, a trumpeter (failing a real one, a recorded version will do nicely).

Begin by picking up the newspaper and reading out a few headlines. Talk about this being one of the ways we use to get other people to hear our news. People used to use a town crier. (You could ask a loud-voiced volunteer to demonstrate. The news they bellow is written on a piece of paper: 'There is only one real God. He made us and he loves us!') Pick up the remote control and explain that now we don't have to shout so loud because we invite the town criers into our homes and sit them in the corner to tell us the latest news. We can even switch them off!

Another thing people used was a trumpeter. (Have this demonstrated briefly.) That got people's attention so they would listen to what you were saying. Now we have this to get people's attention, and get them listening to us. (Demonstrate the mobile phone.) People used to send their news by pigeons, and now we send it on a metal bird. (Show the airmail letter.)

What has stayed the same all through the years is that people always want to pass on their news. And today we are being told that the news the town crier shouted to us (they can do it again) is such good news, not just for us but for everyone, that we need to make sure we pass it on. Like honey or peanut butter, we are not to keep the good news to ourselves, but spread it!

We can tell people about God's love by behaving in a kind and loving way, by being generous with our time and money, by praying for our friends and for difficult situations, by living by God's rules, and by bringing our faith into the conversation instead of only mentioning it among our church friends. And who knows, God may also call some of you to tell the good news as newspaper reporters, in government, on television or as a famous sports star. However you do it, do it!

All-age ideas

- Have the items used in the talk arranged in front of the altar with the sign: 'The Lord is God! (Don't keep the faith, spread it.)'

- Have a clapping message passed all around the church: 'The real God loves you, pass it on.' As you say it you do these claps: clap your own hands, right with your partner, your own again, left with your partner, clap your sides, clap your own hands and then both hands with your partner. When someone has clapped it with you, you find someone else to do it with until eventually everyone has caught the message.

TENTH SUNDAY OF THE YEAR

1 Kings 17:17-24
Psalm 29
Galatians 1:11-19
Luke 7:11-17

Our God is full of compassion; he hears our crying and it is his nature to rescue us.

All-age talk

Bring with you a pair of balance scales. These can be either a heavy-duty kitchen type or a children's educational toy. You could even use a small portable seesaw and have two children to demonstrate it. It's the balancing of weights that matters.

Demonstrate the scales/seesaw with the help of some children, reminding everyone of the way the scales are balanced when there is the same weight both sides. Sometimes our lives can feel like a seesaw or a pair of scales. We might be really happy, and everything is going well, and our team is winning, and we passed our driving test on the eighth attempt, and our operation was successful, and someone has just changed our nappy and fed us. However old or young we are, we all know what it feels like to have the 'joy' side of the scales full up.

Other times we may feel that everything is against us. Our best friend is moving away to another town, our team has lost for the third time running, the washing machine floods the kitchen, and you fall over and graze your knees. Sometimes the pain is so deep that we can hardly bear it – like when someone we love dies, or we are suddenly let down by someone we thought we could trust, or we are faced with serious illness. We all know what it feels like to have the 'sadness' side of the scales full up.

We heard today about the way God looked after a widow and her son through Elijah. And we heard about another widow, beside herself with grief, whose dead son was brought to life by Jesus and given back to her.

So does it look as if our God is only interested in us when the happy side of our scales is full to

343

bursting? No, it proclaims loud and clear that our God is tenderly interested in us all the time, during those terrible times of sadness we sometimes have to go through, as well as the times of great joy we dance through. And that is because he really loves us.

All-age ideas

- Have different voices to read the story of Elijah.

- Show slides or acetates of faces from all over the world which focus our compassion on the greed, poverty, pain, violence, vulnerability and loneliness of many. This can be done in silence or with music suggested by the young people. They are particularly good at putting together pictures and music with sensitivity. If slides and OHPs are not suitable for your church, have the pictures mounted and carried around the church, or fixed on the walls, and encourage the congregation to move around and pray.

ELEVENTH SUNDAY OF THE YEAR

2 Samuel 12:7-10, 13
Psalm 31
Galatians 2:16, 19-21
Luke 7:36-8:3

God has the authority and the desire to forgive our sins completely and set us free from guilt.

All-age talk

During the week collect a few well-known parish voices on tape, perhaps from choir practice or children's liturgy. If you can have some photographs taken at such things, these can be displayed as people come into church. (See All-age Ideas.) You will also need a length of string with a Lego person tied on one end, and a pair of scissors.

Begin by playing the tape and letting people experience the 'Good heavens, that's me!' factor. Remind everyone of how you feel when a raffle ticket is called and you suddenly realise it's the same as the number staring at you from your own hand, or when you catch sight of yourself unexpectedly in a mirror when you're out shopping.

David and Simon were both given that shock in our readings today. They had all done wrong, and yet hadn't really recognised it. Now, suddenly, they are shown the truth about themselves, and it isn't a pretty sight.

Like them, we don't always know when we've done wrong or sinned. We might have had a little tug of conscience but quickly stamped it out so we could go on doing what we wanted to be doing! If you're in doubt, think to yourself, 'Am I happy for God to see me saying this, or doing this, or thinking this?' And if you're not happy with God seeing how you behave at school, or with particular people, or at work, or at your club, then the way you are behaving is probably wrong, and you need to change it.

Sometimes we will need to point out gently to one another where we are wrong. That's all part of

345

loving one another and helping one another to live God's way.

Show the piece of string with a Lego person tied on the end. Explain that whenever we fall into sin, we cut ourselves off from God (cut the string and let the person drop). God longs to put things right, but he can't, unless we call out to him and say, 'I've fallen down! I'm sorry!' As soon as we turn to God like that, and ask him to forgive us, he ties us on again so we're not cut off any more. And the funny thing is we end up closer, if anything, because being forgiven is so wonderful that it makes us love God more than ever.

All-age ideas

- The Gospel story is an excellent one to act out, with different people speaking their parts, either reading them or studying the text first and saying the words.

- Have a sheet of paper with the shape of a cross cut out of it, and fix it on to a mirror, so the effect is of a cross made out of a mirror. This can be used at the Penitential Rite, to remind people that Jesus' love will reflect back to us the state of our inner selves, just as a mirror shows us our outer appearance.

TWELFTH SUNDAY OF THE YEAR

Zechariah 12:10-11
Psalm 62
Galatians 3:26-29
Luke 9:18-24

Following Christ means daily taking up our cross.

All-age talk

Ask two people to come out and stand at least three metres apart. Ask one of the people to walk down to reach the other. Was there any problem with that? (Hopefully not.) Now ask both people to get to you, only this time with one condition – they mustn't move. Can they do it? (No, it's impossible.) If they want to get across to reach you they will have to go on a journey to do it. Is the journey easy or difficult? (They can try it to find out.) They probably did that with no trouble at all.

But suppose the journey is made very difficult? (Tie all four ankles together with a scarf and walk away from them.) Can they get to you now? (Let them try.) As they are moving along, explain that they can certainly do it, but only with quite a struggle.

Stop them half-way and explain that being crucified was like a terrible journey that Jesus had to make to rescue us. In the middle of his journey people shouted at him to come down from the cross and save himself from the suffering.

Ask the people if they would be capable of untying the scarf and walking freely. (Presumably they could.) So could Jesus have come down from the cross and avoided all that suffering? In which case, why didn't he? He did it because he knew that there wasn't any other way to rescue us apart from accepting all the chains of our sin and carrying them for us, even though it made his journey so difficult. Instead of opting out, he chose to carry on (the volunteers can carry on as well) until the journey of rescue was finished, so we can all be set free. (Untie the legs of the volunteers.) And as followers of Christ, we are called to follow him in the kind of loving which led to that terrible journey – the loving which doesn't take the selfish or easy way out, but carries on loving and forgiving however difficult it is.

All-age ideas

- Play some haunting, sad music either to surround the first reading as a background to it, or played afterwards as a reflection upon it.

- At the offering of the gifts invite everyone to re-commit themselves to following Christ, marking their foreheads with the sign of the cross.

THIRTEENTH SUNDAY OF THE YEAR

1 Kings 19:16, 19-21
Psalm 15
Galatians 5:1, 13-18
Luke 9:51-62

When we are called to follow Jesus, that means total commitment, with no half measures.

All-age talk

You will need someone who can do gymnastics or dance. Ask them to prepare a sequence of moves which need total commitment in order to work, such as somersaults and cartwheels, pirouettes and arabesques.

Begin by asking the gymnasts or dancers to perform their demonstration. Briefly interview them, thanking them and asking whether they could do these things first time, or whether they had to practise. Draw attention to the commitment that has to be given to anything you want to do really well. You can't 'half do' some of those moves, or you'd probably fall flat on your face.

As Christians we are called to that same kind of commitment. We can't 'half do' it. When we commit ourselves to following Christ, it's going to affect the way we talk, the way we behave with our friends and our enemies, the way we spend our time and our money. It's going to affect all our thinking and the choices we make. So it's a bit like deciding to do a double somersault, or a triple pirouette – it takes a lot of dedication and courage to launch off.

Imagine if you were just launching yourself into a triple somersault and all your strength suddenly wasn't there. You'd certainly notice it was missing! In fact, you wouldn't be able to do any of those clever moves without strength.

In our Christian life, God's Holy Spirit is the strength. It enables us to do those triple somersaults of caring love for those we don't much like, and the double pirouettes of co-operating when all we want is our own way. Real loving is very hard

349

work, and it takes lots of dedication. With God's strength we can do it, and then we will be moving freely and beautifully through life, in the way God called us to, and knows will make us, and others, truly happy.

All-age ideas

- In a time of prayer, ask various groups of people to stand so that the others can pray for them in their ministry – all those, for instance, who are involved with learning, teaching and education, those in industry and commerce, those caring for children, those who have time during the day to pray, and those whose sporting or leisure activities bring them into contact with people who don't know Jesus.

- Have a display with a list on one side of good works, or things in the parish that need to be done. On the other half, list excuses why they can't be done. Next to this have a list of the things Jesus did, and a list of the excuses he might have used, but didn't, not to do them.

FOURTEENTH SUNDAY OF THE YEAR

Isaiah 66:10-14
Psalm 65
Galatians 6:14-18
Luke 10:1-12, 17-20

In Christ we become a new creation.

All-age talk

Beforehand write out clearly on different colours of paper, six or twelve (depending on numbers of children expected) healings that may well have taken place when the seventy were sent out. (For example, a blind woman got her sight back; two children were dying of a disease, and now they're playing outside; a young man can now walk again; a boy who stuttered can now speak clearly; a family feud has been sorted out.) Give these to different adults to hold in different places around the church when the talk begins. Also give each adult some food to give the children who come to them. Some will be given a sweet each, some a bun each, and some a piece of dry bread.

Begin by reminding everyone that Jesus sent out seventy of his disciples in pairs, to different towns and villages. Let them suggest some reasons for the disciples being sent in pairs. (Friendly; supportive; safer.) So you are going to send people out around the church in pairs, on a mission to find a notice the same colour as the slip of paper you give each pair.

Before they go, tell them to be careful, travel light, not stop to speak to strangers on the way, eat what they're given, say 'Peace be with you' to the person holding their colour, and tell them the kingdom is very near. Get the pairs to repeat the instructions. As they go off around the church, some people can try to make some of the older ones talk on their way. As they reach their paper, the adult there can remind them of their message, if necessary, and give them their food and the notice. The pairs return to you and you can enthuse with them over all the wonderful things that have happened.

351

Thank them for all their hard work, and tell everyone about Jesus wanting everyone to be restored and like a new person. But we're still short of workers in this harvest of people. We need to pray that God will send more workers. And we need to make ourselves available, in case it's us he can use!

All-age ideas

- Have a flower arrangement like a cornfield, with wheat and grasses, poppies and cornflowers, and have a scythe beside the arrangement with the words from Luke: 'Ask the Lord of the harvest to send out workers into his harvest field.'

- As a background to, or reflection upon, the first reading, have some gentle nursery music played, possibly from a music box.

FIFTEENTH SUNDAY OF THE YEAR

Deuteronomy
    30:10-14
Psalm 68
Colossians 1:15-20
Luke 10:25-37

Straighten your lives out and live by God's standards of love.

All-age talk

Bring with you an egg cup, a whole egg in its shell, and a boiled egg which someone has eaten, so that just the shell is left, with a spoon hole at one end. Put this into the egg cup upside down so that it looks like a complete egg ready to eat. You will also need an egg spoon.

Begin by talking about those times you've desperately needed help, like missing the bus when you're already a bit late, or being caught in a downpour on your way to school, and you're hoping one of your friends will happen to drive past and see you. Perhaps the man who had been mugged in Jesus' story felt a bit like that, if he was still able to think after the beating-up he'd been given. Perhaps in the daze of his injuries he heard each set of footsteps coming nearer, and hoped that now he'd get some help. But no, the footsteps quickened up when they got nearer and then went off into the distance again. And the man still lay there, unable to move.

Perhaps he had almost given up hope when the Samaritan, a foreigner, stopped and came to peer at him to see what was wrong. Perhaps, as he swayed in and out of consciousness, he was half aware of being carefully given first aid, of being comforted and reassured that he was going to be all right. Those are good things to feel and hear, when you're in great need. You have no power at such times to make anyone care for you, so all you can do is rely on other people choosing to treat you well.

And that's what we're being taught today: that as Christians we are people called to treat others well, whether we're told to or not, whether anyone sees us or not, whether we want to or not. Why? Simply because our God says that this is the right and good way to live.

The man in today's Gospel, to whom Jesus told his 'good neighbour' story, could recite the rules he was supposed to live by off by heart: 'Love the Lord your God with all your heart and with all your soul and with all your strength and with all your mind. And love your neighbour as yourself.' But for him and for lots of others, those words are like this boiled egg. It looks wonderful and full of goodness. But if I start to dig into it (do that) with my spoon, I find that all the inside is missing, and there's nothing of any goodness there at all.

We must be brave and dig into the words we sing and pray together today, and look at what we find inside. Perhaps there will be rich meaning, and you will know that the words your mouth says are backed up with the way you live. Perhaps you will find the words are just a shell, and your life doesn't back them up at all. If so, come to God today and ask him to fill the shell with new meaning. He can do that, and he's waiting for you to ask.

All-age ideas

- Print out the first reading so that everyone can join in with the questions in it, which you print in bold. (Who will . . .?) Have a narrator and Moses to read the rest of the passage.

- Have a group acting out the story of the good Samaritan, but make sure the first section – the conversation with the expert in the Law – is included in the acting.

SIXTEENTH SUNDAY OF THE YEAR

Genesis 18:1-10
Psalm 14
Colossians 1:24-28
Luke 10:38-42

Attentive listening is all part of serving.

All-age talk

Beforehand make a pair of large card ears, about 30 centimetres high, and a pair of large card hands, about the same size.

Start by asking for two volunteers, one of whom holds the ears to the side of her head, and the other who has the hands fixed to her own hands with large rubber bands. Remind everyone of the two people in the Gospel for today, both very good friends of Jesus. Their names were Martha and Mary and they were sisters. Jesus often went round to the home where they lived with their brother Lazarus, and they all enjoyed one another's company.

(Alice) is like a cartoon picture of Mary, because what she liked to do was sit and listen to Jesus and she could listen to him for hours. She probably liked listening to all sorts of people, and may have been the kind of person people could talk easily to because they could see she was interested in them. Mary's idea of cooking a meal was probably beans on toast, and she probably didn't notice the dust creeping up until she could write in it.

(Laura) is like a cartoon picture of Martha, because what she liked best was doing things for people and making sure they had clean shirts and well-balanced meals. Her idea of cooking a meal would be something like roast chicken with all the trimmings. If you wanted something done, you'd ask Martha.

Now people sometimes get upset by today's Gospel because they think Jesus is saying that everyone ought to spend their time listening like Mary, and that busy, practical people like Martha aren't somehow as good. But, of course, Jesus isn't

355

saying that at all. His own life was full of work and activity, travelling, preaching, teaching and healing, and none of that would have got done if he hadn't been a doer.

But he also spent hours late at night, or early in the morning on his own with God, talking things over and quietly listening. And he knew that this was a really important part of the doing. He knew we need to keep the right balance between input (the ears) and output (the hands). On that particular visit to Martha and Mary's house, the listening was more important than the doing. What we all have to do is notice when we need to listen, and be ready to stop what we're doing and listen.

All of us need to set aside a quiet time to be with God morning and night, every day. It doesn't have to be long, but it has to be there. If we neglect that, our ability to discern right behaviour will start to slip, and we risk sliding into the kind of life that hurts God so much. Spending time quietly with God is not an optional extra for people with time on their hands, it's an absolute necessity, as well as being refreshing, rejuvenating and problem solving! (If there is a parish or diocesan retreat planned this year you can mention that as well.)

All-age ideas

- Have the first reading acted out while being narrated, with the three visitors walking up the aisle, and Abraham and Sarah welcoming them and providing thorougly for their needs.

- Ask people to hold first their ears and then their hands as you pray for God's blessing on every-one's listening and activity in the week ahead.

SEVENTEENTH SUNDAY OF THE YEAR

Genesis 18:20-32
Psalm 137
Colossians 2:12-24
Luke 11:1-13

Keep asking for God's Spirit and he will keep pouring out his blessing on you.

All-age talk

Bring along some strips of bedding plants, or a packet of seeds and a flourishing plant of the same or similar variety.

Proudly show the results of your horticultural exploits, and talk about what your hopes are for the seed or the tiny bedding plants. You don't really want them to stay as they are because, although the pictures on the labels show wonderful flowers or fruit, at present they are only dry dusty things, or boring leafy things, in spite of your recent planting efforts. What you are hoping is that they will eventually grow and flourish, until they flower and fruit as you know they can if all goes well.

That's how God feels about us. When he plants us into life, he knows we have lots of potential, lots of good possibilities. Since he loves us, he really hopes that we will grow, spiritually as well as in our bodies. He doesn't want us to stay the same as when we first begin in our Christian life, because he knows that if all goes well we shall one day be full of flowers and fruit that will help the world.

If I want my little plants to grow I will have to give them things like water and food, and make sure I give them plenty of light. And, being plants, they will just sit there and let me give them the things they need to grow nicely. I also need to talk to them!

God wants to give us lots of things to make us grow. He wants to drench us in his Spirit, warm us with the light of his love, and feed us with his word and in communion. He also wants to talk to us! But because we are humans, and not plants, we sometimes turn away from his light, and put up

357

huge umbrellas against the rain of his Spirit, and refuse to let him feed us, and block our ears to stop ourselves hearing what he says. And when that happens, we stop growing and we wilt and weaken, and we never get to bear any fruit.

Today God is saying to us, 'Let me give you the gifts you need to grow as Christians; keep asking me for them, keep looking for me, and I promise that you will receive everything you need to grow into strong, healthy plants with beautiful flowers and fruit.'

All-age ideas

- Use the Lord's Prayer from Luke today.

- Decorate a door with flowers around it and a notice on it from Luke 11:9.

EIGHTEENTH SUNDAY OF THE YEAR

Ecclesiastes 1:2;
  2:21-23
Psalm 94
Colossians 3:1-5, 9-11
Luke 12:13-21

True richness is not material wealth; true security is not a financial matter.

All-age talk

You will need the packing boxes for various consumables, such as a computer, electronic game, microwave, brand-name shoes, or luxury biscuits. You will also need such things as a CD, gardening and teenage magazines, and a film carton. Choose the items to suit the interests of the people in your congregation, and have enough for one person to hold all at once with great difficulty. Finally, you need a pocket Bible and a tiny spray of flowers.

Remind everyone of the story Jesus told us in the Gospel today, about the farmer who thought that having a bumper harvest, and therefore a financial windfall, meant total security, so that he could just do as he liked and take no care of his soul. His greed had made him foolish. As it happened, he was going to die and face God that very night, and he wasn't in the least prepared for death.

Ask for a volunteer to help you explain something. Explain how all the advertisements tell us that if we get a particular brand of yoghurt or car or shampoo, everyone will like us and fancy us, and we'll be really happy. Sometimes we get taken in by this lie, and start wanting to have things so we'll be safer or happier or better liked.

Go through the things we like to get, piling the packages into the arms of the volunteer as you talk. When they are completely loaded up, and have no hands left to hold anything else, point out the problem with all this 'having' being important to us. It means that when Jesus offers us his Word and his Love (offer the Bible and flowers), we simply haven't room to take it, and we turn it down, because

359

our minds are too full of what we've got and what we want, and how we're going to hang on to what we've got.

And that is a tragedy that lasts not just for a few years but for ever. We need to put down our wanting and having, so that we can take the really important wealth that God offers us. (The volunteer is helped to unload, so they can hold the Bible and flowers.) These are the things which will make us content and happy and secure, whether we have all the other good things or not.

All-age ideas

- Have a flower arrangement in a cash box. Or have buttercups and daisies in a simple and generous arrangement.

- Use this short sketch.

  A I've got a new bike with 36 gears.
  B Well I need a new bike with 36 gears. I'll ask my parents.
  C Why shouldn't I steal a decent bike? I'll never have the money to buy one.

  A I'm going to Florida again this year.
  B We might go to Florida if I can persuade Mum to work more hours.
  C It's not fair. Everybody else goes to Florida. We stay with Nan at Clacton.

  A I am a rich, complacent fool.
  B I am an envious fool.
  C I am a resentful fool.

  A, B, C   And we're all trapped by money!

NINETEENTH SUNDAY OF THE YEAR

Wisdom 18:6-9
Psalm 32
Hebrews 11:1-2, 8-19
Luke 12:32-48

Have faith in God, and get yourself ready to meet him.

All-age talk

You will need a pair of swimming flippers. Have ready a couple of large freezer labels with the words 'I believe in God' written on them.

Ask for a volunteer to walk up and down the church, so that everyone can see the way this person normally walks. Now give them the flippers to wear. As they are being put on, explain that today's readings teach us about how our faith in God affects the way we live. Remind them of Abraham and the way he was ready to get up and go when God asked him to, even though he didn't know exactly how the move would work out. He trusted God to want the best for him, and had faith that God would look after him.

Now that the volunteer is wearing flippers, is he going to walk in the same way as before? Well, let's see. As the person walks up and down, point out that we can all see the effect the flippers are having on the walking – it's a very distinctive flipper walk!

Put the freezer labels on the flippers, explaining that when we decide to walk with faith in God, that is going to affect the way we walk through life. It will give us a very distinctive faith walk. The readings today tell us the kind of things to expect. We will be stopping doing what is wrong and learning to do what is right. We will be noticing the needs of those around us and in our world, and making sure we help out with our time and prayers and money. We will be building up treasure in heaven by our loving kindness, patience, honesty, thoughtfulness and self-control.

All-age ideas

- The parables in the Gospel can be mimed while it is being read.

- In a flower arrangement express the idea of treasure by the container chosen, and have treasure items included in the arrangement. Have the text of Luke 12:34 beside it.

Twentieth Sunday of the Year

Jeremiah 38:4-6, 8-10
Psalm 39
Hebrews 12:1-4
Luke 12:49-53

When we fix our eyes on Jesus our lives will reflect his nature.

All-age talk

Beforehand prepare a number of heavy carrier bags and a rucksack, and have a sack or strong dustbin bag. Label the bags 'I want my own way', 'It isn't fair', 'So what?', 'I'll never forgive them' and 'No one will notice'. Also bring the local school's PE kit.

Begin by showing everyone the PE kit and draw from them what it is, who wears it, and why we do PE dressed like this instead of in our best clothes, or in bridesmaids' dresses, or Mickey Mouse suits. Establish that it's more practical and comfortable to wear light clothes like this which don't get in the way of our running and jumping.

Refer to the letter to the Hebrew Christians in which following Jesus through our lives is said to be a bit like running a race: we need to look where we're going. That means keeping our eyes on Jesus and his way of living. This will keep us on the right track in our own lives, reminding us to be honest instead of telling lies, thinking of other people's needs instead of just wanting our own way, and sharing our ideas and fears with God instead of ignoring him most of the time.

But often we run our Christian life in very unsuitable clothes. At this point ask for a volunteer, and load them up with all the bags, explaining what each represents, and how we weigh ourselves down with all this luggage. As you hand over the sack for them to stand in, point out how difficult we make it for ourselves by hanging on to all these attitudes which make Christian living extra hard. The volunteer can try running to prove the point.

Today we are being given a useful tip for

Christian living: get rid of all these unhelpful habits (name them as you take them from the volunteer), so that we are free to run God's race-track uncluttered and 'light'. Then we can concentrate on Jesus, and learn to live his way – the way of love.

All-age ideas

- Have a display, linked with a flower arrangement, of a PE kit or an athlete's running kit and trophy.

- Collect newspaper pictures and headlines from the week which direct people to pray for the needs of our world. These are held, or fixed on pew ends, the floor, pillars and doors, and people are invited to walk slowly around the church building, being the Church in action as they pray for the concerns they see. The choir or music group will help people's prayer if they sing something like *O Lord, hear my prayer* (Taizé) while people are quietly moving around the church praying either silently or in small groups.

TWENTY-FIRST SUNDAY OF THE YEAR

Isaiah 66:18-21
Psalm 116
Hebrews 12:5-7, 11-13
Luke 13:22-30

At the great and final gathering-in, it will be a question of each person's chosen life direction, and each response to the way of God.

All-age talk

Beforehand collect four shoe boxes, and in one of them place a pair of binoculars.

Ask a volunteer who wears glasses to help you with the talk. Ask her to stand where most people can see her, and put four chairs around her, not quite near enough for her to touch. Blindfold the volunteer, or ask her to keep her eyes shut. On each of the chairs place a box, and in the box containing binoculars also place her glasses. Turn the volunteer to face an empty box.

Point out how (Helen) needs her glasses, and life is very difficult for her because we've taken away her glasses and even covered her eyes! We may sometimes feel that God has done this to us – when everything we hoped for or felt sure of suddenly seems taken away. Or perhaps our best friend moves away, or there are rows at home, and suddenly we don't know exactly where we are or which way to turn. Perhaps we feel let down by God.

Today's readings tell us that God doesn't let us down. Ever. Sometimes he draws back from us a little to encourage us to walk in faith – like when we encourage our children to walk or cycle by moving away from them.

Sometimes the hardest times we have are the times we learn most or get closest to trusting God our loving Father. The secret is to turn in the right direction, because God is the One who has both power and inclination to help. His motive is ardent love for his precious child. If we turn any other way and walk in that direction, we will face emptiness and disappointment. (Help Helen to turn in each wrong direction, open the shoe box and not find her glasses.) But if we turn in God's direction and walk his ways (turn Helen the right way), then we will find fulfilment, just as Helen has found her glasses. And it's often far more than we would have dared hope. Helen has actually found more than just her glasses – there's binoculars here as well, so she can see much further than usual!

All-age ideas

- The Isaiah passage works well read chorally, with voices of different tones – low, medium and high. Work through copies of the passage, experimenting with what combination of voices best brings out the meaning and the poetry. Aim to emphasise the sense of a great gathering in of all the nations.

- Have large letters – N, S, E and W – fixed on the appropriate walls or on the floor of the church.

Twenty-second Sunday of the Year

Ecclesiasticus 3:17-20,
  28-29
Psalm 67
Hebrews 12:18-19,
  22-24
Luke 14:1, 7-14

When we live God's way, both individually and as a community, we will be greatly blessed.

All-age talk

Beforehand prepare two chunks of wood, which should be quite different from each other. From each cut a small chip.

First give out the two chips of wood and show everyone the blocks they came from. Ask a cluster of people round each chip to decide which block their chip came from. How can they tell? (Perhaps by the way it feels and looks and smells; by the colour and the grain.)

In our readings today we are hearing quite a bit about humility, and there's a good reason for this. We are made in the image of God, which means we should be like chips off the old block. People should be able to look at us and the way we think and feel and behave, and see that we are children of our heavenly Father. And one of the great hallmarks of God is *humility*.

Jesus, the Word or Expression of God, had been present when our universe first began. He knew all about the excitement of stars bursting into being, planets being formed and all the ideas of creation taking shape. But in order to put us right and give us life that doesn't end, he was quite prepared to put all that aside and become a human baby, starting at the weakest level. God was humble enough to become one of the creatures he had made.

Like these chips of wood, whatever kind of people we are on the inside will show in the way we behave on the outside. So rather than working on doing things we think will impress people (even

367

humble things like taking the lowest place), God is inviting us to work with him on a transforming process from the inside. He can make us the kind of people who are naturally full of humility, simply because we are more and more like God himself.

All-age ideas

- Make some tiny posies of flowers which match up with the colours of the main flower arrangement. Have the children carrying these little arrangements at the offering of the gifts, so they are clustered around their 'parent' arrangement.

- As part of the Penitential rite, or following the Gospel, provide space for people to reflect on where they are in their spiritual growing, and where they need to recognise areas that require attention. This can either be silence, or a time with quiet music playing.

Twenty-third Sunday of the Year

Wisdom 9:13-18
Psalm 89
Philemon 9-10, 12-17
Luke 14:25-33

Following Jesus is expensive – it costs everything, but it's worth it.

All-age talk

Bring along some catalogues with items which would appeal to the different ages and cultures of those likely to be present. Read out several of the items on offer, and ask people to raise their hands if they think each is a good offer. The more varied and unusual, the better. You might try, for instance, the latest sports car, an electronic game, a lawn mower and a Disneyland holiday. Would the items still be good bargains if you had to give up eating, hobbies or driving in order to pay for them? Establish that if something is important enough, we are prepared to give things up for it. If we're not prepared to change our habits to pay for it, we won't be able to have it.

We are called to follow Jesus. We are offered a fulfilling and rewarding life, inner peace and joy, and life that lasts for ever, even beyond our bodily death. That's quite an offer. But what does it cost? What would we have to give up to pay for it?

Have a long and a short piece of card, or two sticks, and show the long vertical one on its own. This looks like the word 'I'. Place the shorter piece across it. Following Jesus costs us the cross – it means deciding to give up the 'I want' way of living, and putting the sign of God's love (the cross) right at the centre of our lives. (Hold the cross you have made against your own body.)

That means that following Jesus is going to cost us quite a lot. It isn't a cheap, throwaway thing like a paper cup. We need to think very carefully about it before we decide to go for it. Is it worth it?

369

Yes, it certainly is! God made us, so his way is exactly right for us. No one but God can give us the lasting peace and happiness and complete forgiveness we long for. With God we can become more and more our true selves, selves we can face in the mirror and love. With God we can reach out to other people, and be brave enough to stand up for what is right and loving. Although our life as Christians may lead us into some difficult or dangerous situations, we will always have our friend Jesus with us, and that makes it all possible and all worthwhile.

All-age ideas

• Incorporate in a display or flower arrangement some money and a personal finance planner, or some flyers advertising financial advice. The text reads: 'If you wanted to build a tower, you would first sit down and decide how much it would cost ... In the same way, you must give up everything you have to follow me.' Luke 14:28, 33.

• The passage from Wisdom can be read chorally with the questions read by a single voice.

TWENTY-FOURTH SUNDAY OF THE YEAR

Exodus 32:7-11, 13-14
Psalm 50
1 Timothy 1:12-17
Luke 15:1-32

Jesus does not avoid the company of sinners but befriends them.

All-age talk

Gather a mixed group of 'sheep', and appoint a shepherd who is given a crook. Talk about the way the shepherd looks after sheep, finding fresh water and fresh grass, and protecting them from the dangers of wolves and bears. Sometimes a sheep will wander off on its own. (Send one of the sheep to go off and hide somewhere in the church, ensuring that enthusiastic sheep are prevented from going right outside.)

Jesus thought the way we wander off from living good lives was rather like sheep wandering off and getting lost. He loves all of us, and doesn't want any of us to be lost, so, like a good shepherd, he checks that all the rest of the people in the church are OK. (Are they?) Then he sets off to search for the one who has wandered off.

As the shepherd searches for the lost sheep (tell him/her to wait with the sheep when it is found), give some examples of what makes us wander off from God. Perhaps other things crowd God out and take over our life; perhaps we want to disobey God's rules and please ourselves; perhaps some tragedy in our life shakes our faith, and we think God has caused the pain instead of realising that he is weeping with us. Whatever it is, once we realise we are a long way from God, we feel very lost and alone. Sometimes we have got ourselves trapped in habits we can't break out of on our own.

Thankfully Jesus, our good shepherd, is out looking for us, and he will search and search until

371

he finds us. We can help by bleating – which is praying, calling out to God from where we are.

It is very good to be found. As the shepherd brings the wandering sheep, hand in hand, back to the flock, talk about how wonderful it is to know that we are forgiven, and that God loves us enough to forgive us even when we ran away from him. When the sheep comes back to the flock everyone can clap, as, with all the angels of heaven, we celebrate the truth that our God is such an excellent rescuer, full of understanding and mercy, and willing to give up his life to get us back home again.

All-age ideas

- Have an arrangement of model sheep, or a picture or poster of sheep on a hillside.

- If possible, have a pictorial display and explanation of a Middle Eastern marital head-dress, and other examples of something of similar value from other parts of the world – for example, wedding rings.

Twenty-fifth Sunday of the Year

Amos 8:4-7
Psalm 112
1 Timothy 2:1-8
Luke 16:1-13

If you cannot be trusted with worldly riches, or even small amounts of money, then you will not be trusted with spiritual riches either.

All-age talk

You will need to prepare this talk with another adult. The two of you will be bosses, standing at either end of the church.

Begin by asking for a volunteer who doesn't mind doing a few jobs. This person stands halfway down the church, and you introduce them to the two bosses they are to work for this morning. They are to serve both people as well as they can.

First one boss gives an order, such as to put three chairs out in a line in the middle of the church. As soon as this is done, the other boss gets annoyed that the chairs are arranged like this and tells the servant to put only two chairs out, facing different ways. The first boss tells the servant to put a hymn book on each chair. The other boss tells the servant to put the hymn books away and put a kneeler on each chair. Continue the orders so that the poor servant is running about the church pleasing no one.

Thank the volunteer, and explain how Jesus said in today's Gospel that it is impossible to serve two bosses like that. Either you end up loving the first and hating the second, or hating the first and loving the second. It is the same with trying to serve God while we are still bound up with materialism, money and possessions. (Have two signs: 'God' and 'Worldly Riches'. These can include appropriate symbols, such as a cross and some money.) It simply can't be done. While God is whispering to your conscience to live simply and generously, Worldly Riches is

373

insisting that you get the latest fashion in clothes or music. While God is expecting you to commit time to prayer and Bible reading, Worldly Riches is expecting you to commit that time to reading the latest magazines and watching the latest videos.

If we choose to serve God (display the 'God' sign) we have to choose not to serve Worldly Riches. (Tear up the 'Worldly Riches' sign.)

All-age ideas

- The Gospel works well with several different voices.

- Instead of the usual collection plate today, invite people to get out of their seats and bring their offering to a plate which is placed before the altar.

TWENTY-SIXTH SUNDAY OF THE YEAR

Amos 6:1a, 4-7
Psalm 145
1 Timothy 6:11-16
Luke 16:19-31

Wealth can make us complacent so that we fail to notice the needs of those around us.

All-age talk

Arrange for the following items to be in church today, giving different people responsibility for them, so that they will emerge from various people all over the congregation: a pair of sunglasses, some well-known expensive brand of sun cream (the bottle can be empty), a luxurious, squashy cushion, a bottle of champagne (or a champagne bottle) in an ice bucket, and a tape/CD player with some easy-listening music in it ready to play. You will need one of those comfortable sun-loungers. Arrange for another person to walk quietly to the middle of the aisle with a begging bowl and sit down there.

Get the sun-lounger out and invite someone to be cosseted and pampered for a few minutes of the morning. They can lie on the lounger, and various people from all over the church bring them all their comforts. Enthuse about each item as you make the volunteer really comfortable. Leave them snoozing in luxury as you pose the question: 'Is there anything wrong with living in wealth and luxury, and pampering ourselves?'

In itself, no, there isn't. Of course it is good to have times of rest and relaxation, and it is fine to enjoy the good things of life. But if we use wealth to cushion ourselves from the real world, shield our eyes from the harsh glare of suffering, protect ourselves from feeling people's pain, block out the sound of people's crying, and deaden our sense of duty, then we run the danger of rejecting all the needs, and not feeling we have any responsibility

375

to do anything about them anyway. (Hold a 'speech bubble' of card over the volunteer, which says, 'What problems?')

In Jesus' story, the rich man was probably a nice guy, and there is no mention of him doing anything really evil. But he simply hadn't noticed the beggar who sat at his own front gate every day. Point out that all the time we've been enjoying indulging ourselves up here, there has been someone begging down there.

It's all too easy for us to ignore the needs. Jesus reminds us to check that our lack of poverty doesn't prevent us from doing the practical caring love we are called to.

All-age ideas

- Use different voices in the reading of the Luke passage.

- Involve the congregation in this, printing it on the handout or showing it on the OHP.

    A Being wealthy is having a meal every day.

    B Being wealthy is having a bicycle.

    C Being wealthy is owning a house.

    D Being wealthy is having lots of exotic holidays.

    E Being wealthy is not having to work, and collecting Rolls Royces.

    All Being wealthy is all relative.
    Being poor is all relative.
    Having needs is part of being human.

Twenty-seventh Sunday of the Year

Habakkuk 1:2-3;
  2:2-4
Psalm 94
2 Timothy 1:6-8, 13-14
Luke 17:5-10

God hears our distress and our crying, and feels it with us.

All-age talk

Bring along a football, a musical instrument, a cross and a Bible. Choose someone to come out and give them the football, telling them that you are letting them borrow this so that you can watch them on television, this week, playing in the next (Liverpool) game. Give someone else the musical instrument and say you'll be looking forward to hearing them on Classic FM tomorrow morning, then.

Are these things really possible? Why not? Obviously it doesn't really happen like that. Just having a football doesn't mean you can get out there and land the goals against fierce opposition. For that you need lots of training and lots of skills. Just having a musical instrument doesn't mean that you can join a top orchestra and get all the notes and phrasing right. For that you need years of training and practice, and a musical gift.

We know about this in football and music, but we sometimes forget it when it comes to our faith, even though it's still true. Give someone the cross and the Bible. Just because they now have these things doesn't mean that they have arrived as a Christian, and can now make all the right decisions, and be perfect in every way. Living Christ's way will take us a lifetime of training and practice, and we are bound to make mistakes and get into scrapes along the route.

So when the going gets hard work, and we find it's a challenge and a struggle to live by God's rule of love, we mustn't get discouraged. Jesus never promised us it would be easy all the time. All train-ing, whether it's in tackling or goal defence, vibrato on the violin or overcoming the break on the clarinet, forgiving wholeheartedly or conquering self-indul-gence – all these things are difficult to learn and require dedication and perseverance.

When you are finding it's hard being a Christian, don't give up or decide it's too difficult; go to God and ask for some more help. Throughout your whole life he will provide all the training, practice and gifts you need for the work he asks you to do, whether that work is preaching to thousands, or helping your next-door neighbour.

All-age ideas

- The mood of sadness in the Old Testament reading can be expressed well in dance. Look into any dance contacts you may have with groups using the church hall, and consider inviting them. Some of the Scottish strathspey dances are very poignant, for instance, or the slow Greek dances. A local dancing school might welcome the challenge. Or, for a home-grown dance, while the choir sing or recorded music is played, a group of people from the congregation can move slowly up the centre aisle, hands at their sides, doing a slow *pas de basque* in formation, in the style of a folk dance. At the front they link hands and circle first left and then right, then move into the centre, raising their arms, and back again. They all turn outwards and sway from one foot to the other, before moving back down the aisle again. Keep the steps simple and controlled.

- Ask the flower-arranging team to create an arrangement expressing grief and sadness, with a centre of bright hope, perhaps using purple and dark red colours and cascading foliage.

378

TWENTY-EIGHTH SUNDAY OF THE YEAR

2 Kings 5:14-17
Psalm 97
2 Timothy 2:8-13
Luke 17:11-19

God can always use even seemingly hopeless situations for good.

All-age talk

Ask for ten volunteers and dish out 'bandages' for them to wear on arms, legs and head. Explain that they are lepers and, because the disease is thought to be very catching, they can't stay with everyone else here but must go and sit somewhere else. Direct them to a place separate from the rest of the congregation. As they go, tell everyone how the lepers of Jesus' day had to leave their homes and live right away from the villages and towns, and look after themselves. How must they have felt? Lonely? Left out? Guilty? Unacceptable? Frightened?

We may not have the disease of leprosy, but there are lots of people in our world, in our country and in our town – perhaps even in our church – who feel lonely, left out, guilty, unacceptable and frightened, like the lepers. People cry themselves to sleep and wake up feeling sad about the day ahead. People who have lost contact with friends, or whose loved ones have died, try hard to be cheerful when they have a big ache of sadness inside them. Lots of people are hurting, and longing for their life to be different.

That's how these ten lepers felt that morning when they saw Jesus walking along the road on his way to a village. They couldn't come too close to him, but they came as close as they could, and shouted to him, 'Jesus, Master, have pity on us!' (This can be written on a sign so the ten 'lepers' can shout it out.) People still cry out to God in their hearts like this. Does God hear?

He certainly does! Jesus shows us what God is like, and what Jesus did was to tell the lepers to go and show themselves to the priest. Why ever did he tell

379

them that? Because if you were a leper and you were healed, you had to show yourself to a priest, so he could check you over and pronounce you fit and well.

Send your lepers off to 'the priest', who has ten cards saying, 'I declare this leper is now CLEAN. Signed: Fr (John Hayward).' Tell them that when they have their certificate of health they are free to join the other people in the congregation.

If any of the volunteers decides to come and say 'thank you' you can of course use this and praise it. However, since they haven't actually been healed of anything, they will probably all sit down in their places. Tell everyone how one leper (choose one) came back to Jesus to say 'thank you'. All the others had been keen to talk to Jesus when they needed something, but they forgot him once he had sorted them out.

Let's make sure that when God answers our prayers, we don't forget to say thank you – even if his answer is not the answer we expect.

All-age ideas

- Give out small pieces of bandage (cut from old sheeting) to people as they come in. At the Penitential Rite ask them to hold their bandage and wrap it round their hand. Just as the lepers were cut off from their community, so our sin cuts us off from God. Ask them to bring to mind the sins that they need God to heal them of, so that their relationship with him can be restored. At the words of forgiveness they can unwind the bandages and throw them away.

- Involve both sides of the congregation in these responses taken from 2 Timothy 2:
  A If we died with him,
  B then we shall live with him.
  A If we hold firm,
  B then we shall reign with him.
  A If we disown him,
  B then he will disown us.
  A We may be unfaithful,
  All but he is always faithful,
  for he cannot disown his own self.

Twenty-ninth Sunday of the Year

Exodus 17:8-13
Psalm 120
2 Timothy 3:14-4:2
Luke 18:1-8

Don't get side-tracked; always pray and don't give up.

All-age talk

Bring along (or ask someone else in the congregation to bring) something which you have made or are making, which requires lots of persistence and perseverance (such as a garment or model, diary or recipe). Talk about the struggle you have had keeping going with it. Use parts of the church building, particularly if it is an ancient one, and draw everyone's attention to some piece of stained glass or carving, and all the persistence and hard work that went into making it. Emphasise the value of doing these things, even though they are difficult.

Jesus tells us to keep going with our prayer, and never give up. Suggest a pattern of praying when you wake up, before you eat a meal, and before you go to sleep at night, showing large posters of logos for these (as below). Or they can be shown on an OHP. If we get into a prayer habit like this, we will be deepening our friendship with God, and getting to know him better.

There is another good habit we need to have as well as praying, and that is reading the Bible every day. There are lots of books and schemes to help us, and we can choose one which suits our age, interests and experience. Show a few of these and draw attention to the display suggested in the All-age Ideas. If we don't know much about the Bible there are people in the parish to talk it over with.

However we read it, it's important to pray and read God's word in Scripture so that we really can have God's law of love remembered in our minds and written on our hearts. That way we will be ready for any jobs God asks us to do, and we will be better able to hear him speaking into our lives.

All-age ideas

• Have a display of Bible study aids for all ages and characters, and also a selection of different Bible translations, with recommendations.

• In a flower arrangement have an open Bible and a picture or model of 'praying hands', with the arrangement titled 'Daily prayer, daily Scripture reading'.

• Use this short sketch to reinforce the Gospel reading, or prepare people for it:

Woman   Knock, knock.

Judge   Who's there?

Woman   Winnie.

Judge   Winnie who?

Woman   Winnie you going to do something about that money I was cheated of?

Judge   Oh don't worry, that case will be coming up very soon. Now if you don't mind, it's my day off and I'm going to play golf.

(Sign held up saying 'Next day')

Woman   Knock, knock.

Judge   Who's there?

Woman   Winnie.

Judge   Winnie who?

Woman	Winnie you going to do something about . . .
Judge	OK, you don't have to say all that again. I remember. I'll deal with it, madam. Leave it to me. *(Aside)* But not yet because I'd rather watch telly and have a snooze.
Woman	Knock, knock.
Judge	*(Sounding sleepy)* Who's there?
Woman	Winnie.
Judge	Winnie who? *(Aside)* Oh, hang on, I won't ask! I don't know, there's no rest for the wicked. Wretched woman, I'd better do what she asks or I'll never get any peace! *(Shouts)* All right, Winnie, you win. I'll come with you and sort it out *now*!

THIRTIETH SUNDAY OF THE YEAR

Ecclesiasticus
35:12-14, 16-17
Psalm 33
2 Timothy 4:6-8, 16-18
Luke 18:9-14

When we recognise our dependence on God we will approach him with true humility and accept his gifts with joy.

All-age talk

Involve a couple of children in constructing a tower, using building blocks or large packing case cartons. When it is really high, suggest that now they won't need the big block at the bottom any more. Take it away, and of course the whole lot falls down. Be surprised, and protest that you only took one brick away! Then point out that it was the important brick you took – the foundation stone – and everything else depends on that.

Our whole lives depend on God. It's God who gives us life for a start, and provides our planet with what we need to live on. It is God's rain, sunshine and earth which we use to grow our wheat for bread and pizzas. We might sometimes forget to think about God, but he never ever forgets to think about us. He looks after us through our whole lives as we grow up and get old.

We heard another of Jesus' stories this morning, with some more cartoon-type characters. There's Pharisee Ferdinand and Tax Collector Ted.

Both of them have gone to pray. Let's look again at how Pharisee Ferdinand prays. (Display the picture, while a pompous voice reads the part. He needs to

384

sound really smug.) Let people give their ideas of what's wrong with his prayer.

Let's listen in on Tax Collector Ted. (Show the picture, and have someone saying his prayer. This should sound quite genuine.) Comment on the way this person knows he needs God's mercy. And it was this person, Jesus said, who went away right with God, rather than Pharisee Ferdinand who did lots of good things but didn't have any idea of how much he depended on God, thinking that doing good things could earn him a special place in God's Kingdom all by himself.

We owe our whole life to God. Let's not kid ourselves that we don't need him.

All-age ideas

- Act out today's Gospel, or use different people for the different voices.

- Have a display or a banner with words taken from Psalm 33: 'The humble shall hear and be glad'; or from the Gospel: 'For everyone who exalts himself will be humbled and everyone who humbles himself will be exalted'.

THIRTY-FIRST SUNDAY OF THE YEAR

Wisdom 11:22-12:2
Psalm 144
2 Thessalonians
  1:11-2:2
Luke 19:1-10

Jesus came to search out the lost and save them. Through him we come to our senses and make our lives clean.

All-age talk

Bring along some wallpaper, paste and brush, and some foundation make-up. Introduce these items, talking about what a difference they can make to the look of a room or a face, and how we carefully choose and apply them.

Point out that much as we may want to make our faces and rooms beautiful with what shows, like wallpaper and make-up, we always have to start on the hidden hard work. We need to make sure our faces are completely clean before we go on making them even more beautiful; we have to make sure our walls are properly repaired and strong before applying the wallpaper.

In our spiritual lives it is just the same, and in our first reading we heard how God patiently and lovingly helps us with the whole process. He understands the way we want to rush, or miss out the boring but necessary bits, and gently he trains us to be better at this. He knows that if we don't attack the root problems of sin in our lives it will be like using nice wallpaper to cover a crumbling wall, or make-up to cover a spot. It certainly doesn't help the problem and may well make it worse.

Zacchaeus knew something was wrong in his life. When Jesus came to his house, he helped him to sort out the problem properly, instead of just covering it over and hoping it would go away. Sin never goes away unless we deal with it properly. It isn't any good trying to make it look pretty or covering it over with excuses. Like Zacchaeus we need to invite Jesus in and deal with it.

All-age ideas

- Have a group of people to read the Wisdom passage, some lines with a single voice, others with two or three voices together. Work through the reading and try out different voice groupings to bring out the meaning and the gentle mercy of it.

- Act out the Gospel, using a narrator and other people reading the different parts.

THIRTY-SECOND SUNDAY OF THE YEAR

Maccabees 7:1-2, 9-14
Psalm 16
2 Thessalonians
  2:16-3:5
Luke 20:27-38

Life after death is not wishful thinking but a definite reality.

All-age talk

Bring along some tasters of a particular cheese, tiny chunks such as those you find in most supermarkets from time to time. Bring also a block of the same cheese, labelled.

Show your tray of tasters for the cheese you have brought to recommend. Since these tasters came off the main block of cheese, you can guarantee that they will taste as good as the main block.

Although we haven't been to heaven, God gives us lots of little 'tasters' which help us find out what it is like. Whenever we sense Jesus giving us peace of mind or joy, or the lovely knowledge that God really loves and cares for us, we are getting a taster of life after death. Jesus lives in heaven so when he comes into us, he doesn't leave heaven behind but brings it with him. So the more we live in God's company and follow Jesus, the more of heaven we will have in our lives even before we die.

Explain that lots of people think Christians are crazy believing that there is life after death. Since they can't see beyond death, they don't think there can be anything like heaven. If I had never seen the yellow daffodil flowers in spring, I would probably think people were crazy burying dry bulbs in their earth at this time of year. But because I have seen what happens to those bulbs, I trust that they won't just rot in the ground. If I were a caterpillar, I would probably laugh at anyone suggesting that one day I would be flying about with colourful wings. It isn't true that the only real things are those we can see.

It is sometimes difficult to trust that what we can't see is still there, but we make the effort to do it whenever we drive in fog, walk along looking around instead of at the path under our feet, or wash our backs. So it is quite possible. And Jesus has told us that there really is life after death, and lots of people saw him alive after he had died. So we aren't crazy for believing there is life after death; we happen to know it's true, and we've already tasted little bits of how lovely it is.

All-age ideas

- Play a recording, or suggest the choir sing *I know that my Redeemer liveth*.

- Decorate the church with brightly coloured flowers and dried flowers, to make it all look bright and beautiful, even in November.

- Make a colourful 'Welcome!' for everyone to walk through as they come into church.

THIRTY-THIRD SUNDAY OF THE YEAR

Malachi 3:19-20
Psalm 97
2 Thessalonians 3:7-12
Luke 21:5-19

There will be dark and dangerous times as the end approaches, but by standing firm through it all we will gain life.

All-age talk

Prepare some large card road signs, and a cereal packet which is labelled 'The last age' on the front and has 'Warnings and advice' with a copy of today's Gospel stuck on the back. Bring these along, together with a packet of cigarettes, and something packed in a plastic bag with the warning of suffocation printed on it.

Begin by asking volunteers to hold the road signs at intervals down the aisle, and ask a couple of people to 'drive their car' among the signs. Talk them through, getting people to say what the signs mean as they come to them, and encouraging them to react appropriately. (If a roundabout sign is used, for instance, they can drive round an imaginary roundabout.) Point out how useful the signs are in warning us so that we are better prepared as we drive.

Show the cigarette packet and read out the warning on that, and on the plastic bag. Lots of things have warnings and good advice printed on them – hair colouring, pain-killers, frozen pies and skateboards – the manufacturer wants customers to be warned of any dangers and know how to avoid them.

Now pick up the prepared cereal packet, and show the 'product name'. Today's Gospel is doing the same thing. It's offering us some warnings and advice for living through this: the last age. We are in the middle of this at the moment. It's the time between Jesus dying on the cross and coming to

390

life again and going to heaven (which has already happened) and the Day of Judgement, or the Second Coming, which will mark the end of things as we know them. (That hasn't happened yet.)

Jesus knew this would be a very difficult and dangerous age to live in, and he told his disciples to watch for the signs and be prepared. (Turn the packet of cereal round and show the warnings and advice.) Compulsive cereal packet readers will find it may put them off their breakfast. It's the section of Luke's Gospel that we've all just heard this morning.

Pick up on some of the phrases to remind people, and help them see that these things are indeed happening in places all over the world. The signs are there. So what are we to do about them?

Our job as Christians is to stand firm and not get fazed when these terrible things happen, but be in there helping, comforting and doing our best to show and proclaim God's love by our words and actions, even when we get laughed at, despised or persecuted in the process.

Perhaps you are thinking that sounds very hard. Well, you're right, it is very hard and we may feel like giving up. But God promises to be there with us through it all, and will make sure we have all the courage we need to do it. We are warned and prepared specially, because God wants us to be able to stay firm to the end and be saved.

All-age ideas

- As a reflection on the Gospel, try this mime. Play some music from Delirious? ('Sanctify' from *King of Fools* works really well) as a background, or if your parish has more traditional tastes, try some Taizé music, such as *O Lord, hear my prayer*; if tastes are classical try some Shostakovich. Have groups of people all over the church ready to jeer and buffet two or three people who are starting at the back of the church and trying to make their way through the persecution and terror of the last days. One of them gives up and stomps off to the back, but the others make it all the way to the front, reaching out to others along the way in love and comfort, in spite of their treatment. One or two of the jeerers are persuaded to join them. As they reach the front they raise their arms in praise and joy, and everyone in the congregation can applaud. Make the actions slow and deliberate.

- Read part of Psalm 97 in parts using the whole congregation, like this:

Men	Let the sea and all within it thunder,
Children	the world and all its peoples.
Women	Let the rivers clap their hands *(all clap)*
Men	and the hills ring out their joy
Children	at the presence of the Lord.
Women	For the Lord comes, he comes to rule the earth.
All	*(to one another)* He will rule the world with justice and the peoples with fairness.

CHRIST THE KING

2 Samuel 5:1-3
Psalm 121
Colossians 1:11-20
Luke 23:35-43

This Jesus, dying by crucifixion between criminals, is the anointed King of all creation in whom all things are reconciled.

All-age talk

Beforehand prepare a flock of large card sheep. Numbers will depend on your congregation; there need to be at least six.

Begin by talking about the way sheep get easily scared, and will scuttle away a few metres and then stop and eat, and then scuttle away again and eat again. That's why they can easily get lost, because they don't realise how far they have scuttled! Children with little experience of sheep may have noticed a similar 'scuttle, eat, scuttle' pattern in rabbits, who also get scared very easily.

Introduce your flock of sheep, with a volunteer holding each one. Those who are holding them can give them names, or they can be given the names of the children. All through the Bible we read that people are rather like sheep. We get scared (though we usually try to hide that and pretend we aren't scared at all) and we follow one another into all sorts of rather silly and dangerous places and ideas, and we tend to wander off and get lost. (Send the sheep to do that now.)

God promised that he would be sending his people a king – a good king, whose kingdom would last for ever. Ask for a volunteer and place a crown on their head. But he also knew that his people were like sheep, so this king would not be the kind of king who bosses everybody around and makes them give him all their money so he can be the richest person in the world. God decided that this

393

king would be a shepherd. (Give the king a crook.) And he would go and search for all the lost sheep and bring them safely back to their pasture again. (Send the shepherd king off to do that.)

When the shepherd king has brought all the sheep back, explain that Jesus, the Christ, is our King, and he is the sort of king who knows us each by name, and searches for us when we are lost, and looks after us when he has found us.

In the Gospel today we heard that even when Jesus was dying on the cross he was still searching for lost sheep, right up to the moment he died. Two criminals were being executed with him that day, and one of them, only hours before he died, turned to him and asked for help. Straight away Jesus assured him of forgiveness; he had just brought another sheep back home to its pasture.

Ask the shepherd king to stretch out his arms. Point out that when Jesus, our King, was on the cross, his arms were stretched out like this, so he was in the shape of a cross, and this is the shape of welcoming love.

All-age ideas

- Lay the card sheep from the All-age Talk on the floor around the altar or some other place where everyone can see them.

- Focus attention on the cross today, surrounding it with flowers, and hanging a crown around it. Or have an arrangement of flowers which expresses the idea of a Shepherd King, with a crown and a crook.

SPECIAL FEASTS
YEARS A, B, C

MARY, MOTHER OF GOD – 1 JANUARY

Numbers 6:22-27
Psalm 66
Galatians 4:4-7
Luke 2:16-21

Jesus Christ, the Son of God, is born of a woman.

All-age talk

Ask everyone to raise their hands if what you say applies to them. (For example, they are sitting on the end of a row, ate cornflakes for breakfast, watch *Coronation Street*, and, finally, were born of a mother.) Although the first few things would have applied to some but not to others, everybody on earth in every generation, however young or old, has been born of a mother. That is something we all share as humans. We were all carried around inside a woman, where we were provided with all we needed until we had grown big and strong enough to survive out in this world. That's when we were born.

Over Christmas we have been celebrating Jesus being born into this world, and today we are looking at that from the point of view of Mary, his mother. It was through Mary saying, 'Yes!' to God that Jesus, the Son of God, could be born into the human family as a baby, born from a woman. It is when *we* are prepared to say, 'Yes!' to God, as Mary did, that God can use us and work through us for the good of the world.

We have such a lot to thank our mothers for. All that time we were in the womb, growing in the darkness, our bodies taking shape, it was our mothers' bodies that kept us safe and healthy, protected from the outside world, warm and nourished, so that when we needed energy, particular minerals or vitamins, we got them. As we got larger, our mothers found it quite tiring and needed to put their feet up sometimes. As we took up more space, our mothers found it harder to bend down and could feel us kicking about inside.

And then it was time for us to be born, and our mothers worked, or laboured, hard at that with us, so that we could live out here in the world we now know so well. The mothering didn't stop there, of course; when you are a mother you go on with the loving and caring for the rest of your life, helping your children gradually to grow into the independent persons God planned them to be.

So as we think today of our own mothering, and thank God for it, we remember with love and affection Mary, the woman who agreed to mother the Son of God. It was in the darkness and security of her womb that Jesus Christ grew and developed; it was through her labour that he was born, and it was her mothering that enabled him to become the adult who was and is the Saviour of the world.

All-age ideas

- Have mothers and their young children taking the collection and offering the gifts today.

- Make a collection particularly for children who need mothering, or for women and children in refuge homes.

- Decorate with flowers the Lady Chapel or a statue of the Mother and Child.

THE PRESENTATION OF THE LORD (CANDLEMAS) – 2 FEBRUARY

Malachi 3:1-4
Psalm 23
Hebrews 2:14-18
Luke 2:22-40

In accordance with Jewish tradition, the Light of the World is presented as a first-born baby in the temple at Jerusalem.

All-age talk

Today is a good opportunity to celebrate the elderly faithful and build relationships between young and old. Beforehand arrange for an elderly man and woman to sit at the front with a microphone to answer a few questions put to them by the children about what life was like when they were children. Gather the children round their feet and introduce the elderly people. Since they have been alive a long time they have picked up lots of wisdom. They have lived through things the younger ones here have heard about in history. Invite the children to find out what it was like being a child 70 or more years ago – they can ask about clothes, toys, school, church or food, for instance. After a few questions thank the volunteers and have the children escort them back to their seats.

In today's Gospel we heard about Joseph and Mary bringing the baby Jesus into the temple. All Jewish families did this when their first son was born. They came to give a present, or offer a sacrifice to God and dedicate the child. We've had two wise, elderly people answering questions today. And when Mary, Joseph and Jesus came into the temple there were two wise elderly people there. Their names were Simeon and Anna. They had both loved God all their life, and if any of us do that, we will end up wise and lovable in our old age. You can't love God all your life and end up crabby and narrow-minded.

Jesus didn't have a big label tied round his

swaddling clothes saying 'I am the Messiah'. Joseph and Mary didn't wave flags or shout to everyone, 'Look! This is the baby you've all been waiting for!' From the outside he looked just like any other baby, and Mary and Joseph looked just like an ordinary, fairly poor set of parents, rather dusty after the journey.

So how did Simeon and Anna know that this baby was the one they were waiting for?

Simeon had been told that he would see the promised Messiah in person before he died. He had been listening to God all his life, and because he was used to listening to God, he was able to recognise that this particular baby was the Messiah, God's chosen one.

When we spend a lot of time with another person we get to know how they think, and we understand them better and better. If we spend time with God every day, starting from today, and carry on doing that right into our old age, we will get to know him better and better, and it won't be long before we are able to hear what he speaks into our hearts. It is astounding that the powerful creator of this universe is happy to communicate with individuals like this, but that's God for you. He's hoping there will be some wise and faithful elderly Christians in the future – twenty, thirty, forty, fifty, sixty, seventy or eighty years from now. There could be. It could be us.

All-age ideas

- Have a grandparent and grandchild bringing up the offertory gifts.

- Act out the Gospel as it is narrated, using a young family with a real baby if you have one available!

- Have a display of photographs of those who regularly receive communion in their homes, with space for people to sign their pledge to pray for a particular person daily. It is important that these frail and elderly faithful do not become forgotten by the rest of the church.

Saint John the Baptist – 24 June

Isaiah 49:1-6
Psalm 138
Acts 13:22-26
Luke 1:57-66, 80

John is born with a mission to prepare the way for the Messiah by calling people to repentance.

All-age talk

Begin by explaining that to prepare for the talk today you will need everyone in each row to sit in reverse order from how they are sitting at the moment, so that those nearest the centre will end up nearest the sides. And they will have to do it cheerfully! (Give everyone some time to organise this. It should create mild chaos for a while which gradually settles into order again.) Thank everyone for their co-operation.

What they have just experienced is an important truth – when God prepares his people for his coming, that is bound to cause disturbance. Prophets are there to cause disturbance. The Holy Spirit disturbs us in order to prepare us and change us.

Today we are celebrating the birth of a great disturber: John, known as the Baptist because of the way he baptised people with water as a sign of their washed and changed lives. His calling was to alert people to the way they were living and to challenge them to sort themselves out in line with God's standards. When our own lives are challenged like this we have to set about checking the way we are living – are we in line with God's way of love and God's values?

There may be drastic changes needed (as there were today for those sitting on the ends of rows), or there may be minor changes and fine tuning to be done (as there were for those few who have ended up sitting in the same place as before). But either way we need to get up, spiritually, both individually and as a community, and take a candid look at the way we speak to people, and how we spend our time and our money. We need to look at our relationships and our attitudes, and at the extent we allow our Lord to reign in us.

Now, as they realign themselves in their rows, ask them to do so in silence, opening up their lives, both in thankfulness for John the Baptist, and in readiness to be realigned with God's will.

All-age ideas

- In the entrance to the church have some large display boards with such signs as 'Get ready to meet God's Son!', 'How does your way match up with God's way?' and 'You can be free – God's love can set you free!'

SAINTS PETER AND PAUL – 29 JUNE

Acts 12:1-11
Psalm 33
2 Timothy 4:6-8, 17-18
Matthew 16:13-19

Through the dedication of the apostles Peter and Paul, the Gospel of Jesus Christ spread and the Church was rapidly established.

All-age talk

Bring along a length of cotton and a length of rope. Around the church place some keys, a fishing net with fish in it (a piece of net curtain is fine), a writing pad, envelopes and pen, and a map.

Today we are celebrating two great saints together – Saint Peter and Saint Paul. It is largely thanks to the work of these two that we are all here today, because when the Church was very young and very new, Peter led it and Paul spread it!

Send some volunteers to find and bring back the keys and the fishing net. What do these have to do with today? Simon Peter was a fisherman when Jesus walked along the beach and talked to the people there. He was impressed by what Jesus said and did, and Jesus called Simon to fish for people instead of fish. Instead of casting his nets into the water, and bringing in lots of fish, he would be working where Jesus led him and in charge of bringing lots of people into God's kingdom.

What about the keys? Later, when Jesus asked the disciples who they thought he was, Simon knew: 'You are the Messiah,' he said, 'the Son of God.' And Jesus gave him a new name – Peter, or Rock. He said that on this rock he would build up the new Church. As leader, he would be in charge, and a good sign of being in charge is having the keys. Peter was going to be in charge of who should be let into the kingdom of God, and that's a very responsible job.

402

Send other volunteers to find the notepaper and the map. What do these have to do with today? Paul travelled a lot, all around the Mediterranean sea, sometimes on land by foot and sometimes by ship. He was shipwrecked three times, and was often in danger. Why did he spend his time doing that? He was spreading the good news about Jesus, setting up small churches in all the main cities and teaching them the faith. Once they were strong enough, off he'd go to start another church somewhere else, but he kept in touch with all these church communities by letter, helping them grow and sort out their problems.

(Hold the cotton.) Both Peter and Paul were ordinary people, with their faults as well as their strengths. They had made big mistakes in their lives and let Jesus down. (Break the cotton.) But what made it possible for God to use them for so much good was that both of them were open to God and willing to learn; they were prepared to trust God with their whole life. (Hold the rope.) They knew that, however much they had let God down, God would never let them down. (Tug the rope to show that it holds.) By the end of their lives they could both say that, although they had been through such a lot of adventures and so much danger, and faced lots of angry people, their God had always been there, and never let them down.

And when they were eventually killed for their faith in Jesus, they were welcomed into the joy of heaven for ever.

All-age ideas

- Have the symbols from the talk displayed near the altar so that people are reminded as they come to receive communion.

- Have twin flower arrangements side by side, one expressing and celebrating Peter's life and the other Paul's life.

403

THE TRANSFIGURATION OF THE LORD – 6 AUGUST

Daniel 7:9-10, 13-14
Psalm 96
2 Peter 1:16-19
Matthew 17:1-9

Jesus is seen in all God's glory, and as fulfilling the Law and the prophets.

All-age talk

Bring along a piece of coal.

Show everyone what you have brought – a lump of black, hard shiny stuff which burns well. It's called coal. Coal is dusty and dirty and not that wonderful to look at. It used to be burnt in people's fireplaces and in steam engines and steam ships and factories all over the world as fuel. To get coal, the miners are taken deep down under the ground into coal mines to cut or blast the coal from the rock. They are covered in dirty coal dust when they come up at the end of their work and need hot showers and lots of soap to get them clean again.

So it is quite a surprise to find that a diamond, like you get in jewellery, is made of the same carbon that coal is made of. Ask people to show around to one another any diamonds they may be wearing, especially so that all the children can see the clear sparkling nature of diamonds. Sometimes the light splits into lovely rainbows through a diamond, and they cost a lot of money to buy. They are precious jewels, and they play with the light like clear water, yet they're so strong that they are sometimes used in industry to cut things that nothing else can cut.

Why are we looking at coal and diamonds today?

Today we are celebrating the Transfiguration – the time when Jesus took Peter, James and John up the mountain, and while he was praying with all his heart and soul, he suddenly looked completely different. The disciples saw him not as the human friend and teacher they knew well, but filled with all the bright glory of God, shining with God's majesty, power and love. If we imagine seeing a familiar piece of coal suddenly shining and sparkling like a diamond, and we suddenly realise that actually both coal and diamond are the same thing, that's a bit like how it must have seemed for Peter, James and John when they suddenly saw that Jesus was both human *and* the Son of God.

As we think today of that experience they had on the mountain, we can see, with them, Jesus, the wandering teacher and healer from Nazareth, shining with all the glory of the living God! It would not always be showing in that way, but even during the terrible, humiliating process of crucifixion, the glory would still be there, seen in the beauty of love and forgiveness that goes on and on and never gives up on us.

All-age ideas

- Have lots of candles, flowers and reflected light in church today.

- At one point read *The glory of God* by Gerard Manley Hopkins.

THE ASSUMPTION – 15 AUGUST

Apocalypse 11:19;
   12:1-6, 10
Psalm 44
1 Corinthians 15:20-26
Luke 1:39-56

The Almighty has done great things for me!

All-age talk

Ask if anyone ever dreams, and collect a couple of examples of dreams. What about daydreams and wishes? Collect some examples of these, too. We all have wishes that are close to our hearts, whether they are ones we are brave enough to share in public or not! Sometimes a dream can spur us into action. If we dream of being a supermodel, we'll probably start experimenting with clothes and make-up – and with our expression in front of a mirror to perfect that essential pouty look! If we dream of becoming a rock climber, we might start on the stairs, going up three or four at a time. If we dream of joining a band, we might start practising by singing loudly in the bath. Often it is those whose dreams keep them focused who end up by achieving what at one time seemed almost impossible.

As Christians, we have a great and wonderful hope – that we will one day come to know for ourselves the glory of heaven, and live with God in that life which lasts for ever, sharing with Our Lady and all the saints the joy of worshipping God with our whole being, at one and at peace with our Creator and Redeemer, and with one another in the community of heaven.

As with our other dreams and hopes, this hope may sometimes seem a long way off. Perhaps we are tired and scratchy with the children; perhaps we are winding our brothers or sisters up and can't seem to stop; perhaps we have once again let slip our habit of daily prayer, and there seems so little time to fit God in. Will we ever make it to that dream of heaven?

Today's celebration of the Assumption reminds us to hope again. As we think of Mary, our spiritual Mother, taken into the glory of heaven, the full impact of Christ's resurrection hits us with all its power. Christ raised from death spells victory! It is not we who are going to earn that place in heaven, but Christ who has won it for us and graciously offers it to us. All we have to do is trust Christ, hang on to Christ with our hopes and dreams, and let him clothe us with righteousness and new life. It is God's pleasure to give us the kingdom, and he will use every opportunity this life provides to transform us into heavenly citizens, so that, one day, we shall be able to realise that dream, and join Mary and the saints in the full joy of heaven.

All-age ideas

- Have several arrangements of flowers moving upwards from dead wood at the bottom to gradually increasing colour, so that the top arrangement is a burst of colour and joy of new life.

THE TRIUMPH OF THE HOLY CROSS – 14 SEPTEMBER

Numbers 21:4-9
Psalm 77
Philippians 2:6-11
John 3:13-17

Through Christ's loving obedience, even to death on a cross, he has opened up the way for us to eternal life.

All-age talk

Beforehand cut a number of teardrop shapes out of paper and leave one of these on each row. Also have a bunch of flowers, hidden until later.

Today we are celebrating the Triumph, or victory, of the Cross. Direct everyone's attention to a crucifix. When we look at the cross what we see is the good Jesus, nailed on the cross in great pain. How can that be a victory, when it looks like a terrible, evil thing happening to such a good and loving person? It doesn't look much like a victory. The cross seems to be about pain and disappointment and failure.

Sometimes we feel disappointed with God, too. Perhaps he doesn't answer our prayer in the way we would like him to. Perhaps things aren't working out for us in the way we hoped they would, and we feel God could have done something about it. Perhaps there has been a tragedy or natural disaster, and we feel God should have stopped it happening.

One thing the cross shows us is God, suffering. We don't worship a being who sits a long way off from our real, painful world and isn't interested in whether we are hurting or sad. The true God loves us so much that he came to join us and join our suffering, whatever it is. It would not be loving to control us completely, so that we were like robots. God knows that the best kind of world means we will sometimes suffer, and not understand why. His answer is to be there for us and with us with unlimited loving, which we can see in the cross.

Ask people to find the teardrop on their row

408

and, as they pass it along to the aisle, to look at it and think of their own personal disappointments and regrets. Have a couple of people to collect the teardrops in a basket and walk up in silence to lay them at the foot of the cross. In a way, that is what is happening as Jesus hangs dying there.

Send a young volunteer to get the flowers and stand holding them in front of the cross. The great triumph of the cross is that this love, which goes on and on and never ends, manages to turn death into life, and bring good out of evil.

All-age ideas

- Surround a cross with garlands of Michaelmas daisies.

- Use the following for the Penitential Rite:
  Love stretched out on the cross exposes our indifference.
  Lord, have mercy.
  Lord, have mercy.
  The generosity of the cross shows us our meanness of spirit.
  Christ, have mercy.
  Christ, have mercy.
  The humility of the cross challenges our vanity and pride.
  Lord, have mercy.
  Lord, have mercy.

ALL SAINTS – 1 NOVEMBER

Apocalypse 7:2-4,
  9-14
Psalm 23:1-6
1 John 3:1-3
Matthew 5:1-12

Lives that have shone with God's love on earth are filled with joy as they see their Lord face to face.

All-age talk

Today we are celebrating the festival of all the saints of God. Saints are God's close friends, and there are lots of them around, as well as all the famous ones like Our Lady and Joseph, Peter and the other disciples, Francis, Benedict, Clare and Catherine.

What makes a saint?

Suppose your car breaks down on the motorway, and, as you drive skilfully on to the hard shoulder, smoke pours out of the bonnet. At this moment there is no doubt in your mind about it – you know that you need the AA or the RAC to sort you out. Suppose you've fallen down in the playground and find you can't move your ankle without terrible pain. At that moment you know without doubt that you need some help from the teacher on duty and the first aid people in the school office.

Show everyone a large arrow on which is written 'We know our need'. As soon as we know our need that points us towards getting it sorted. (Have 'Get help' written on a large piece of paper or card.) But what if we don't know or realise our need?

Suppose you have got some spaghetti sauce on your chin and you are just going out to meet an important client, or a new boyfriend or girlfriend. If we realise we have the sauce on our chin (show the arrow), then we'll probably go and wipe it off. (Show the 'Get help' sign.) But if we aren't aware of the sauce on our chin (show a sign without an arrow which says, 'Don't know our need') then we won't do anything about wiping it off. (Turn the 'Get help' sign over so it's a blank sign.)

410

If we don't realise our need of God (show 'Don't know our need') then we won't go to him for the help we urgently and desperately need. (Keep the blank sign up.) But if we *do* realise how much we need God (show the arrow) then that will lead us to seeking God's help in our lives. (Turn over the 'Get help' sign so it shows.)

Saints are ordinary people like us who realise their need of God (show the arrow) and spend their lives close to him so that he can help them in all they do. (Show the 'Get help' sign.)

All-age ideas

- For the reading from the Apocalypse, ask several people to read it chorally, preparing it prayerfully and deciding how their voices can best express the sense of the heavenly.

- Ask different groups and clubs to prepare banners celebrating different saints, so that the church is full of their witness and example.

FEASTS OF THE DEDICATION OF A CHURCH

2 Chronicles 5:6-11,
   13-6:2 or
      Acts 7:44-50
Psalm 83
1 Corinthians 3:9-13,
   16-17
John 4:19-24

The church building symbolises the spiritual temple, being built of the living stones of God's people.

All-age talk

Draw attention to the decoration of the church. Today we are celebrating the anniversary of our church being dedicated. In (1900) a lot of bricklayers, masons and glaziers, plasterers and painters created a space which was set apart for God. At that first service of dedication the people of this area gathered. Talk about the kind of things they might have been wearing, how they might have travelled and so on, to build a picture of that day when the church began its life.

One of the most important things those people did that day was to offer the building for God's work and dedicate themselves to be the living stones of Christ's Church here. Now we are here today, still gathering to worship God, still dedicating ourselves to his service in this area. And the church building is like a picture of what we are all called to be – built up as living stones into the spiritual temple of God.

Week by week we bring in with us all the people and situations we have met and enjoyed and wrestled with; all the griefs and joys, heartaches and hopes of those we have talked with and whose lives have touched ours. Here we offer all that in the Mass, and it is gathered up with our praise and love to be accepted and transformed. So we do not worship here for ourselves alone, but on behalf of all who are not here and would never think of coming; on behalf of all those our lives have brushed against.

412

Through our worship, their worries and fears are brought into the healing love of God.

The name of our church reminds us that the whole Church includes the saints in heaven as well as all of us on earth, and they are here with us, too, cheering us on and praying for us as we worship God in our prayers and our work each day. As we thank God for this place, which holds precious memories for many of us, we dedicate ourselves freshly to living as God's people, and ask God's blessing on our neighbourhood and all who will visit this place during the coming year.

All-age ideas

- Have banners and posters showing the date of the church's dedication and other significant dates in its history, together with reminders of the saint in whose name the church is dedicated.

- Gather a collection of photographs and have an exhibition celebrating the ministry of the church both in the past and in the present.

APPENDIX

Come, Spirit, come, prise open my heart
(Eighth Sunday of the Year, Year C)

2. Come, Spirit, come, take charge of my mind.
   Show me the darkness that you find.
   Help me to trust you, even with my shame,
   till I freely acknowledge where I am to blame.

3. Come, Spirit, come, bring life to my soul.
   Your forgiveness makes me whole.
   Then from the pain and stress of sin set free
   I am dazed by the awesome love you have for me.

Text: Susan Sayers
Music: Susan Sayers, arr. Donald Thomson
© Copyright 1997 Kevin Mayhew Ltd.